MISSING PERSONS

MISSING PERSONS

A Memoir

Gayle Greene

UNIVERSITY OF NEVADA PRESS *Reno & Las Vegas*

University of Nevada Press | Reno, Nevada 89557 USA
www.unpress.nevada.edu
Copyright © 2018 by University of Nevada Press
All rights reserved
Cover design by TG Design
All photographs courtesy of the author, except photo on page 8, courtesy of Al Schwoerer.
"This Ole House" Stuart Hamblen, © 1954, renewed 1982. Hamblen Music Co./ASCAP (administered by ClearBox Rights); "Big Yellow Taxi," words and music by Joni Mitchell, © 1970 (renewed), Crazy Crow Music, exclusive print rights administered by Alfred Music; "Walking the Wrack Line," by Barbara Hurd, courtesy of University of Georgia Press.

LIBRARY OF CONGRESS CATALOGING-IN-PUBLICATION DATA
Names: Greene, Gayle, 1943– author.
Title: Missing persons : a memoir / Gayle Greene.
Description: Reno, Nevada : University of Nevada Press, [2017]
Identifiers: LCCN 2017005580 (print) | LCCN 2017041072 (e-book) | ISBN 978-1-943859-46-7 (pbk. : alk. paper) | ISBN 978-0-87417-646-9 (e-book) |
Subjects: LCSH: Greene, Gayle, 1943– | Greene, Gayle, 1943—Family. | Literary historians—United States—Biography. | Critics—United States—Biography. | Families—Psychological aspects. | Loss (Psychology) | Grief.
Classification: LCC PS29.G74 A3 2017 (print) | LCC PS29.G74 (e-book) | DDC 818/.603 [B] —dc23
LC record available at https://lccn.loc.gov/2017005580

The paper used in this book meets the requirements of American National Standard for Information Sciences—Permanence of Paper for Printed Library Materials, ANSI/NISO Z39.48-1992 (R2002).

FIRST PRINTING

Manufactured in the United States of America

Frontispiece: *1900 Foothills of Saratoga*, created by John O. Trucker. Courtesy of the San Jose Public Library.

To Janet Adelman

January 26, 1941–April 6, 2010

A friend who was family

And loss, after all, is mostly a story about what happens next.

—Barbara Hurd, *Walking the Wrack Line*

CONTENTS

MISSING PERSONS

MOTHER COUNTRY

Home is a place you grow up wanting to leave,
and grow old wanting to get back to.

—JOHN ED PEARCE

"WHAT NOW?" Sammy's question snaps me to.

We're at the picnic table out back, Sammy and Joey tucking into burgers and fries, me sipping coffee, not quite awake, gazing for what feels like the first time at my mother's garden. I swear I've never seen this garden before.

She planted that tree—as tall as that redwood is, that's how many years she lived in this house; it towers, two, three times taller than the house. A trumpet vine winds through the branches, lacing streaks of scarlet through dark, feathery green; a bird of paradise, bristly as a cockatoo, only oranger than a cockatoo, oranger than the oranges on the tree beside; purple lilies of the Nile ring a turquoise pool, and—good grief, a giant clam shell! Off of what wild barrier reef did she get *that*, and didn't there used to be a flamingo, can I be remembering right?—yes, a tall pink flamingo she placed so it was sipping from the shell. We thought it was so hokey, Billy and I, we made such fun of her for that, such wise-ass kids...

"Such a *dahling* woman, such a *lovely* disposition..." Sammy's voice jolts me back—*Mother,* is he talking about? No, Aunt Paddy. "Well, they're at rest now. Fortunate that they went together. Fortunate you were here." Of my mother he says, "I only wish she'd been happier. But you gave her a good death, you did that. Whatever else you did, you atoned."

Atoned? What the...fuck?

3

Dahling, he says, that exaggerated way theater people talk, *thee-ah-tah*. Sammy used to be in the theater, and he still does volunteer work for the little theater downtown, and for the Stanford VA, which is where he met Joey, a large lunky fellow messed up by Vietnam. What a pair—Sammy is thin, wiry, pert, wearing the red and orange Hawaiian shirt he wears always; Joey slouches in an oversized plaid work shirt, eyes swimming benignly behind thick glasses. "The Boys," Mother called them, though Sammy is eighty-five, nearly as old as she was. They've lived here, how long, twenty years, more, renting the back rooms, making do with a microwave oven and the bathroom sink.

They sit, munching french fries, smiling encouragement. My turn to speak.

What now?

I cast a baleful look at the house. There it stands, solid, implacable, and oh-so pink. *Sunset pink*, she called it, when she had it painted a few years ago. *Peptodismal pink*, corrected Keith, the good-humored, burly Brit from down the block, who she called on whenever something broke.

No answers there, only *things*. Things piled in closets, under beds, things stacked to the rafters of the garage, things stacked *on* the rafters of the garage. Everyone's things have landed here. This house is the end of the line. I am the end of the line. She warned me about this, or tried to, "such a small family," she'd mutter—as though I couldn't count, Paddy, her, me. Now me. As though it was my fault we'd come to this.

And the photographs, acres of photographs, on shelves, tables, sills, in boxes, drawers, trunks, achingly beautiful photos of old California, people whose names I don't even know. She and Paddy always meant to organize the photos, now it is left to me. I've sat in the house these days since they died, trying to sort out the photos, only I don't know what order they go in, when they were taken, or where. Or *why*.

Lake County, c. 1912. I think that's my grandmother in the dark dress; the kid next to the driver is my mother.

"How about a garage sale?" Sammy says.

"I dunno." Language has left me. How would I know what to sell, what to toss, what to pack up and take with me, and where to and what for? How would I know what any of this stuff is worth? These things so priceless and so worthless. This priceless junk.

This priceless irony. I was so eager to get away, I bolted out, barely seventeen, put a continent between us. Now it feels like I never got out, like there's been nothing between then and now—men I thought I loved, friends I thought were mine, courses taught, books I wrote, plenary lectures given in large, drafty hotel ballrooms...feels like none of it ever happened. I wore my professional identity like a magic cloak, a talisman against her, against being her. I wore it like a coat of mail. Plucked off me now like a shell off a snail.

Sammy clears the table, Joey gets up to move the hose to the orange tree. I should go in and deal with the photos. But it's good to sit out here, taking in the garden, scent of woodchips baking in the sun. I swear I've never looked at this garden before.

You would never in a million years recognize this place for the patch of dirt it once was. 1953, when we moved here, the yard, the house, the block were fresh hacked from an orchard. Los Altos had only the year before been made into a town. There were two apricot trees spared by the developer and a chicken wire fence between us and the orchard behind. I'd sit here and gaze through the chicken wire, imagine the whole of that orchard was our backyard, the earth, plowed in deep, loamy furrows, trees stretching far as the eye could see, branches bent with plump, velvety, pink-orange fruit.

We were the south end of town, toward Mountain View, with its poultry farms, vegetable patches, canneries, not the posh end, toward

...imagine the whole of that orchard was our backyard.

Palo Alto, and we were the wrong side of the tracks—there were still railroad tracks those days, they'd be torn up a decade later to make an expressway. A prune orchard at the end of the block kept the street closed to through traffic and there were no sidewalks, so it felt like a country lane. A path through the orchard led to my school, Loyola, where I was in sixth grade, and a block beyond that was the Rancho Market, where the BookMobile parked Saturdays, high point of my week. Probably nobody knows what a BookMobile is anymore. A van full of books that traveled around to out-of-the-way places, like this was then.

The *Valley of Heart's Delight*, it was called, a place so paradisiacal that people flocked from miles around to see the blossoms in the spring. First came the almonds, decked in white, then the peaches, pears, cherries, apricots, gossamer petals of the sheerest pink, then the plums, their scent so strong it wafted in through closed windows. In summer, apricots and prunes were laid out in long wooden trays to dry, orange and purple swaths against the dark, rich soil, and the pungence of fruit stewing, fruit canning, fruit drying filled the air, so the whole of the valley smelled sweet as our kitchen when Mother had a pie in the oven.

These images bubble up now like the juices in those pies, luscious, delicious, dripping with nostalgia. This was my world when I was a kid, a world I roamed freely by foot and bike, this and the little downtown a mile to the north, that had Clint's Ice Cream Parlor, Al's Barber Shop, a mom and pop hardware store, and Mac's Tea Room, the bar where my friends' mothers hung out.

For whom the valley was not such a delight.

Lost Altos, she called it. She was forty-six, I was ten, my brother Bill was five, my father having set up house with his Younger Woman, one of his younger women, in San Jose, eighteen miles south. He got his new life and he got us, too, near but not too near. Mother got us, a fragment of a family in a decade that centered on family. She got

Downtown Los Altos, 1954.

an allowance, a car, and the house, which he kept in his name. And the trap sprang shut.

Sundays he'd come up and they'd quarrel. His voice would go low and growly, hers would go shrill, my throat would get tight, I'd scuttle down the hall, slam my door, dive into a book. He was at her about the bills, though she spent nothing I could see, bought our clothes, furnished the house from the Salvation Army. She'd scream and rage and order him out of the house, out of her life—*slam* went the door, *screech* went his tires as he sped off into the night. She'd cry that she was headed for the loony bin, she wished she was dead, she'd kill herself, she would. Billy and I would try to calm her down, "Ah, Ma, please don't."

By Tuesday she'd stop crying. Then Sunday, he'd come up again.

She railed at the block, *dead end* like her life, swore she'd take us back to Miami, where we'd lived before. I'd stomp and yell, *no more moving!* Before Miami, there'd been San Jose, after Miami, San Jose again, and before that, Oakland, the Santa Cruz Mountains, Campbell. I'd gone to six schools in six grades—we'd moved enough!

She railed at the house, *such a small house, just like every other house in California.* A ranch style, like all the other houses on the block and for blocks around—two small bedrooms in the front, a larger bedroom to the rear, a bathroom at the end of the hall. A window above the sink let her look out while she did the dishes, though there was not much to look at: a patch of dirt trying to become a lawn, a twig my father planted, saying it'd be a cherry tree someday, a house across the street just like ours, where a lady lived who refused to speak to my mother because she was a divorcée (she wasn't, really, there was never a divorce). In 1950s suburbia, it seems, if you were a woman alone, people felt it was their business to make you feel more alone.

Nobody wants to know me, she'd say. At the time I thought she was being *paranoiac,* a word I was too young to know, but knew. Now I think probably nobody did want to know her. She was prettier than the other mothers, with her black hair, olive skin, and startling blue eyes. Not the Vivien Leigh sparkle I saw in the old photos but those same movie-star cheekbones, that unsettling smile, and a play of irony about her too-blue eyes that suggested more in her thoughts than was in her words—you never knew what she was thinking but you knew *that* she was thinking. She was far too attractive to be invited to the homes of the few married women she knew, and there were no single people in Los Altos, it seemed. She was nothing like the mothers we saw on our new TV: they wore pearls and high-heeled shoes and showed off sparkling dishes and spotless floors; she wore peasant blouses and a silver bracelet with a Mexican rose. And her appliances did not gleam—pots got banged, dishes got dropped, desultory dinners got shoved across the kitchen table, hamburgers, french fries, frozen peas, same thing every night.

The kitchen table was formica fabricated to look like wood; secondhand like everything else in the house, it tipped and wobbled on wrong-sized legs—put something down on that table, you might never see it again, it would disappear into a mulch of papers, bills, books. *Why can't you children pick up after yourselves, put things back where they belong?* she'd complain, and we'd laugh because she never did, and she'd try to look stern but her eyes betrayed her—she was never sufficiently on her own side to discipline us effectively. She'd sit at that table mornings, typing away at an old Underwood; a foot tall and gunmetal gray, it went "ding" at the end of each line, the "dings" coming faster as she rapped out letters to her congressman, the president, protesting the arms race, the Rosenberg executions, and later, Vietnam.

At the far end of the living room, where other mothers might have made a dining room, she put a grand piano, not a baby grand but a giant grand. The house rang with it, my ears rang, too, the great, rolling chords of Schumann, Rachmaninoff, Chopin, Liszt surrounded me as I stomped down the hall, slammed my door, dived into a book, but there was no shutting it out—it filled our small house with yearning, twining its tendrils through my heart, unspeakably sad, unspeakably beautiful, and the stronger it tugged, the harder I pulled to get away.

Head in a book, she'd yell, *come down to earth, join the human race, be a part of the real world.* I never believed her bit about *the real world,* couldn't see it had done much for her. *Escape,* she said my novels were, *an excuse for not being here.* Of course they were, that was their point. I read weekends and after school, on the school bus, in the back of the car, at the dentist's, at the dinner table, pausing only to turn the page. They took me twenty thousand leagues under the sea, to the center of the earth, to the snows of Kilimanjaro, *From Here to Eternity, East of Eden, Exodus...* anywhere but here.

She got up at dawn, I stayed up till dawn; she put on weight, I starved myself thin. She was fearful, fretful, and the more fretful she, the more foolhardy I. She was terrified of fast driving, I drove fast. The first thing I did with the little sports car my father loaned me was head over the hills to Half Moon Bay, up the coast to San Francisco, down to Santa Cruz, Carmel, Big Sur, as far away as I could and still get back by night.

Her rages were *operatic, histrionic*, words I was too young to know, but knew. One night, I looked up to see a pan of sudsy dishes hurtling across the room, crash, splat, it landed at the foot of the bed where I lay reading. *Brat, ungrateful brat, why can't you help around the house for a change, care about something besides yourself?* "Care about *me!*" is what I heard. She didn't make that easy.

You'd look so much prettier if you'd put on a skirt, stand up straight, get your hair out of your face.

Mother. Shut up!

Don't you dare use that language with me, young lady, don't you dare take that tone with me, we'll see what your father has to say...

My father. Much on my mind these past months, though for so long screened out. I wrote a story in high school from the point of view of a woman locked in a loony bin for killing her husband. I guess anger was easier than anything else I dared feel for this complicated man. But what dreams I had...a man, a woman, a child, we stand, holding hands, a family tableau, except that the man has no head and we are drenched in blood—we are missing our head, glued together by his blood. Yet I was pleased when people said I looked more like him than her. She was the beauty, he was *the doctor*—he got *out*. Is that why I became one? Not a *real* doctor, as he said—"in all the time it took to get that PhD, you could have become a *real* doctor." A doctor of English literature—what was *that*?

She hated New York, I moved to New York, the city he'd left behind. I fashioned a self as much like his as I could imagine. *Don't push yourself so hard*, she'd say; I pushed. *Never fall for a man*; I fell, and fell again. *Cruel*, I was, she said it often enough, and I guess I was; I kicked and clawed like a cornered creature, hacked my way out—but it was my life I was fighting for, or so I felt. And it may have been, given what happened to Bill. (Where would he have been, brother Bill, those shouting scenes, best not think; her shots were aimed at me, but shrapnel fell his way; but no, no thoughts of Bill.)

Sitting here now in my mother's garden, missing her so much, it's hard to remember what any of that was about. For there was that other mother, the mother I found at the kitchen table one morning, reading the words I'd copied out the night before: *When to the sessions of sweet silent thought, I summon up remembrance of things past...*I'd copied those words to feel what it felt like to write Shakespeare. "Oh, Gayley," she said (only she ever said my name so it sounded like *gaily*)—"that's beautiful! Did you write that?" That's my ma, I thought, she thinks I can do anything. The mother I overheard snap at a friend who dared criticize her daughter for not helping around the house: "She can learn to do dishes when she needs to, it doesn't really require a great deal of talent."

I could do no wrong, I could do no right. Contradiction was at the core of us, it seems anything I can say about her, I can say the opposite. The woman trapped in the house, mourning her unlived life, the woman who made the walls ring with music; she could be a black hole in her depression, she could be the buoyancy I counted on when I was down, and she could flip, one to the other, swift, sudden, no warning. The images I have of her, images are all I have of her, split, splinter, spin—how can I see anything through all these tears? The mother there in the voices in my head, she will always be there in the voices in my head—*you can't, you can't possibly, you can, you must*—so much a part of me that I'm afraid...

She is taking too much of me.

For it happened that, in the course of time—not sure exactly when, or how—that furious adolescent morphed into middle age, and my mother, the sting gone out of her, or mostly gone, took to making chicken soup and muffins. Aunt Paddy, well, she just went on being Paddy, but for Mother and me, what a transformation, a late-life rapprochement, a gift of age. And I found my way back. I'd drive down from Berkeley, my car full of books and papers, which I'd spread out on the long black table in the big front room, set up my laptop, set to work. And the times became longer times, and the house came to feel like…home.

So it was that on a day last summer, nearly a year ago, I was sitting at the kitchen table, the birds raucous in the cherry tree, sun flooding the kitchen. I was reading *The Making of the Atomic Bomb*, one eye on Mother as she backed the Cadillac out of the garage. She shot out the driveway in a puff of black smoke, clipping a garbage can, sending it clattering to the ground, then turned the long, low sedan and gunned it down the block.

She and Paddy were headed for a garage sale. That's where you'd find them summer mornings, bent over walking sticks (not all that bent for their eighty-eight and eighty-nine years), rummaging through shoes clothes pots pans waffle irons, the detritus of decades, other people's decades. From a distance, you'd take them for twins, with their poodle wigs and bright polyester blouses. Up close, you'd see differences: Paddy, paler, stouter, looked older, though she was younger by a year and a half.

Agnes and *Paddy*. The Paterson sisters. Greenberg and Greenspoon. They both married men named *Jack*, Jack Greenberg and Jack Greenspoon, strange congruences of the sisters' lives. Paddy lived in a retirement inn near San Jose, where she moved when her Jack died a decade or so before. Mother, still here, this house become her house since my father died a few years back; this house become a handsome property, what with the fortunes of the valley and the rooms added on, which she rented to The Boys (though she had to go back to *Greenberg* to inherit—she'd changed our name to Greene when they split up).

I wandered out to the street to set the garbage can upright, wondering vaguely if she ought still to be driving. The traffic's got so bad. This is not the *Valley of Heart's Delight* anymore—*Silicon Valley* is what it's called today. Each time I come back, I run a red light that wasn't there before, I get lost on a road newly dead-ended into a freeway embankment, a cloverleaf dumps me somewhere I have never been, I lose all sense of direction in the maze of highways and expressways. Now eight lanes of hissing asphalt rip through the hills where I once rode a horse and Apple Computer stands on the patch of ground where Paddy's Poodle Rancho used to be.

Nah, she'll be okay, I'd tell myself, dragging the garbage can out of range. She has these amazing routes all around town, knows how to get anywhere making only right turns.

I glanced up the block at the hills, the Santa Cruz Mountains that border the valley on the ocean side, fog on their crests like a shaggy silver crown. The park at the end of the street where the or-chard used to be keeps the block closed to through traffic, making it an enclave where trees and foliage flourish, full, lush, fragrant. Two lacey willows fringe our front yard, and the twig my father planted has become a cherry tree that arches over house and lawn, its branches heavy with heart-shaped, pinkish-gold fruit, cherries more succulent than a supermarket ever sold.

I filled my pockets with cherries, wandered back to the kitchen, back to *The Making of the Atomic Bomb*. I was a long time reading, when the scrunch of tires brought me to, and there they were, strug-gling out of the car with shopping bags from Andronico's, the new yuppie supermarket that stands where the Rancho Market used to be. I help them unload—"What's this?"—a jumbo sack of potato chips, a salami, a packet of cupcakes frosted in day-glo pink—"Jeez, you guys are living proof—eat junk and live long!"

My mother had been remarkably healthy all her life, though she'd been complaining lately that her joints ached so badly she couldn't play the piano. I'd remind her that she was, after all, nearly ninety and took no medications, though even I couldn't help notic-ing how bony she'd become, and that swollen stomach she said was a failing liver from the hepatitis she'd had decades before. She swore it'd be the death of her, I assured her she'd outlive it. *"Outlive a liver?"* she'd say. "Ha! Nobody outlives a liver—you'll see," but she'd said it so often it lost its sting. And there was Paddy, who'd had a bypass a few years before, slathering mayonnaise on her sandwich—I grabbed the jar, she grabbed it back. "Humph!" she snorted, "I made it all the way to eighty-one with that fat in my arteries, had a marvelous time putting it there, and I'd do it again, by god. I know," she said, giving me a wicked wink, "I'm on borrowed time. Aren't we all?"

Borrowed time. It was a thing she said—*we are all of us only ever on borrowed time.* Paddy, the younger sister, the sibling in the shadow—Mother got the good looks, Paddy got the good nature, it was said, though beneath that sweetness lay an iron will. Before Poodle Rancho, she'd worked at the Soviet Embassy and sung lead roles in Gilbert and Sullivan. "Never tell her I told you," Mother told me, whispering it even as we sat at the kitchen table, "your aunt was a member of the *Communist* Party. She had visits from the FBI." So many secrets in our family, things we were supposed not to know, not really secret, only secret from each other that we knew.

So we sat at the kitchen table, my aunt and mother tucking into their sandwiches, me nibbling cherries, and I'd thank god or whatever it is that makes stuff happen, for long life, and thank time, that takes away but sometimes tosses back, that we had time to come to this, the three of us at the kitchen table, no longer chafing to be somewhere else. For the years covered the scars with forgetful snow, not all of them, of course, not the gash left by my brother, not that smoking hole—that, there was no forgetting or forgiving. Mother was seventy-two when he took his life. I don't know how she survived it, but she did. We the women, we came through.

They nattered on about the garage sale, about the outrage of health care, terrible injustices, right here in the valley—homeless sleep under freeway ramps, we never had homeless before, monster mansions going up, right here on this block, obscene...They stayed tuned to these late-night talk radio shows, which kept them remarkably well informed and indignant. They chatted on about their ailments, their remedies, their doctors, some of whom they knew from the days my father had his practice in San Jose. They had enlightened views about assisted suicide, there were living wills and no-nonsense instructions written down somewhere, I didn't know where, didn't want to know.

"I'm not afraid of death," said my mother, reaching for a potato chip. "I think of the year 1906—how did I feel in 1906?" (She was born in 1907.) "Well, that's how I'll feel once I'm gone." I took her at her word, being a firm believer in denial where death is concerned.

So here I sit, in my mother's garden, watching a squirrel leap from the redwood tree onto the house, thunk and scuttle of squirrel on roof, amazed at my powers of denial. How could I not have heard the sadness in their voices as they told me of friends who had died, of parts of their bodies that were aching and failing, how could I not have prepared…planned…something? And how could I not have worried that I still thought of this as *home?*

Denial. The failure to imagine. The need *not* to imagine.

My friends, all two who have driven down from Berkeley, say *get out, go on home.* But I don't trust myself to drive—distances feel different, the sky seems too high, like the roof's been ripped away, everything exposed, this deep disorientation about where things are. I'm not sure where *home* is. My house in Berkeley? a way station I used to repack on my way somewhere else, and the woman who lived there, a stranger to me now. Here is where I remember, here is all I have ever been.

I decide to get up, I sit rooted to the spot, spellbound in a fantastical garden. Sammy's raking the leaves, Joey scooping them into the wheelbarrow, it goes on. I stare at the house, it stares back, its long plate glass window reflects the purple lilies of the Nile, the turquoise pool, a bronze-green Buddha in the bamboo. How can it be standing there so sure and firm? it feels like it's tumbled down around my ears.

But no, it's not the house that has toppled, it's my own walls that have fallen, crumbled like clapboard in a lava flow. *Slow down*, she'd say, my father said that too, *you're going to really hurt yourself someday if you don't slow down.*

So now I've slowed down. Ground to a halt. Now what?

I make myself get up, wander into the house—how can it be so empty yet so full of things? I sit down to the long black table by the window where I used to work. It is covered with photos. A trim, white-haired man in a three-piece suit, the sepia so faded I can barely make his features out, formal and distant and from another age. A girl in bloomers and a rakish hat stands, bold on a boulder in a rushing stream. Two little girls astride a horse, two little girls peer coyly from behind fans, gazing into a future now turned to dust.

Two little girls sit astride a horse.

A California story.

Who *are* these people? I never asked, and they never offered. They came west to leave the past behind—that's why people come to California, to leave it all behind. *A California story.*

Where to begin? The story of a life makes a kind of sense when your mother's there to know it. But when she dies, the narrative threads unravel, the self itself's undone, for there can be no self without a story, no story of a life that makes a life make sense. When a family dies, all stories end. No family now to help me through, no faith, not a shred. Oh god, I'd like a god right now, any god would do.

I stare at the faces for a clue to the people gone missing. I see it's not just their lives gone missing, it's my own.

ENDING

And what would comfort be?

—ADRIENNE RICH, "In the Wake of Home"

THE VOICE ON MY PHONE MACHINE is nervous, raspy, an old man's voice. "Gayle, this is Sammy. Call when you get in." A second message: "Gayle, are you there?" And a third: "Please call."

When? He doesn't say. Yesterday? Last week? I've been gone two weeks, finishing the semester at the college where I teach. I look at my watch, it's midnight, I phone anyway, I can tell I woke him up, though he says no—he doesn't know what it was, he wasn't with her when it happened, she started shaking all over, convulsive-like, could hardly dial the phone to call Reggie from next door. She's better now, we found a walker in the garage, she's getting around on that, but she's weak, I should come down.

I ask him what he thinks it is; he repeats, he doesn't know—"just come." I need him to tell me she'll be okay, though I know it's not the point, what Sammy says. "But she's better, you say. I'll be down in a few days."

"I dunno," he says, doubtful.

I get off the phone and sink into a chair—not now, please not now, this can't be happening, I can't deal with it now. I haven't slept in my own bed for weeks, my tooth is throbbing, I need a dentist. I've been feeling lately that this way I live is not sustainable, teaching in southern California, living in northern California, Mother an hour south of where I live, Bob, the new man in my life, three and a half hours north, in Mendocino, crazy, this far-flung geography, and did it just happen or did I somehow make it happen, so nobody gets hold of me—please, please just a few more days, not now.

In the morning, I get her on the phone. Yes, she's okay; yes, she had a spell; no, she doesn't know what it was, but she was shaking so badly she could barely dial the phone; no, no need to come right away, Sammy will drive her to the doctor. I can tell she's being brave, but I need to believe her, so I do.

I hang up, the phone rings.

Sammy: "Gayle, get down here."

"But she said…"

"Just *come!*"

It is evening by the time I get on the road, 880 south through Oakland, the same freeway I drove up from the airport the night before, narrow lanes, nasty, blight on both sides, but better not risk the Bay Bridge through San Francisco with its colossal snarls. So much traffic, I mutter, darting in and out between the SUVs and killer trucks that grind close on my tail, hiked up high, and mean.

I turn onto our street—Christmas on Clinton Road, a splash of twinkling lights, white lights and red lights, blue, green, and purple lights, lights looped like icicles over hedges, houses, trees, reindeers on rooftops with blinking red nose lights. Ours is the only house that has no lights, only a gold glow through Mother's bedroom drape.

Her drape is open a crack. I tiptoe to the window, peer in. She is lying on her bed, propped up on pillows, hair thin and white, face pale and shrunk, her eyes blank and sad, so sad, just lying there, not reading or watching TV, not like her at all. I let myself in the front door—"Hi, Ma." "Oh, Gayley, is that you?" surprise in her voice, and relief, I can hear. But she doesn't get up—usually she gets up, no matter how late, sits at the kitchen table while I haul in suitcases and supplies. "Your life as a *peripatetic* scholar," she'd say, clearing a shelf for me in the refrigerator, enjoying an opportunity to show off one of her big words, and we'd sit and chat, sometimes till dawn. Not to-night. I find a chair and draw it up to her bed, shoving aside the commode, which—I notice—has become a regular fixture in the room.

"I came down early."

"That's nice, Gayley," she says, still not offering to get up.

I haven't seen her for a month, but I see now: her stomach is huge, her legs swollen, her cheeks flushed, not a healthy flush. She says she's tired, so I leave her and unpack the car—no, this way of life is not sustainable—all the while there's a clamoring in my head, that's not her stomach, that swelling, that's her liver, she always said it would kill her, I didn't believe…this can't be happening…she'll pull herself together, she can do it, she always has, she can do it now. I need her to pull herself together, I need her to be…my mother.

And there's a small, mean voice, *no, not again,* her needs, her claims, *please don't clutch,* sucking me back, *I'm unhappy, fix it, you could fix it if you would,* pulling me under. *Fix it yourself!* I'd snap, *get a grip,* and usually she could. I have a mad impulse to say it now, but it's lunatic now—*dammit,* you *get a grip,* I say to myself. *You're* the grown-up, *act like a grown-up.*

I will, I will. *But the book,* comes a wail, I'm so close to finishing the book, I've been pushing so hard to get it done. Alice Stewart, the crusty old anti-nuclear warrior whose story I'm writing—I need to get it written while she's still alive, while I can still read my notes, remember the interviews I did last summer, all those books I read on radiation science, the nuclear industry, it'll all fly out of my head if I don't get it down. I've been saying, whenever somebody tells me I'm working too hard, that writing the biography of a ninety-year-old woman gives meaning to the word *deadline.* But it's not just Alice's story that's at stake, there's so much of me invested in this book, this story that has weight in the world, politics, science, power, so much more heft than anything I've written. Now I see, *this* is the real deadline, this story unfolding here.

Please let her hang in there till I can deal with this. Yeah, right, comes another voice, and when do you think *that* might be?

So I take over the shopping, cooking, errands. We try to pretend it's a lark that I came down early, make like a holiday, though we're both terrified in an unspoken way, *nobody outlives a liver.*

Christmas morning, Paddy arrives, bearing food. Mother has told her not to bother with dinner, but as in most clashes between the sisters, my aunt prevails. My dog Nellie goes into sheepdog paroxysms at Paddy's arrival, barking and running circles around her until she has to sit down or be knocked down. Paddy adores Nellie, sneaks her scraps from the table; Mother, not so delighted to have this ninety-pound woolly mammoth leaping about, looks on, exasperated, amused. I think she's resigned herself to Nellie as the closest she'll have to a grandchild, but I see that wry look of hers, and I'm not sure. "Sit!" commands Mother, then scolds, "Look at that coat of yours—looks like something you slept in!"

"Well, what *else* am I supposed to sleep in?" says Paddy, speaking for Nellie. I breathe a silent thanks for that moment, Nellie, the genius of comic relief. I leash her to the doorknob, out of harm's way.

Paddy sets about fixing the meal, moving slowly, deliberately, refusing offers of help. It is reassuring, the way she makes her way around the kitchen, pouring maraschino cherries into green liquid jello, layering marshmallows onto sweet potatoes. Sammy and Joey are out back, sweeping the patio, raking the leaves; they drag the garbage can through the side gate to the front, always managing to leave it where Mother will clip it with the Cadillac. Ever busy, eager to help, I don't think she ever raised their rent. But they're more than renters by now; this is their home.

My odd little family, my odd and original yet strangely *functional* family, far more functional than the family I grew up in.

Before the boys come in, Paddy and Mother and I exchange gifts. Mother looks puzzled at the present I give her, a set of no-stick pots and pans. I didn't think it was such a great idea, either. It was Paddy's idea, she said a set of matching cookware might cheer her up, but it is so clearly not what we'll be needing. Mother shuffles to her bedroom and back on swollen legs, returning with a string of pearls. "These were given me by my father," she says, "or was it your father? maybe these were the pearls Jack gave me. Well, never mind—now

My odd and original yet strangely functional family…Sammy and Keith.

they're yours." She moves around the kitchen slowly, her stomach so swollen that her nubby white cardigan won't stay buttoned, Paddy and I trying not to meet each other's eyes. "The other pearls," she tells Paddy, "will be yours when I die."

"Shh, shh, not for a while yet," clucks Paddy.

Sammy and Joey arrive, Paddy produces dinner, nobody has much of an appetite, all of us casting about for something to talk about besides Mother's health.

Paddy sleeps over that night. This is new. My aunt never stays over, has a thing about not staying over, told me she'd never live with her sister, they'd tried that once, twice, never again. Close, the sisters are, and rivalrous, as only the closest can be. Born without a mean bone in her body, it is said of Paddy. Maybe she was born that way, maybe she cultivated sweetness as a way of claiming ground against a beautiful, overbearing elder sister, I don't know, but she is easy in a way Mother is not. "Your aunt steals all the love," Mother would say, as though there's never enough to go around; maybe there never is. Twisted into strange knots, the family ties.

So Paddy's staying over tells me, this is serious.

I try to get her to take my bed but she insists she breathes easier sitting up, the big chair in the front room suits her fine. Stubborn she is, Mother always said her little sister is the stubbornest person alive, and I see that short of picking her up and physically transporting her, there'd be no way I'd get her to sleep in my room. So I leave her dozing in the big chair and go to my room, the chatter and jabber of late-night talk shows following me down the hall—*You're on, Burlingame, Ritchie from San Leandro, you're on the air.*

I am used to the sound of these talk shows, Mother has them on all night, but this night she and Paddy land on different stations and there comes a cacophony, like a cackling of voices from outer space clamoring to get back to earth. I get up to shut my door, when suddenly I hear a different sound, O *Holy Night, the angels are all singing*—they've tuned in the same station, it must be heaven they've tuned in, only a choir of angels could sing like that; except nobody in this house believes in angels. I stand, transfixed, transported to a moment when *all is calm, all is bright,* a dream of a Christmas that never was, not with us, no heavenly hosts here. From down the hall, the kitchen lamp casts a purplish glow, and I am back...where? The three of us haven't slept under the same roof since I was a child—to when I was a child, then, a stab of longing, of premonition, and I think, this is what I'll remember as I lie dying, this will be my light at the end of the tunnel, the gleam at the end of the hall and my mother and aunt, *sleep in heavenly peace.*

Later, I leash Nellie for a walk. As I tiptoe past Paddy sleeping in the chair, she raises her head and smiles, an old crone's smile, sweet as that song—how old she looks without her teeth and wig, how'd she get so old?

Oh god, I'm all they've got. They're all I've got.

I am trying to get things under control, only three weeks before school starts again, three weeks to get things back to where they were so Mother can carry on. But there is no getting hold of this situation— Christmas dinner has brought on uncontrollable runs—there is not even any talking about the situation, *nobody outlives a liver.*

Mother needs to see her liver specialist, but for this to happen, I need to figure out the New Health Plan she's got herself onto. It is cunning, how complicated it's been made: we need a referral from her primary caregiver, Dr. Goldstein; the referral has to be okayed by the insurance company, then sent back to Goldstein, who will forward it to Dr. Landers, the liver man—then she can make an appointment. Or at least that's the way I think it works.

So we go see Goldstein. I drive round and round the parking lot till a space opens up near his office, help Mother out of the car, hand her her cane, hold the umbrella over her. The sidewalk is slick, she leans heavily on my arm, we inch along, Aunt Paddy drawing up the rear, toting our purses. All heads turn as we clatter into the waiting room, two ancient ladies in bright flowery blouses and poodle wigs, fumbling with walking sticks and umbrellas. Paddy digs into her handbag, produces a list of questions written in her elegant, old-fashioned hand.

Goldstein's office is thronging with people, secretaries, nurses, patients, a receptionist directing the flow, phones ringing off the hook, feels like an empire he's got going here. He greets Mother with an effusive show—"Hello, Aggie, how *are* you? But Aggie, you look terrible, how'd you let this happen?" trying to make a joke of it, he always *did* charm her, she never could resist a bedside manner (quaint term—do doctors even visit bedsides anymore?) Yes, of course, he'll send a referral.

But Landers never gets the referral, Goldstein doesn't return my calls, and when I finally reach a human being at the New Health Plan, she's as bewildered as I am about how it all works.

Finally, we get in to see Landers. He prescribes a battery of drugs that take the swelling down but take Mother down, too, make her sleep all day. I think we should cut the doses in half, but I've been told these meds are tricky, must be kept in balance, I need advice. I call Landers, who, to my surprise, calls back. Mother picks up the phone out of a drugged sleep. "Hello, this is Agnes Greenberg"; then she says it again, still not quite awake, "Hello, this is Agnes Greenberg." "Well, I don't have all day," he huffs. When I cough to let him know I'm on the line, his tone turns polite, but I am shocked—this is a doctor who knew my father when he had his practice, Mother spoke of him so warmly. Then he can't seem to understand what I'm asking, like it's so complicated, reducing the dose; seems like he's not trying very hard.

Abandoned doesn't begin to describe the feeling of these days. Did I imagine all doctors were like my father, an old-style doctor who'd be at a patient's side in a flash; I guess I did. This longing for my father surprises me.

Mother, I see, is not dealing with the medications. She forgets to take her pills, then takes too many, then can't remember if she's taken any at all. I tell myself, it's just that she's never approved of medications, that's why she forgets; but then I see, she is really not dealing with this. It takes me awhile to take this in. This is the moment, the moment you dread, when you realize you can no longer count on a parent to be competent. You understand, she will never return to that place in the universe you counted on her to fill, could count on because she was your mother. I see. I'm the parent now, I who have never been a parent and don't know how.

So I try to make a game of it. I buy envelopes and a giant box of crayons. I draw, MONDAY MORNING, a big, smiley yellow sun for morning meds; MONDAY AFTERNOON, a drooping purple flower; MONDAY NIGHT, a silvery moon in a dark blue sky—and so on for a month of medications. Mother chuckles at my lopsided suns and moons and implausible flowers—"Oh, Gayley, you used to be such a *good* little artist—what happened?" The rainbow of bright colors, the waxy, crayola smell, take me back—I could be a kid again, sitting at the kitchen table, scribbling away.

But kid time is over, and so is winter break over, and I have nothing in place.

The last day I can be here before school starts again, I drive her to the hospital. There's been blood in her stool, they've scheduled a test. I stand by her side, holding her hand, watching the screen as the tube makes its way down into her body, poking, probing. She endures this indignity like a little lamb. When it's finished, she lies, sedated on the gurney, curled on her side. I stand, holding her hand, waiting for her to come around, and such sadness floods me that I have to sit down, and such guilt. I'd been awful that morning. I'd timed my sleeping pill to the alarm, but she didn't trust me to wake up, she shook me out of a deep sleep before I needed to be awake, putting me into a grog and a grump for the whole day, her anxiety feeding my anxiety, making it worse, it always did; I'd snapped at her, then the guilt.

Landers beckons me outside into the hall. "Listen, we have to talk," he says, leaning against the wall, crossing his arms. I have a mad urge to punch him out, paunchy, pasty-faced little man, so he can't say what's coming next. "There are lesions, something bad is going to happen—I don't know what or when."

"I know," I say. I do not know, really, I have no idea what a lesion has to do with a liver, but I'm not eager for details and he's not eager to give them; we both know, *nobody outlives a liver.*

"What did they find?" says Mother, coming out of the sedative, placing her hand in mine, her fingers frail as bird bones that once moved so strong and sure on the piano.

"Oh, a few lesions, nothing much." But I know she can see, even with her old eyes, the tears I can't keep back.

I am trying to hold things together till spring break, to make it through February, the first weeks of March…

I fly down to southern California Tuesdays, I teach Tuesday, Wednesday, Thursday, fly back Thursday night, drive down to Los

Altos. Down and back, back and down, sleep or no sleep, brain or no brain, I slog on.

Mother is trying to be good, trying to remember to take the pills in the envelopes marked with suns, moons, and flowers, to eat only the unsalted rice and vegetables I leave for her. Valiant and plucky, she is—on the good days, that is; not all are good.

One Friday, I reel in and find Paddy at the sink doing dishes, Mother at the kitchen table muttering, "Can't you hurry it up? 'Slow as molasses, slow as molasses,' that's what Mother said you were." Oh, no, this can't be happening—"Mother!" I snap, school-marm stern, "that's no way to talk!" Silence in the kitchen. Mother looks chastened, Paddy looks grim, her jaw set, she stabs at a pot.

"Why does she say such hateful things—she has, all her life," Paddy grumbles, as I drive her home that night. "I can't clean up those messes. She belongs in a home. People like that belong in a home." *People like that*—she is furious. No, please, not a home, but then, I haven't been the one to clean up the messes.

"I don't think she realizes how hurtful she can be," I say, springing to Mother's defense, our roles reversing. Paddy has always been so protective of my mother, would never let me speak a word against her. "I know, but my mother used to wonder, too, who she took after..." She is breaking the silence of a lifetime, beginning a conversation I'd like to have—what is it about Mother, can you tell me, help me understand? I would like to ask, but there is too much pressing for us to stop and look at the past.

Infirmity isn't bringing out the best in her, that's sure. Gone is the lively lady so full of interest who'd sit chatting with me at the kitchen table till dawn. We talked about...me, mainly, I guess it was me we talked about, my teaching, my trophies, my troubles, my love life; it was assumed by both of us that my happiness was her happiness. But no, we'd talk about her, too, her friends, the neighbors, her ailments, and if she was in the dumps I could jolly her out of them, or so I thought. Or so she let me think. She'd tell me about

We'd sit and chat, sometimes till dawn.

things she heard on the radio, the boys coming back from Vietnam, the Gulf War—"they're in terrible shape, the boys, the government isn't owning up"—underground knowledge gleaned from those late-night shows.

Now there is only her liver, her symptoms, her anxieties. She has no more care for the world's problems, or for mine.

We reel on through January and February. I make it to Los Altos every weekend but two.

One of those weekends, Bob comes down from Mendocino. He pulls up to my house around 3:00 AM, dazed from hours on the road. Bob, the new man in my life, not so new actually, we're a few years old; in fact, we seem lately to have settled into being a couple. What started out with the *sturm* and *drang* I've always confused with love has smoothed into a taken-for-granted sort of thing, welcome after the drama in my life. His hair is long—he's been months up the coast. "You look like Nellie," I say, tousling his shaggy head. "You moving out, or in?" he says, stumbling over a backpack as he steps in the door to give me a hug, widening his eyes at the mess of books and papers on the stairs. We've done okay on the phone, we're used to time apart, we talk every night; but now I remember how I love looking at his face, it's like looking at a fire, playful, interesting, intense—his mind's like that, too, full of play. He's tall, hollow-cheeked, an Abe-Lincoln kind of angularity, sensitivity etched into the lines of his face.

He has news, his landlord is selling his house—not good news, that storybook house of his by the sea, soon not to be his house. There is, of course, this house in Berkeley, he could move in here with me, this small workaday house left me by Uncle Ted, but we neither of us leap at this—there's barely room for me here, a bedroom for sleep, a bedroom for work. I can't drag him in to what's going on with Mother, he'd be no good at it, he doesn't even know her, I'd have him to worry about and her, too. I'm not sure we'd survive his living here. I need us to survive.

We spend the weekend talking about what to do. There's a place he can go, an old farmhouse in a remote corner of France, empty for the next few months, a place he can work. He's desperate to get hold of a software project he's just begun, all that stands between him and penury—if he loses his work, he loses himself, I know how that goes. I am desolate at the thought of his being so far away, I try not to let it show—*act like a grown-up, if you can't feel like a grown-up,* I tell myself. It's the sort of thing I tell students—act the way you'd like yourself to be and you may actually begin to *be* that way. Nice idea, sometimes it even works.

I say nothing to Mother about his coming down. I tell her I spent the weekend working, which is pretty much what we do, he at the dining room table staring into a computer, me in my study staring into a computer, but then I feel guilty, then resentful at the guilt, then guilty at the resentment, then confused—surely I have a right to this much to myself.

The other weekend I don't go to Mother's, I fly to Denver to meet Alice Stewart, who is there testifying against the Rocky Flats nuclear facility. Alice, whose biography I've been trying to write, is my hero. She discovered, in the 1950s, that if you x-ray pregnant women, as doctors did those days, you double the risk of a childhood cancer—for which she was demoted, defunded, defamed. Nobody wanted to hear the bad news about radiation, especially not the physicians, who went right on x-raying pregnant women. Alice dug in her heels and spent the next twenty years proving her case—which is why doctors don't do fetal X-rays anymore. Then when she was in her seventies, she was called in on a study at Hanford, the facility that produced plutonium for the Nagasaki and Trinity bombs, where she discovered that the cancer risk to nuclear workers was about twenty times higher than was being claimed; this made her anathema to the nuclear industry and the governments of the US and UK—though it made her a hero of the anti-nuclear movement.

I would like to be like Alice, living a life of derring-do, flying around, taking courageous stands. I would like to have a mother like Alice, and I've probably let that show, boring everyone into a stupor with my nonstop talk about Alice. But whatever jealousy Mother has felt, she's kept a lid on—in fact, she's been keen on this book. I think she's seen my efforts to rescue an unknown woman from obscurity, a woman as old as she, as a sort of gallantry.

Denver sounds easy, since usually I have to travel to England to see Alice, but it's not. The flight is delayed, my friend can't meet me, he loans me an old VW bug that has a hole in the floor through which the road is alarmingly visible, though it's barely visible through the windshield, what with the blizzard and the wipers not working. When I finally get to where Alice is staying, there are reporters and lawyers buzzing around—it's always a circus with Alice, people vying for her attention, me angling for a few uninterrupted moments: Was the radiation risk greater or lesser than…? How did the Department of Energy respond to that…? Did the new Hanford study find a publisher…? I jot down notes in a spidery scrawl that I hope I'll be able to decipher at some future time, stash the notes in a folder I hope I'll be able to find, so I can write it up later, making it read, making it real, making it matter, this strange, satisfying shaping that makes a book.

That weekend, I do tell Mother about, though I still can't shake the guilt, a load she lightens, however, when she lashes out, "you'd better get down and take care of business here—it's worth more to you than anything that'll come of that book of yours." Damn—why *does* she say such things? I thought she was on my side with this, then she comes out with that—get back here where you belong, here is what matters, *I* am all that matters. I bristle and get off the phone.

But maybe she's right, maybe I should not leave her side at a time like this, I don't know what's right, what's *my* right, what's her right, I never have known my rights from hers.

Why, I ask myself, don't I ask for the term off? Well, it's not so easy to find someone to take over a course, once it's set up. C'mon, Gayle, people take over other people's classes all the time, you're not irreplaceable. The truth is, work is how I know I exist, it has always been, but especially now, work is how I know it's not me dying in this house—if I lose it, I lose myself, if I lose myself, I won't be able to deal with what is happening here. Or so I tell myself.

We make it to spring break. I do the usual mad dash down the 880, rushing to avoid the rush, to find Mom and Paddy at the kitchen table, dressed for the doctor's. Mother has on a red and purple flowered blouse, rakishly off-shoulder, a painfully sharp shoulder blade poking through—gads, has she lost more weight? "You see?" she says, seeing my dismay, is that triumph in her voice, or am I imagining, *I told you I am dying, have been telling you all along…* "Well, Gayle, I suppose I'm interfering with your trip to Mendocino. You know, you have to deal with this only once—you have the rest of your life to go to Mendocino."

Bull's-eye, nail on the head, nail through the heart—she does have a way of saying things. But she's wrong, there won't be a way back to Mendocino, to that house of Bob's by the sea, soon not to be his. I'll never get out of here—you've won, you've got me back. I am, as a matter of fact, holding a hope of getting to Mendocino at the end of spring break; I keep this to myself.

I drive her to Dr. Landers, help her and Paddy out of the car, we edge down the long slippery walk. Mother is chipper, the doctor will find out what is wrong, the doctor will fix it, that touching confidence she has in doctors, you'd think she'd know better, having been married to one. I go into the examination room with her, Landers looks her over, avoids my eyes. What *can* they be thinking, I know he's thinking; but we can't not do this, we have to go through this, for hope, for the fiction of hope. "Nothing new," he says. He'll have a nurse assigned to us, to check in from time to time.

"Oh, how nice to be out, how long it's been since I've been out, how lovely the blossoms," says Mother, as we drive past a row of plum trees in bloom, pink, woolly puffs against the winter sky. "Can we take the long way home, see if the old apricot orchard is in bloom?" So we drive past the vacant lot that still has trees. She used to know how to get all the way to San Jose on back roads, had elaborate routes through the orchards, knew which trees were bearing what, and when. We'd pull over to the side of the road, the cherries plums apricots yielded, warm and dusty to the touch, we'd pick bag after bag, more than we could eat, she'd put up preserves, the big glass jars bubbling fiercely in vats of boiling water, she'd line them up on the counter to cool, the lids went *pop*, scent of sugar and fruit flood the house, ambrosial.

But now there are no blossoms, only bare black twigs against a darkening sky.

That night, I am preparing for classes in the living room, when the phone rings and I can tell it's Paddy. The two of them talk two or three times a day, Mother propped on her bed, legs crossed at the ankles (still shapely legs, when the swelling goes down). "Yes," I hear her say, "yes, that's wonderful, dear, yes, that would work—well, bless your heart," and I know, before she gets off the phone, that my aunt has offered to move in. What a relief—now they can be together and I can stop shuttling between here and San Jose, Paddy can be here to oversee, we'll get someone in to help…we'll make do.

What a bail-out, what a reprieve—what a champ Aunt Paddy is!

I call her right away: "But, Paddy, you are taking my room—no argument." She agrees. She says she had a hard time making this decision. "I never thought it would come to this, but changed circumstances mean changed plans." It's a big deal for her to move in—she likes it where she is. She has a life at the retirement inn, responsibilities; when somebody fails to show for a meal, she checks up to make sure they're okay. There's a garden and a duck pond, she feeds the ducks.

She asks me if there'll be room for her desk and books. I assure her I'll make space; though how, I do not know.

I set about clearing out my room, the room that's been mine since I was a kid, the room I shared with Pick-Pocket Pete, a little black poodle named for his skill at nuzzling kleenexes out of pockets. A small room, a corner room that looks out on willows and plum trees. My junior high school self lay here, scribbling in diaries and reading *My Friend Flicka*, *Black Beauty*, and every Black Stallion novel and Laddie and Lassie novel ever written. My high school self lay here, reading *Gone with the Wind*, *Look Homeward, Angel*, *You Can't Go Home Again*, and later, *Wuthering Heights*, *Madame Bovary*, *Anna Karenina*.

Here I lay, eighteen and broken-hearted, thought I'd never recover from that breakup—tall, handsome David, first love, loomed as large in my adolescent imagination as his father's plant loomed over the valley, that huge Hewlett-Packard plant on the edge of the Stanford campus. I had no idea what they did there, could not have imagined that what they were doing was even then transforming the valley, I knew only that David was gorgeous and wildly funny. He'd sing Tom Lehrer songs as we drove to the Sierras, and one time, he recited the entire first act of *Julius Caesar*; we tossed sleeping bags down on a field in Tuolumne Meadows, spent the night. Here was the prince who might kiss me awake, and I did need that magic kiss, oh how I needed it—without it, I was nobody, with it, I might be somebody, somebody I could not imagine being on my own.

And a decade later, I came home for the summer from New York, crash-landed from another breakup, heart heavy as the Renaissance tomes I'd hauled across country, massively blocked on the dissertation I was supposed to be writing. I was taking the books out of boxes, a sinking feeling, all this work to get through, how can I possibly, when I came across a paper I'd written on... *Julius Caesar*. Not the subject I was supposed to be writing about, but I thought, maybe I can turn this into an article, and I sat down and started tinkering, and when I looked up, the shadows were long, and I knew I'd be okay, I can work. Next day, Mother took me downtown to the new typewriter store, bought me a state-of-the-art Smith Corona electric, portable so I could carry it back to New York, and by the end of summer, the paper had grown into a dissertation, and by spring I was sprung from Columbia, a newly minted, unemployed PhD.

Work is my friend is an insight I trace to this room, to that day in June. Work is the way I know I am not my mother, work is the way I can come back to be with my mother, my mother and my work, so at odds yet so oddly intertwined. Work turned out to be my way in the world, not David or Michael or Edward, or any man. It seems an idyll now, that summer day so long ago, though of course it was no idyll then—I was anxious about that dissertation, about getting a job, and ambivalent, as always, about being home with Mother. But it takes me away to think about it now, and away is where I want to be, away from the moans and bedsprings creaking through the wall.

I turn to the chest of drawers, they're crammed with things. A baby's hospital bracelet, *William Greenberg* in tiny blue alphabet beads, it pains me to see that name of a brother I once had. What must she have felt, tucking these beads into the drawer, I have never dared imagine her sorrow, I walled off her pain along with my own— how, really, did she survive? *Greenberg* was my name too, when I was a kid. She didn't want my father's name, didn't want us to have it, didn't dare push for a divorce, but she could ditch the name, a way of denying his part in us, I guess. And here's a photo of her and Billy on a cruise in the Bahamas, where she picked up the hepatitis that lodged in her liver—one of the few trips she ever took, and look how she paid. There they are in silly party hats, he no longer a boy but not quite a man, she no longer young but not old, *old and ugly*, she said she was, *ugly and old*, but she's not ugly in this photo, and not old, well, no older than…I am now, I realize with a start.

Grampa's harmonica, his gold watch, old keys, old key rings, and every scrap of paper that ever related to me—report cards, my award-winning high school story about the woman locked in the loony bin for killing her husband, a ticket stub for *The Cherry Orchard*. I took her to see this play when she visited me in New York, I thought she hated that evening, she was fearful of the stairs, fretful about the seat, complained of a draft—yet she saved the ticket stub, along with every postcard and birthday card I ever sent her, every essay or article I ever brought or sent home, all the little trophies I'd drop like doggie bones at her feet. "Oh, Gayley, that's wonderful," she'd say, not always knowing exactly what she was approving; it didn't matter, her approval gave it meaning.

Who'd have thought a chest of drawers could hold so many things that would reach out and grab and bite? I am weeping as I upend the drawers into cartons. I tiptoe into her room, find the keys to her car, back the Cadillac into the driveway, haul the boxes to the garage, no more able than she to throw out a single thing.

I drive back to Berkeley that night, hoping to take off for

Mendocino next morning, one last time with Bob in that house by the sea. But in the morning, the phone rings. It's the nurse Landers assigned us, Nurse Barbara, telling me Mother is unable to get out of bed, I should get back.

I'm back in an hour. Paddy is waiting at the window as I pull up to the house. We sit at the kitchen table. We need a new plan.

Later that day, Mother is well enough to get out of bed. She and Paddy and I are at the kitchen table, when suddenly she drops her soup in her lap and begins to wail. We help her back to bed, try to calm her down. She is terrified—she can't work her hands.

I am terrified, too. I give in and call an agency, which I hadn't done because I wanted some choice about who we got, and with an agency, you take whoever they send; but I can no longer be choosy. There are other issues too, it is dawning on me. I call the lawyer who handled my father's estate, and the next day, his secretary drives up from San Jose. Mother has rallied a bit and is sitting up in bed. I steady the clipboard and help her with the pen, which she can barely hold, her neat, precise writing turned to a scrawl, the *berg* sliding crazily down the page—"on this 18th day of March, 1997, Agnes Greenberg designates Power of Attorney to her daughter, Gayle Greene."

I don't like this Power, don't like it at all.

That night, as I drive Paddy back to her apartment, I become aware she is making strange little snorting sounds like a pig. I am slow to take this in, I'm even vaguely irritated at the sound, then it hits me—"Paddy, what's going on?" She doesn't know, she says, she's been having trouble breathing, she's scheduled for an angiogram in the morning, she was supposed to have it last week but she put it off. She asks if I can arrange with the college to take the semester off, and I feel the noose tighten—it's like everyone is saying, *get back here where you belong, should never have left,* sucking me back, sucking me under. It's like nobody ever assumes I have a *real* job, *legitimate*—always this sense of wrongness about attachments to anything out there, *the outside world. Never trust the outside world,* Grampa said; Mother said it, too, Paddy, too, they were in cahoots.

I tell Paddy the semester is more than half over, my room is cleared out, I still think we can manage, just a few more weeks.

In the morning, I'm in Mother's room, when the phone rings and it's the hospital—Paddy has had a heart attack. I am too surprised to know how to conceal this from Mother, I've picked up the phone in her room, she knows it's about Paddy. "Hang on," I say, "I'll be back."

I dash out back to tell Sammy and Joey, rush to the hospital, find Paddy in intensive care, sitting up in a ruffly nightgown. She grasps my hand, "Oh Gayle, let me go—my heart is old, I'm old, I'm tired, it's okay if I die." Her hand is clammy, her forehead damp, she keeps drifting off, I put my arms around her—"don't go, Paddy, *please* don't go…"

She had sat in her apartment and let it happen, just sat there and let the pain wash through her, waves and waves of pain. Why hadn't she called 911, out of what reluctance to go on? she knew how it ended—why live on to see her sister die, the pain, the ignominy, the hurt creatures clinging to the twig—let it go, get out first. She'd put in her years nursing, her mother, her father, her husband Jack, she knew the end of the story. Only when she could stand the pain no more had she called for help. But now she's come through, though her heart is badly damaged—she will never again be able, my independent aunt, to care for herself, care for others. No more thought that she'll help my mother, she is going to need help herself.

I can see her putting this together. She is, miraculously, stabilizing, and by the end of the week, she's released from intensive care and moved downstairs to a regular room. I sit by her bed, on the end of her bed, we sit waiting, wondering—*what now?*

I call the dean and tell him to get someone to take my courses for the following week.

I have a new plan: there's a place near Mother's where Paddy conva-
lesced after her bypass. I call and inquire—yes, they have a room. For
sisters? No, they can't share a room, not if they're coming in on different health plans, the system won't allow it. I go over and check the
place out. The room they have for Mother reeks of fresh paint, looks
out on a wall; I know she'll hate this place, she'll be terrified, confused, sick from the paint. I hate the thought of bringing her here—
but how else will she ever be with Paddy?

I tell Paddy about this plan, yes, she says, absently, sounds like a
good idea, but she has other things on her mind. She asks, will I go
to her apartment, get her bathrobe and slippers, make sure there's
nothing valuable lying around. I drive down to San Jose, let myself
in. Her furry gold bedspread is twisted off the bed as though from a
scuffle, a nitroglycerin bottle on the floor. I search through her jewelry boxes—the precious pieces, she gave me through the years, opals
and diamonds, gifts from admirers
I had no idea she had, always a
sense of treasure associated with
Paddy, presents lavished on Billy
and me, packages within packages
wrapped cunningly, so we had to
work to get them open.

When we were kids, she lived
in the orchards, a shack at the
end of a dirt road, far away so she
could keep dogs. Take Stevens
Creek Road down toward Cuper-
tino, right at Homestead, keep on
toward Saratoga till there are no
more houses, watch for the big

Always a sense of treasure associated with Paddy...

mailbox, careful or you'll miss it, turn right onto the dirt road, but *slow!* the road's caked in gullies, the car heaves and tosses, hold on tight, roll up the windows, the dust is in your teeth, between your toes before your foot touches ground, the dark valley soil turned to summer silt—and *hot*. We arrive in a cloud of dust, pull up alongside Paddy's wood-bodied station wagon with *Poodle Rancho* and a dancing pink poodle painted on the side, park in the shade of the big fig tree. The dogs yelp and leap and hurl themselves at us, Paddy shouting, "down, Bo, down Pete." After dinner, we sit out on the sagging porch, swatting mosquitoes till it's cool enough to go in. She makes a bed for me on the couch, the dogs jump up, lick my face, snuggle down under the covers.

Those old Paddy shacks, floorboards that swayed and creaked, sashless windows that fell like guillotines, uncertain plumbing, an upright piano that moved wherever she moved. She sang, Mother played, Gilbert and Sullivan:

Sue and Gayle, Poodle Rancho, 1955.

A wandering minstrel I
A thing of shreds and patches,
Of ballads, songs, and snatches,
And dreamy lullaby!

That was Paddy, a dreamer, a wanderer.

Poodle Rancho was where she stayed longest—*"no more moving!"* Grampa said, he'd dragged across country, west to east, east to west, once too often—no more! Grampa was good with the dogs, she was good with Grampa, they all kept each other going, though he was quiet those days, long gone the wild man who outdrank Jack London, mainly he withdrew, in more pain from the cancer than he let on—big as a grapefruit, my father said it was, amazed that he'd endured it so long. When he died, she gave up Poodle Rancho, swapped the station wagon and some puppies for a purple Lincoln Continental, got a new hairdo, blond and curly, packed the three remaining poodles into the Lincoln, and headed for Miami. The Lincoln kept breaking down, and when she got to northern Florida, she swapped it for a VW bug and a few lots on the Gulf of Mexico; she wrote Mother, telling her she'd deeded them over to Billy and me, they'd be worth something someday (they were, too, became the down payment on my house). When she got to Miami, she looked for a house, and that's how she met Jack Greenspoon—he found her a house and showed up to her housewarming with chocolate and champagne, a charming, wooing widower. Surprised us all, my maiden aunt, finding the man of her dreams in her fifties.

When Bill died, they came back to California to be with Mother. When Jack died, she couldn't bear the loneliness and moved to a retirement inn, then to another, then here, to this room, where I am stumbling around in search of a light switch—which, when I find, I lock eyes with the eyes of my grandmother, Christine Heuser, the grandmother I never knew, one of the grandmothers I never knew, her delicate features framed by soft, dark curls, beautiful in an ethereal nineteenth-century way. Always that portrait hung on Paddy's wall, now it will hang on mine.

I find a brooch, a necklace, a ring, which I take back to the hospital, asking Paddy to tell me the history of each piece, something to do while we sit waiting for a doctor to issue orders, to say what's to become of her. She keeps nodding off and clutching her purse, I swear it's the same white plastic handbag she carried when I was a kid, source of sweets she'd dole out to Bill and me. We decide to go through it and take out her money so she can rest easy—four dollar bills and three Hershey kisses and two butterscotch candies, oh Paddy, not with your diabetes! She drifts off, I curl up on the foot of her bed and fall instantly to sleep.

I am packing my car, the things I am packing are old and precious, I can't fit them in the trunk—I keep taking them out and wedging them in, trying to find a way of arranging them so they won't break, but there's no way I can make them safe. Mom and Paddy stand by, wringing their hands, weeping.

I jerk awake—my car has no trunk. Bill's car had a trunk, the car he drove over a cliff, is it his car I'm packing, is that where I'm headed, over that precipice? I shake my head to clear it of the dream—don't do this, Billy, don't come back now, not now.

Next morning, Paddy seems confused. She's tried to make a list of things for me to get from her apartment, but her writing's a scrawl, her speech is slurred. There are dozens of people milling about, wandering in and out of the room, on and off shifts, nobody paying her any attention; they look at her chart, take her temperature, go back to their computers, engage with their screens.

Paddy looks down at her scrawl, dismayed. "Oh, I don't know, I can't say what I want, just bring—all of it, I guess. Just move me out."

"Okay, Paddy, I was going to do that anyway. Don't worry—I'll get it all."

"My, you're a smart girl," she says, beaming at me that whole-hearted approval she has all my life.

It's clear there's something badly wrong, but I can't get anyone to pay attention. Finally a nurse comes in, takes her vital signs, notices that her blood sugar has dropped, says she should eat. An alarm goes off in my head—"she has diabetes, you know." No, they didn't know. Didn't know? "You've had her in this hospital a whole week, and you didn't...*know?*" "Yes, well, she should eat—it's bad for her blood sugar to drop." No shit, lady, I could do better for her at home. I ask her to bring some Ensure, which I know Paddy likes. She goes off but doesn't return. I find someone else to ask, she smiles, nods, disappears, doesn't come back. I keep trying to get someone to send a doctor, then finally, toward evening, a man in a white coat turns up, takes out a clipboard, begins asking Paddy questions. Name? Address? Name of the president? Well, she knows *that*, all right—she not only voted for Bill Clinton, she canvassed for him. Yes, her memory is fine, no, her speech is not right, he'll order tests for tomorrow.

"Can't we just hold off on those tests?" says Paddy, pretty please, coaxing, like a little girl—"just hold off and see what happens?"

"Tomorrow," he repeats.

She shrugs. "Such a waste of money—I'll die anyway."

I, meanwhile, have been told that her health insurance will pay for only three days in a convalescent home, so I try to get her to tell me where her money is, how much there is, how I can get at it. I haven't told her about this latest glitch, so she has no explanation for my sudden interest in her finances. Her brow beads with sweat, I try to get her to focus—I am making things worse, but I'm not thinking clearly either. She's got it in her head that she took some cash out of the bank to pay for a convalescent home.

"How much?"

"Three or four."

"Three or four what?"

"Oh, I don't know. Thousand, maybe. I don't know." That gets my attention—three or four thousand dollars? It wasn't in her purse, it must be in her apartment. She drifts off, and I drive back to her place and search her file cabinet and drawers. No money, but I find a six-pack of Ensure, which I bring back to the hospital. She is sleeping, I leave the Ensure by her bed with a note in big letters: "I LOVE YOU. Back soon!"

"You are not allowed to bring food to the patients," says a nurse as I'm halfway down the hall. I whirl around, and the look on her face tells me what she's seeing on mine—I will kill you if you try to keep me from leaving this, I mean, *kill*—she backs off, literally, takes a few steps back. "Better write your name on it, then, so the hospital doesn't bill you for it."

Back at Mother's, I phone Bob, keeping my voice low so Mother can't hear (her door's open always now, she wants light), when an operator cuts in, and it's the hospital. Paddy's taken a turn. I alert Sammy and Joey and tear back to the hospital.

When I get there, she seems to be struggling. "It's okay, Paddy, I found it," I lie, "it's okay." "Good girl," she says, and slumps back. I think she was holding on till I got there. She closes her eyes and goes under, but her breathing is rough; I ask them to raise the bed. A nurse asks if she should give her morphine, I say yes, and Paddy settles back. The nurse pulls a screen around the bed, sits down beside me, says she doesn't think she'll last the night. She has kind eyes, not curious eyes like most people, and as she sits with me, she tells me how her husband died of cancer and how that changed her life, she went back to school and made nursing her work. She tells me the stages Paddy's passing through, as she slips away.

The room is cold, hum and beep of machines, shadows on the screen, sound of coughing. I sit, stiff and shivering in the straight-backed chair. The nurse with the kind eyes asks if I'd like to get into the bed with Paddy. I crawl in beside her, wanting to hug her but not daring, she seems far away. The nurse brings me a blanket, tells me to get some rest, I snuggle up beside Paddy, watching her bosom go up and down, holding her hand, thinking what an ample bosom it is, how she'd been a mother to me. I snuggle closer, I'd like to lie here forever, hearing her breathe, just knowing she's here.

The next thing I know, the room is growing light. The nurse with the kind eyes helps me out of the bed, tells me it won't be long. I go back to the chair and take my aunt's hand, it is swollen, I try to squeeze it, let her know I'm here, but she is so far away—this is her struggle, hers alone. Her breathing slows, slower, then stops.

The hospital starts up again, the staff returns to their computers, somebody comes and closes her mouth, composes her head, finds her wig on the bedtable, puts it decorously on. I sit, holding her hand. I need to say something, to tell her something…

…she'd been a mother to me.

Fear no more the heat of the sun, these lines from *Cymbeline* are running through my head—*thou thy worldly task has done, golden girls and lads all must, like chimney sweepers come to dust.* Paddy would like the bit about the chimney sweepers, but it's too arty, I need words for her alone, something to send her off to—where? "Go to where the poodles are!" the words bubble up—funny! dog heaven? But that is where I saw her happiest, that pure, silly joy she had with the puppies. "Puppies!" she'd say, holding out a tiny, wriggling ball of fur for me to take, its eyes shut tight, that milky puppy smell.

Then the words well up, "Thank you, Paddy, thank *you!*"

How could I not have said that while she lived? I thought there'd be time, I thought we would talk (about Mother, among other things), I never expected her to go before Mother—how could I not have thanked her while there was time? I blew away her last hours of life, bothering her about money.

I make myself stand up. *Wait*, says a voice, a real voice, not one of the voices clamoring in my head. A woman, tall, official, holds out a clipboard with papers for me to sign; another woman shoves a business card at me, telling me to call this number to make arrangements. *Arrangements?* There are other words, too, *morgue, mortuary, death certificate.* I try to pay attention.

I stand there stammering, feeling something more needs to be said, but the room is full of strangers, and it's Paddy I want to say it to, not her mortal remains. Finally I get myself to turn, find my way out the door, stumble down the hall, make my way out to the parking lot. The morning is bright, people going about as though nothing has happened, a holiday feel, something special about this day. Then I remember, it's Good Friday. I wander up and down the parking lot until I find my car. In my arms are Paddy's pink bathrobe, her white purse, her fuzzy slippers.

I turn down our block and pull over to the side, trying to dry my tears before I get back to the house. What can I tell Mother?

"Hi, Ma, how're you doin'?"

"Okay," she says, "Mom is—okay." She says the words slowly, drawing out the *o-kaay*. I dread the next question—where've you been? But it doesn't come, she just studies my face. Is she too far gone to realize there's something strange about my coming home at this hour, or is she telling me she knows and she'll be…*o-kaay?*

"How's Paddy?" She stares, her eyes intense, red-rimmed, white hair streaming back like an Old Testament prophet.

"Well, she had a heart attack," I say, letting her know it's serious so there will be a way of explaining her absence.

"Oh!" she gasps, sharp intake of breath, that way she has of registering someone else's pain as though it's her own—it scares me sometimes, the way she is, like she has no skin. "Oh *no!*" Then, after a moment, she states, solemn, "Well, she's going to hurt for a long time."

"Yes," I say. A long time.

I find Sammy and Joey, tell them about Paddy, tell them not to tell Mother, don't ask, don't tell, *consider it not so deeply, it will make us mad,* and they're as ready as I am to stay on the surface. I ask them to keep an eye on Mother. I call Nellie and herd her down the hall, make her get up on the bed, wrap myself around her shaggy bulk, my mind whirring—there's a room at the convalescent home, there's no way I'll take Mother there now, terrible that would have been even with Paddy, unthinkable now, I need to think: when my brother died, she and Paddy did not tell their brother Ted, then in his final illness—they wanted to spare Ted that pain, I want to spare her this. But which would be worse for her, to know or not to know?

I bite off a piece of sleeping pill; when I come to, it's afternoon. I call the dean, keeping my voice low, tell him to get someone to take my courses for the following week.

That night I drive back down to Paddy's and look for the folder marked "Funeral." Her file cabinet is filled with causes: Southern Poverty Law Center, Amnesty International, Earthjustice. I find the file with instructions: "First, make sure I'm dead. No embalming, simple cremation." She names a mortuary on El Camino, conveniently located, not far from the hospital. Leave it to Paddy to make it all nice and easy. The name of the mortuary is familiar—my brother's? I neaten up the room.

We are moving her the next day. I have called Jack Greenspoon's grandson and his wife; I barely know them, but they're Paddy's only kin, other than me. They arrive from Los Angeles around noon. They've dropped everything to come, they love Paddy that much; they're not even blood, but they call her *Grandma* just the same. The relief I feel seeing them is enormous. They're a few years younger than I am, though Cindy's low, raspy smoker's voice makes her sound older, wiser. Alfred is a foursquare, all-American kind of guy who wears a baseball cap. Mother never talked politics with him— "some things are better left unsaid," she'd say, with uncharacteristic tact. Cindy says something like this now, that we'd best leave Paddy's death unsaid.

So we all—Cindy and Alfred and Sammy and Joey and Keith from the end of the block—all convoy down to Paddy's, Keith with truck and trailer, to move my aunt. So many things, how can she have so many things when she moved around so much, two big closets bursting with clothes, blouses, slacks, jackets neatly rainbowed in purples reds pinks oranges yellows greens blues. One, two, three walking sticks. "What does Paddy need three walking sticks for?" says Keith, as he comes across the third. I think this is sort of bad taste, mutter something about her not needing any now, when a neighbor pokes her head in the door, says she's so sorry to hear that Lydia died. Keith whirls around, confused—"Lydia...Paddy...died?" I am shocked, too, I was sure I had told him, or that somebody had told him, but somehow this had not got communicated.

"Holy shit," says Keith, looking for a place to sit down. "I thought we were moving her."

We *are* moving her, these are her things, we move them just as she wished, her carved wooden tables, her jewelry boxes, a suitcase full of...ducks, their little round, glazed bodies and pert, turned-up tails and beaks. When I was a kid, I thought all aunts made ducks, it was a thing aunts did, and they did look more like ducks those days, sober tans, grays, and whites, each with a personality and presence all its own; when she took up ceramics again in her eighties, their colors went wild, flamingo pink and turquoise blue like no duck ever was, their necks got longer, like swans or geese—*Gayley Goose*, she'd say, as she gave me a duck for Christmas, for my birthday, any excuse, she'd give me a duck, as, later, she gave me opals and diamonds wrapped cunningly in tissues and bows.

We shove them all into boxes, load the boxes into cars, van, and trailer, dump everything into Mother's garage. A set of white wicker shelves lands in the middle of the garage, draped with shawls, scarves, and beads, looking like an effort of decoration amidst the deluge, like one of Paddy's arrangements, for she made beauty wherever she lived—no matter how small the room, she'd drape beads on a mirror, arrange shells, fans, flowers on a doily or shawl. There sit her shelves in my mother's garage, made newly empty by the absence of the Cadillac (which I gave to Keith), there's Paddy, her things wedged in among my father's and brother's things, her walking sticks propped by the door alongside brooms and mops, lamps shoes books toasters scissors seashells driftwood thrown crazily together.

My mother calling from the bedroom, when is Paddy moving in?

SCENES FROM A DEATHBED

Death is a fearful thing.

—Shakespeare, *Measure for Measure*

I HAVE HEARD OF THINGS done to the dying, bodies tethered to beds, wired to machines, electric shocks to re-start the heart, plastic tubes poked up nose and throat, respirators pumping air in and out. There is no way I'll let this happen to my mother.

I have heard these things from Inge, a woman sent by the agency, our first bit of good luck. Inge breezes in on a gust of drugstore perfume, takes off her rings and bracelets, rolls up her sleeves, goes in to introduce herself to Mother. A large Polish woman with bottle-bright red curls and chins that jiggle when she laughs, which she does a lot, she draws on a pair of rubber gloves and sets about changing Mother, telling me to pay attention for when I have to do this myself. Mother looks slightly bemused but tries to cooperate, pulls herself over on her side so we won't push and tug. Inge instructs me to buy some short flannel nighties and a quilt, the afghans are too heavy. She tells me what supplies to lay in, vaseline swabs, rubber gloves, nappies. I am so glad to have somebody tell me what to do, relieved to be bossed about.

Later, I'm sitting at the kitchen table, filling out her worksheet, when Inge appears in the door, arms crossed, frowning.

"Why isn't she on hospice?"

"Why...should she be?"

"Yes, because she's terminal."

Terminal. Inge is the first person to say it. I know, of course I know, yet the word shocks. I have a vague idea of hospice as a place people go to die, and if I know anything, it's that Mother's not going anywhere. She's lived forty-four years in this house, she's never been in a hospital except to have babies, she's never been comfortable spending the night out—how could she now, sick and confused, leave home?

"I'm not sending her away."

"No, no, hospice isn't a place." Inge strips off her rubber gloves, sits down at the table, puts her rings and bracelets back on. "It's a service, a set of services—they work with you so you can keep her home."

"How…?"

"She has to be certified terminal."

"*Certified terminal?*"

"Within six months of the end. You need a doctor's order," she explains. My heart sinks. "There's no way we could get a doctor to this house."

"You say there's a nurse assigned to her? Ask her—she'll put in a request to the doctor."

The next morning, I ask Nurse Barbara about getting Mother on hospice. "Perhaps," she says, "that might be a possibility. But we would need Dr. Goldstein to authorize any such request." Her voice is so flat and toneless, it could be computer-generated—once more with feeling, I want to say, try saying it like it matters. She says it hadn't occurred to her to suggest hospice, she hadn't seen Mother as terminal.

"Hadn't *seen?*" cries Inge, when I tell her, cheeks flushing, voice rising—"How could she *not see?*"

"Why didn't her doctors tell me about hospice?"

"They don't…they just don't. I don't think they like admitting there are problems they can't fix."

Where have they gone, those doctors my mother and aunt knew all those years? Vanished into posh offices where they're surrounded by women who run interference between them and the messy, hopeless drama played out here. When I called Goldstein to cancel her last appointment, nobody even asked why she wasn't coming in, nobody said *sorry*. Christ, when my friend Trish's dog died, her vet called to say *sorry*.

"Now you listen to me," says Inge, her voice high and excited— "You don't want the doctors, you hear me? They know nothing about death, nothing!" and she tells me the things she's seen done to the dying—"*heroic measures*," she practically spits out the words.

Heroic, those measures? No, the house calls my father made, the hospital rounds and careful follow-ups, the way he'd sit all night till the patient died or the baby came—*those* were heroic measures. My father, the strength of this longing for my father surprises me.

Goldstein signs the authorization, but it is provisional—tests will have to be done, numbers produced, to verify that Mother is within six months of the end.

I had not known death was so exact a science.

The next day, a woman shows up from hospice, a handsome, helmet-haired blond in a well-cut suit and classy shoes. I'd have pegged her for the corporate world, not end-of-life care, until I notice the brief-case she's carrying, battered and bulging with papers—she wouldn't get far up a corporate ladder, carrying that. She heaves the briefcase onto the kitchen table, takes out a sheaf of papers. She instructs me, above all, *do not call 911*: this would hand Mother over to a system where I lose all control over what's done to her, and *heroic measures* kick in, "stuff they do to cover legal asses," she mutters. I pay atten-tion. I take the DO NOT RESUSCITATE stickers and plaster them on the telephone, the refrigerator, the kitchen table, the nightstand by Mother's bed. I promise to tell anyone working here, in case of emer-gency, *Call Hospice, Do Not Call 911, Do Not Resuscitate.*

Hospice will send a nurse three times a week, Carolyn explains, to maintain contact with the doctors and see that Mother gets the medications she needs. Someone will be in to bathe her a few times a week, and various other things will happen. Only a small part of what she says is getting through to me, and only as the weeks go by do I see how well worked out these services are.

But I still need someone to live in. I've placed ads in papers and interviewed women, but none seems right. I have only one lead, through Inge, who tells me to keep this quiet, she could lose her job for this, but she has a friend here from Jamaica who has experience nursing, should she send her over?

That's all I know—Inge recommends her.

Jenny stands at the door, a short black woman in her early thirties, though her stoutness and seriousness make her seem older. A large, unkempt sheepdog sniffs her over, barking welcome. Jenny grins, pats Nellie's head—good, she passes the first test. She glances around the large front room to see what she's getting in for, I follow her gaze, see what she sees—a pile of dirty laundry on the piano bench, a walker and wheelchair against the wall, a walking stick hanging on a doorknob, dustballs big as tumbleweeds blowing down the hall. "Come meet my mother," I say, cheerily as I can, hoping Mother is with us this afternoon. I lead Jenny into the bedroom, a clutter of medicine bottles, ointments, baby wipes, swabs, disposable diapers, an unused commode shoved in the corner. Mother rouses herself, holds out her hand. "Hello, my name is Mrs. Greenberg, what's yours?" she chirps, blue eyes meeting Jenny's. Jenny's smile fills her whole face.

That's it—Jenny is ours.

It isn't an easy situation, I see that she sees. She asks the right questions—what are her responsibilities, how can she reach me, how long will it take me to get back, does the dog go or stay? Don't worry, I say, Nellie comes with me, which I later realize was the wrong answer—she wanted Nellie to stay.

Do you think you are up to this? I ask. What experience do you have? She nursed her grandmother through the end, she knows what to expect. Are you sure? She is sure.

Jenny moves in the next day. She asks for a broom and the dustballs fly. She rearranges the papers on the kitchen table into neat piles, thereby totally scrambling my system for my mother's bills, but it's a small price to pay. A weight lifts. I have two days before I have to be back in the classroom, I am hungry for the sea, for one last time with Bob in that house by the sea.

I stand in the front door, stammering and torn.

"Go," says Jenny.

"Go," says Inge, giving me a shove, "get yourself out of here. She's not dying, yet. This could go on for weeks, months—get some rest."

"You are going to need it," says Jenny, her voice serious.

It's Saturday night, the traffic is kamikaze, my tooth is really aching. I poke around with tongue and finger, I see it's a different tooth from the one that's been hurting, ohno, I have two bad teeth. After four hours on the freeway, I get to Cloverdale, where highway 128 turns off to the coast. I pull over and crawl in the backseat with Nellie and close my eyes before I can face the twisty mountain road. This is a road I usually love, through orchards and fields and a redwood forest, but I don't love it tonight, the headlights stab my eyes. I take the curves fast, sloppy, driving badly. I make myself slow down for the hairpin turns, for the treacherous bit that snakes up the cliff where the Navarro River enters the sea, then eleven miles up the coast to the town of Mendocino, once a fishing village, now a tourist mecca, though its weathered wooden houses and water towers look unchanged from the 1960s, when I lived here; unchanged, I imagine, from the 1860s, when the town was built.

Two miles north of town is Bob's house, soon not to be Bob's house. I walk in and see that it's true, what he's been saying—he really is moving out. Boxes and crates are piled in the corners, couches up-ended and shoved to the side, movers are coming Monday to cart it all off to storage while he's in France. He's been saying how hard it is to uproot himself from this place he's lived so long, what a wrench, but I hadn't heard—I'd been picturing the house as it was, bright, serene, tall, angled skylights that let in sun, moon, and stars, not chaos, like everywhere else.

"Oh dear," I say, looking around for a place to sit. "Maybe I shouldn't have come."

I go straight to bed. At some point, I become aware of daylight, Bob standing by the bed, fully dressed, watching me. I groan to let him know I'm alive, turn over, go back to sleep.

It's late afternoon when I come to, a chill day, a good day to sleep through. April 6, the day my brother took his life. I pull a chair over to the window and stare out to sea. A high fog, not the misty fog I used to love to watch wisping up the meadow, swirling through Spanish moss, but a gray sky, dull and blank as my mind. I try to think, not think, exactly, just let it seep in, what's been happening. When I went to Los Altos three weeks ago, Paddy was fine and Mother was failing, but she was there. Now Paddy is gone and Mother is…where? A series of strokes, or maybe this is what happens when a liver fails, I don't know, but she is not all here.

So they will go together. I guess that's right. I'd always dreaded which of them would be left after the other. "I hope I never see her like that again, looking so cold and dead," she said, after Paddy's bypass; I felt her shudder, and I hoped not, too. Well, Mother, you never will have to see her like that, and she never will have to see you like that, and that's right—you should go together. You required one another.

But what about *me?* I required you, too. Now who will I have to mourn you with, and who will I have to mourn her with, and where will I be without you, and what will it matter?

I stare at the horizon, the sky seems at wrong angles to the sea, the earth's plates shifting—no, it's no help, this house, husked, too. Bob's halfway out already, his mind's on France, and I'm too deep in myself to reach out.

He tries, in his way, insists that we get out, walk to the lighthouse, he produces food, fusses at me to eat. But the big thing between us, that he is leaving, is unspoken, shoved under the carpet with other things I dare not feel—fear, hurt, abandonment. Maybe France wasn't such a great idea—it seemed to make sense, but will I forgive him.

I drive back to Berkeley the next day and fly down to Claremont the day after. I teach Tuesday, Wednesday, Thursday, fly back late Thursday, repack and pick up Nellie in Berkeley, drive down to Los Altos, and spend the rest of the week with Mother.

Sammy and Joey help me drag Paddy's bed in from the garage so I can sleep in the front room. We struggle with the bedframe, but our combined talents can't get it to stand, so we give up and drop the mattress on the floor, shove it in the corner behind the piano. I find the tall shoji screens Mother used to make her studio when she gave piano lessons, arrange them around the bed—they mark off a space, a sort of shelter from which I can see Mother's room, and hear her. I find Paddy's gold furry bedspread and her bedside lamp, which I put on her night table with her Avon lotion, her smell. I like it here, it feels like a little lair. It feels like camping out in the living room, the way Billy and I did when we were kids, dragging our sleeping bags onto the carpet, draping a blanket over chairs and couch, pretending it was a tent—"couple of giggling idiots," Mother would say, setting us off into greater giggling. Billy, his sweet round face never did fit that square 1950s crew cut, he loved dogs and baseball, so proud of his Little League uniform, he wore it everywhere, Silly Billy, he did great Elvis imitations, too, crooning and strumming an imaginary guitar.

Monday night, I tiptoe out of Mother's room, with its slowed, hushed time, pack the car, drive up Magdalena Avenue on to the 280, north. I pick up speed, edge left, the fast lane, the world's time, through San Francisco, across the Bay Bridge to Berkeley. Back in my house, I gather up books and notes, hunt for a skirt and sweater not too fuzzed with dog hair, lay them out for morning, when I'm on the road again, 880 south to the Oakland airport.

I sit, nose pressed to the window. As the plane loops over San Francisco Bay, I see all the way down the long body of water, the whole length of the Peninsula. I trace the 280 south, find Stanford by its red tile roofs, locate the Foothill Expressway, where the railroad tracks used to be, follow the road to the little clump of blocks that's downtown Los Altos; then, a few roads south, a patch of green that's the park at the end of Clinton Road, where an old woman lies dying, that life struggle so momentous, Silicon Valley takes no note. I see below the huge, rounded aircraft hangars of Moffett Field, the long, low rectangular roofs of the valley's industrial parks, the salt flats of the south bay like green and purple splotches on a giant artist's palette. To the right of the plane are the Santa Cruz Mountains, to the left, the Diablo Range and the round, velvety foothills of San Jose, and over those hills, the vast Central Valley.

Odd and melancholy, this view of life passing before me in the landscape, my life and her life and the valley's, the Valley of Heart's Delight now a gridwork of highways, expressways, freeways.

I trace the 101 south—you could smell the Gilroy garlic for miles, those years I used to drive this route, those many years I'd drive, south to north, to Mother and friends in Berkeley, then north to south and back to work. I'd stop at a fruit stand, load up on melons, peaches, garlic braids, take the winding road through the sage-sweet hills, over the Pacheco Pass and on to Highway 5, the long straight interstate that cuts through California's heartland, north to south, south to north.

Now I am, plunk, in front of a classroom, mind filmy with the sights and sounds of death. *Macbeth*, I go back to. I'm glad it's *Macbeth*, I can find my way around this play, *I have supped full with horrors, life's but a walking shadow*. I have no idea what my students have been told, where they think I've been. I mutter something about my aunt's death, my mother's illness, say we'll play it by ear, not sure I can finish out the term or even the week. Most of them act as though nothing's happened, most of my colleagues do, too, a few offer condolences, formal, polite, sorry for your loss, don't ask, don't

I'd stop at a fruit stand.

tell, *consider it not so deeply, these deeds must not be thought after these ways, it will make us mad*. A few, I can tell from their pained expressions, have been there, too.

A bunch of roses appears outside my office, propped against the door. The next Tuesday, there are roses; there are roses by my door every week for the rest of term, left by a student, I assume, I never do learn who they are from. Each Tuesday, I see the flowers and bite back tears. This silent offering moves me more than words, petals on the dust, gestures of kindness, this is all that's left now, the kindness of strangers.

Then, slowly, in the course of a few days' teaching, the cobwebs disperse, my mind clears, the class comes into focus and these kids, so far from where I've been, so young and so unbroken, begin to seem real. But then I turn around and do it all in reverse, north to Berkeley, unpack and repack, south to Mother's.

I whirl into the house, heart racing, metabolism speeding from days teaching and traveling. I enter this zone like a space traveler decompressing, shed jacket and sweater, her room's kept so warm; even with the quilt, she wants more blankets. I slow myself down, down, to this place where time has a different meaning, not to be used for anything but to minister to the body, the body primal, imperative, its intake, output, digestion, excretion, this is what matters now.

Life centers on this room. A small room, thick with sickroom smells, disinfectants, underlay of something like decay, the surfaces cluttered with the paraphernalia of illness. A few people fill the room, these days there are often more. Two large unframed mirrors hang on opposite walls, facing one another—Mother thought they would make the room seem larger, but they don't, they push in, reflecting us back to ourselves over and over, reduplicating our images back and back again, like the mirrors the witches hold up to Macbeth, stretching out to the crack of doom. I glimpse a face tight with tension, mouth set in a frown, surely not my face, so pinched and old.

I empty my head of everything but her. All of us here, all of us women—for death is women's work—focus wholly on this body which is my mother, which demands our complete attention, wiping, swabbing, changing, cleaning. She is very good at first, tries to cooperate when we change her or bathe her, but then it gets harder for her to move, she sort of absents herself from the scene, simply takes herself away—to be rolled this way and that, tugged at and diapered, best not be present for that. Then she freezes, cries out, as we push and tug, skin breaking at the touch—how can she can be so thin yet so heavy? *Dead weight,* I understand the term.

At the end of four days, I organize myself out the door, up the freeway, unpack, repack, fly back down to Claremont, where I am, plunk, in front of a class again. *Dear daughter, I confess that I am old, age is unnecessary,* Lear, burning his way through the dark wood again— *I gave you all!* Christ, where does he get the energy? With us, there are no fists raised against the heavens, no ranting or raging, no *wisdom in madness,* only a moaning and muttering that makes less sense each day. I do not know what she means, she cannot seem to say. Does it hurt, I ask, where does it hurt, what can I do? She cannot say.

Each time I leave her, I wonder, will there be a next time, will she know me when I return, give me that smile when I walk in the door? I tell myself it doesn't matter to her if I stay or go, but I know it matters—her smile when she greets me is full of joy. Yet each week, I go, tiptoe out the door, turn my back on the moaning that is worse.

Why, I ask myself again, don't I ask the college for a leave? But, if I was going to do that, I should have done it when it might have helped Paddy, now *I'm in so far that to turn back is as tedious as to cross o'er.* Truth is, I'd be terrified to be only here, that old fear of being sucked back, sucked under, this house, her unhappiness, *save me.* The relief I feel each week, putting on grown-up clothes, standing before a class, knowing that I exist—how can she scare me so, my crumbled little mother, so frail, so dear, these are phantom terrors, but no less real for that.

I should stay with her, I should never have left, I will feel this later, I will feel it forever, I don't know when or what it means, but there's *hell to pay.*

Thursday night, 3:00 AM, I drive up to the house. Her light is on always now, gold glow through the drapes. I peer into her room, not knowing whether I hope she'll wake or stay asleep.

She stirs, smiles, that smile could melt stone. "Why, Gayley, what a lovely dress," she says, though it's the same ratty old jacket and jeans I've worn all winter.

"Thanks, Ma. How was your day?"

"Oh, it was wonderful, wonderful. We had a party."

"Really, a party?" I peel off jacket and sweater, pull the chair up to the bed. "What kind of party?"

"Oh, a bunch of old ladies." She wrinkles her nose. Lying there in the low light, tucked under the forest green quilt, she could be an ancient wood sprite, an elf in an enchanted bower. This is the mother

I love, mischief in her grin, complicity. She draws me down close, whispers in my ear, "They shouldn't have bothered, Gayley, really, all that trouble—it's too much for the girls."

"No bother." A hospice volunteer dropped by to play the piano, I later learn—that was the party.

"Yes, it's too much for the girls, tell them to go away—"

"But Ma, they have to be here..."

"No, let's just us talk, the two of us, the way we used to." Her voice turns querulous. It hurts so much that she wants to talk—I'd like that, too, I think I would. I never imagined we'd end up not talking, we'd talked so well, now there is no talking, only fretting on her part, reassurances on mine.

I leave her to unpack the car, she calls me back—"Gayley, Gayley." I come back, stand in the door, "What, Ma? what is it?" She stammers, "well, in other words, *in other words*..." I don't know if I should encourage her to try again, when it will only go the same way "...*in other words*," she repeats and bursts into tears—"oh, to have a brain again, to have a body." I stroke her hair, tell her it's okay.

In the morning I make lists of things to do and things to get, diapers, rubber gloves, baby wipes, baby aspirin, vaseline, q-tips, I cruise the aisles of the drugstore, loading the cart. I am forever rattled, forever misplacing things—I get back to Berkeley and realize I've left a book in Los Altos, I stop in the middle of a lecture to ransack my backpack for a gradebook I've left on the plane, I race down the block, yelling for Nellie, only to find her where I left her, in the car.

One day, I'm sure I've lost the document that gives me Power of Attorney, I call Jenny, frantic with loss, ask her to search the papers on the kitchen table—"it's important." "*I* know," she says. Is it only that West Indian lilt that's so reassuring, or does she really know? Whatever it is, it makes me feel better, the way she says it, not so alone. She ducks into Mother's room on her way down the hall, asks if she'd like a treat, says a few words to cheer her up, sings to her, *Swing low, sweet chariot*—cool cloth on a hot brow, moist q-tip in a dry mouth, vaseline on parched lips, a ministering angel, maybe there are such things.

It's a congenial community that's grown up around my mother: Jenny and Inge and Debbie, who comes to bathe Mother three times a week; Allison, the hospice nurse, a stumpy, iron-gray woman I've come to trust completely; Jo, who drops by to play the piano. And there's a woman who drops by from time to time to check on how I'm doing, who, I finally figure out, is a social worker sent by hospice to make sure I'm bearing up, since hospice knows the caregiver needs care, too. "*Sweet!*" she says, pointing to the poster on the kitchen wall, Koko and the kitten, the gorilla gazing adoringly at the tiny kitten cradled in its giant paws. The kindness of strangers. Sammy and Joey pop in once or twice a day to ask if we need anything. Linda from across the street, tall, athletic-trim Linda with the pixie cut, and Reggie from next door, who, I finally figure out, bears a strong resemblance to Maggie Thatcher; I'd been wondering who she reminds me of—yes, definitely Thatcher, same beaked nose and lacquered red hair.

This little group that's gathered around my mother is also, I realize, supporting me. But what, then, when they leave, will become of me? No, no thoughts allowed, only the day to be got through, the drive, the airport, the class, the urgency of the moment, moments turn to days, to weeks, flatten into the future, and then, what then?… no, no thoughts, *consider it not so deeply, it will make us mad.*

Inge breezes in every other day on a gust of chatter and perfume, takes off her rings and bracelets, goes in to sit by Mother, holds her hand, sings her songs. Sometimes she and Jenny and I chat at the kitchen table and Inge tells us about her ex-boyfriend and ex-husband; neither is very nice to her, yet both want her back. "What's with these guys!" she says, indignant yet unfazed, as unfazed by them as she is by her *terminals*, as she calls them—Mother is not her only.

Jenny talks about Jamaica, how she misses it, misses her sisters, the women in her church, about her children, how she longs to be back with them, but times are hard, she needs to be here. She tells us about her daughter, her dogs, her vegetable garden, says she never had a mother like mine—it was her grandmother who raised her, she misses her to this day. She says that when her grandmother died, her old dog followed her to the cemetery, hung around the grave, stopped eating—"dat dog diminish, dat dog diminish." I know how that dog felt.

"Say, girl, could you leave the dog?" she asks one night, as I'm on my way out. "This house is *lonely!*" So Nellie stays. But, I assure Jenny, this house has been a whole lot lonelier, there's more going on here now than there used to be. "But poor Paddy's missing all the fun," says Mother, and I realize she's enjoying the fuss, and I think, why, *why* do we wait for people to die before we pay them attention, why not make a buzz around them while they're well? The fiction is that Paddy's resting, too tired to join us. Yes, I assure her, she has company too; yes, she had corn for supper too.

I call Jenny when I get to Berkeley, I call her again when I get to my office. "A good day," she says, "she eat all her supper tonight." Or, "not such a good day, she moan a lot. When you comin' back, girl?"

"Pork chop. She wake up this morning and she say 'pork chop.' So I give her some pork and beans. *Marie*—she call me *Marie*. Who Marie?"

"I don't know any Marie. Maybe somebody from her past."

"They brought a bed today—girl, you should see it, the mattress puffed full of air, the machine puff it up."

"What bed, who…?"

Hospice, of course, a mattress to prevent bed sores—nearly every week now, there's a new piece of equipment. The bed has a device to keep the mattress inflated, it makes a strange hissing sound like a large animal breathing. I try to imagine it a friendly creature, since it's here to stay, but I can't shake the sense of a presence, huge, close, wheezing. One week I come back and there's a catheter, a tube that drains into a plastic bag hooked to the side of the bed. I wince at that, poked in to so tender a part. Inge assures me she has to have it, she can't lie there wet, her skin is breaking down.

"She ask for you today," says Jenny; "she say, 'where Gayley?' I say, 'Gayle's at school.' 'Oh, that's good,' she say. Ten minutes later she say, 'Is Gayley coming?' 'When she get home from school.' 'That's right,' she say." That's right, school is where Gayley ought to be, though Gayley is not sure of this, not sure at all.

"Lord, girl, I'm glad you call, we had a day! The alarm go off, the nurse move the bed, what a *noise!* Nellie barking, Lord, she go on, the neighbors come."

"Oh, no, I forgot, she put an alarm in the room—what did you *do?*"

"Sammy come. He punch in the numbers. He shut it off."

"How was Mom?"

"She laugh. She just laugh and laugh."

Way to go, Ma. A thing Bill and I used to say, a term of amusement, of endearment, well, mainly endearment, sometimes exasperation— *Way to go, Ma.*

If you walked into this room, you'd see her photo on the wall. She is so beautiful in the old photos, but they made her sad, so she put them away—all except this, a honeymoon photo, girl on a hilltop, hair in a scarf, a shy, hopeful smile. You'd look at the photo, then at the wild old woman with the streaming white hair, then back to the photo—how can both of these be true?

"Hello, my name is Mrs. Greenberg—what's yours?" she chirps to a new person. "She's my favorite," says Debbie, come to bathe her, "I just love her. You really see what a person is when they die—it all hangs out, who they are."

"Who they…are?"

...a honeymoon photo, girl on a hilltop.

"Most of them just sort of lie there, just sort of blah, know what I mean? Your mom is great." Maybe she says that to everyone, but I bet not.

One morning, Sammy's laughter wafts in through the open window on the scent of blossoms. Mother chuckles—"Sammy, what a laugh!" I brace myself, hoping she won't say something biting (why does she have to be so critical, and why do I have to be so much like her?) "A good laugh," she says. "Funny, they were just—tenants. And now, they're so..." she stops, searching for a word. "Important," I say, relieved there are no barbs.

"What'll it be, Ma—french toast, eggs, cereal?"

She takes her time, thoughtful. "Eggs, I think. Yes, I'd like eggs."

"How about some Christmas juice?" I say, giving Martinelli's, the sparkling apple juice we have at Christmas, a new name. "Oh, d'ye think we could?" she says, her face lighting up. "I don't see why not." I hold the glass up close so she can sip it through a straw, she sucks greedily, soon she is drinking a bottle a day. I know what foods she likes and I know the most efficient routes to them in Andronico's. She craves things with salt, cream of mushroom soup, clam chowder, and at some point I figure, to hell with it, she should eat what she wants. And chocolates, I pick up a pound of See's candy each Friday; by the next Friday, it is gone.

"What good coffee, Gayley!" she exclaims, when I give her a cup of my gourmet brew from Berkeley, and I think—"ha!" She always got at me about my extravagance, insisted that supermarket coffee tasted just as good. And I feed her lemon meringue pie from Andronico's, and Häagen-Dazs ice cream, which she'd never get for herself, and she loves it—"see, Ma, it really does taste better."

So ends a lifelong argument about food.

One night when Jenny is gone and I am changing her, all thumbs and embarrassment, she says, "Why, Gayley, I didn't know you knew how to do that! What a good little caregiver you turned out to be."

"Well, Ma. You did it for me."

But there are the bad days—"I can't think, can't talk," she wails, and bursts into tears. "I used to have a house, a garden, a piano."

"You still do, Ma, they're still here."

"But *I'm* not!" she cries.

"Ah, Ma."

She hates the new bed. The bars, which we keep up to prevent her from falling out, make a cage, she wants them off. We find her mornings, legs twisted through the rails. "Take down those bars!" she commands, "I'm going to walk. Let me out of here—I want to go home."

"But, Ma, you *are* home, this is home." I sound unconvincing, even to myself. Where *is* home, if not here? But maybe she means some earlier home, where they were all together, she and her mother

and sister and brother Ted, or *home* in the song Jenny sings, *comin'*
for to carry me home. I point out the window—"Look, Ma, the cherry
tree," proof positive that this is home. I bring in a sprig of blossoms,
put it by her bed.

"No, no, this is a terrible place, I don't want to be here."

We try to take her out in the wheelchair, show her the piano,
the garden, but it's getting dangerous; she panics at the move from
bed to wheelchair, feet catching, weight toppling, skin ripping. One
day I hear a scream and a thud and I rush in to find her on the floor,
Jenny stands, stammering. "It's not her fault!" Mother cries, "you
mustn't blame Marie, I just fell." *Marie*, that name she calls Jenny.
To the women, she shows respect, to them, she says, "thank you" and
"pardon me," she knows who's in charge—"Just wait till that daughter of mine gets back, I'll tell her!" Inge says she says.

"You could—you have—the power..." she stammers. I have the
Power of Attorney, she knows I have it, she gave it to me. She begins
to focus on *the power* as something I've stolen from her, something
I'm withholding, I who have never felt so powerless, trekking to the
far ends of the valley to find the kind of bandage that won't rip her
skin, the kind of mouthwash that won't hurt her if she swallows, I
have the power, *save me, you could save me if you would. Dammit, save
yourself*—my mind runs to that place, like a tongue to a bad tooth,
I can't help it. I am trying, really trying to be the mother I have never
been, but I am battling ghosts.

"That's no way to act," she says one night, looking at me hard.

"What way, Ma?"

"*What have you done with her?*" That dreadful question. I repeat
the story—Paddy is resting, getting her strength back. "*A fairy tale*,"
she hisses, or is it the mattress that makes that hiss? She knows I am
lying, and if I'm lying about that, I could be lying about everything,
I could be keeping her from Paddy, keeping her in this cage, a prisoner and bound. *A fairy tale*, I feel it too, bound to this house, bound
to each other, *spellbound*.

Maybe she could take the truth about Paddy, maybe she even knows. Cindy says I'm right not to tell her, so does a friend of Mother's I'm in telephone touch with. It's the people who don't know her, Inge, some of the hospice workers, who think I should tell her. I am torn. All I know is, there's family precedent; when Uncle Ted was in his final illness, Mother and Paddy did not tell him that Bill had died. But maybe I'm wrong, maybe it's myself I'm trying to spare.

So there's a chasm between us, she crying for her sister, me, murmuring reassurances, she's resting, she's all right, you'll see her again; she, crying for her mommy, I want to cry for mine.

The hospice workers aren't pleased about my three-day absences. One day Nurse Allison confronts me, asks me what arrangements I've made.

"*Arrangements?*" I echo, the word oddly familiar. She explains, "If it happens while you are gone, there have to be arrangements. Jenny has to know what to do, it's not fair to her otherwise."

"Yes, I see."

I go to Mother's file cabinet and find the folder marked "Funeral"; in it, a living will, brochures from the Hemlock Society, the Neptune Society, an envelope marked Peninsula Funeral Society— "dues paid, membership current." She joined these societies when she read Jessica Mitford's *American Way of Death*, said this was the way to go, no frills, no fuss, no point to that *malarkey, stuff and nonsense, hocus pocus.* I dimly registered it at the time and shoved it in the part of my brain with things not to think about, the many things I choose not to think about. There in the Peninsula Funeral Society brochure, I find a list of participating mortuaries, rates half of what it cost to cremate Paddy.

Way to go, Ma.

I choose a mortuary in San Bruno, near San Francisco. I call and they fax me forms. I am about to fax them back, when I read the small print: "Remains to be released to…" an address in Colma. Where the hell is Colma? I call and ask.

"You don't know Colma?" says the voice on the phone. "The City of the Dead." It seems that a century ago, San Francisco decided it no longer wanted its dead within city limits and designated Colma, just south, as its burial ground.

I fax back the forms, but when I get to Mother's later that week, there's a message saying they hadn't come through. When I finally get a human being on the phone, he's not sure what I'm talking about, thinks I'm arranging to have a body picked up. Finally he gets it—"oh, we're talking about a pre-deceased?"

"Pre-deceased?" A laugh escapes me, snort more than laugh. Silence at the other end.

"Well, yeah, she's right here," I say, and just about offer to put her on the phone. Mother would enjoy this, would have enjoyed it. I realize I am very far from imagining her deceased.

She is still here, no question. I am stroking her forehead, groping for reassurances; "You were always such a good sweet kind mama," I say. Her eyes snap open, intelligence gleams—"I was *not!*" Enough of her to say, *oh no, you don't,* no sappy Hallmark epitaphs for me. No pie in the sky for me.

Enough of her to worry, even, about me. "Poor girl, this must be terrible for you, terrible."

"No, Ma, it's okay. Really."

"Do you have friends?"

"Friends?" It's a real question. I used to have friends, I thought I did, but that was before I got so… busy. It seems I've been busy a long time. "I think so, I think I have friends…enough…" Enough for *what?*

One night she says, as I walk in the room, *"Be kind."* That cuts— what unkindness of mine is she recalling, there have been plenty through the years. Or maybe she's offering me the advice Paddy gave, not long before she died—*"Be kind,"* she said. We were sitting at the kitchen table, probably I had my nose in a book or was grumbling about something, when these words popped out of nowhere—"*Be kind.*" Something in her tone snapped me to, made me pay attention, I could hear, she was speaking from her heart. "Take time with people, Gayle. The rest"—wave of hand—"really isn't very important." But Mother's words, like so much of what she says these last days, are enigmatic.

That night, or was it the next night, time blurs, I'm standing at the end of the bed, rubbing her feet, studying her face as she is studying mine, giving me that quizzical, appraising look. "Do you know who I am?" I say. After a long silence, comes the word, "No." My heart sinks. But then I think she may have heard my question as more complicated than I meant, like it was some complex question about identity, who I really am. I do not think she does not know me.

I try again, tickling her foot. "Hey, Ma—it's me, Gayley Goose," her childhood name for me. She grins. "*Gayley Goose.* Such a cute little rascal."

Her radio, suddenly she wants it on, the voices crackle, fill the room—*Hello, Hayward, you're on the air, Come in, Livermore, a caller from Livermore.* But she isn't listening, so we turn it off. I find a tape Bob made of Schumann, Chopin, Debussy, music she used to play. At first, she's rapt, intent upon each note, then she starts to cry, and so do I.

No more piano, no more radio, only the hiss and sigh of the mattress.

On bad nights, she calls *Lydia, Lydia,* drawing the word out like a moan—*Ly-di-aaah.* She hasn't called her sister by that name since we renamed her *Paddy* half a century ago—*Paddy* for Paterson, also, for *Knick knack Paddy whack, give the dog a bone.* Now *Lydia* echoes from a distant past.

Nurse Allison sends me to Goldstein to get a prescription for a painkiller, a tall purple bottle of syrup. But the moaning gets worse. Nurse Allison sends me back to Goldstein for a prescription for a morphine patch, and from Goldstein's, I trek around to several pharmacies, so dangerous and controlled a substance this is that nobody wants it on their shelves. One night Mother is moaning so much that Jenny and I apply a patch—"wear rubber gloves when handling," say the instructions, very strict directives, "flush down the toilet, do not dispose of where a pet can reach." The next morning, I have trouble bringing her around. By afternoon, she's slept it off, but I think, *Whoa...this is the way...*The hospice people have said, "If you think she's in pain, do not let it go on."

That night, she draws me down and whispers, "This place is full of bugs, look there—on the walls, on the floor. Oh, Gayley, it's dirty, *terribly.*"

"Ma, there are no bugs."

"Don't you see them? Oh, Gayley, did you feel it?"

"Feel what, Ma?"

"Last night, the crack, terrible—didn't you feel it?" Terror in her eyes. "Oh, I'm sure it's broken! Let me out of here, I'm not ready to die." I up the dose of Ativan and painkiller, still trying to keep it low, still trying to keep her here, though it makes no sense. I know that in a nursing home, a hospital, they wouldn't be measuring out the medications by halves and quarters, they'd have her completely drugged by now, and maybe they'd be right; but she is fighting for her life, and I am, too.

"Paddy sleeps, Pappy sleeps, I think I'll sleep, too," she mumbles as I tuck her in one night. Meaning, she knows they are gone and knows it's her time too? A metaphor or a mad mutter? I never can tell.

Sometimes she thinks Paddy is upstairs (there is no upstairs)—"Paddy, did you have corn for supper?" she says to the ceiling, "Did you have pork chop?"

"Oh, yeah, she go on like that," says Jenny, then, narrowing her eyes, "where was Paddy buried?"

"She wasn't buried, she's..." I stop, remembering her box of ashes is in the closet of the bedroom where Jenny is sleeping. Damn, Jenny's probably been nosing around. I know she has strong ideas about the spirit world, I can't have her getting spooked. But I have nowhere else to put it—I can't risk the garage, where everything's so chaotic, or the front room, where everything's so exposed.

One Thursday, late, I walk in, and Mother asks for her blue bathrobe. I see that she's tucked in under her quilt, her face flushed with warmth. "But Ma, you don't need a robe." She begins to fret.

"Oh, I just give it to her," says Jenny, the next morning, "she ask for it all the time."

So the next time she asks for the blue robe, I give it to her, and she hugs it to her. "This is something you know nothing about," she says, "*nothing to do with you.*" Much that is on her mind these days has nothing to do with me. At one time I'd have welcomed not being the center of her universe, now I just feel dumb, like what was that all about, that long struggle between us, that tug of war, I feel like I'm standing, stupid, a slack piece of rope dangling in my hand, nothing to hold me up.

Most of the names she says are names I've never heard, but when I try to get her to talk about the past, to call forth a scene from an old photo—remember Lake County? remember the swimming hole, remember the pony?—she smiles but says nothing.

She has lost so much weight, she is so shrunk, but she is still beautiful. Her brow is high, pale, unwrinkled, though there's a line between her eyes, a furrow where there wasn't. Her eyes, ice blue, focus, intent upon a place just beyond my head, staring at…what? She cannot tell me what she sees.

I would like to photograph her but I'm afraid it might freak her out. So I snap shots in words, not writing, exactly, just jotting down images, phrases, pieces of dreams.

I study her, try to take her in. Her skin, remarkably clear despite the sun she loved, the beach places she lived, California, Florida, Hawaii. Her face has held together, not pulled loose in jowls, but her

Remember the swimming hole, remember the pony?

nose has arched—she used to joke that it had grown, made her look like a crone. I think it looks regal.

I study her, *bone of my bone, flesh of my flesh,* the body, flesh, bones that shaped mine. Good bones, old bones, I wonder if I will make bones so old. I wonder if I want to.

I stroke her forehead, touch the pulse at her temple, feel the strength of her will to live. The doctors always said she had the heart of a young woman. Her belly, Buddha-like, like the Buddhas in the backyard. I can't bear to think what the swelling means, I don't want to know, her skin is breaking down, there is no arresting these processes. We keep an eye on the plastic bag by the bed—if it turns dark, says Nurse Allison, the kidneys are failing. I'm not sure what good that does to know.

If she dies soon, I think grimly, she won't need this body. It feels like a race to beat the breakdown of the body. DO NOT RESUSCITATE says the sign on the refrigerator door. As though *resuscitation* were a possibility now.

Probably it's better that she's not all here to take it in. But it means we never talk. I thought we would talk, we'd talked before. She always said death was a natural part of life, nothing to fear. She

left books around for me to find, *Final Exit, Let Me Die Before I Wake.*
I told her I would never let her come to this. But that was another
mother, who knew nothing of the body's tricks, and that was another
daughter, who knew nothing at all.

Should I try to get her to talk about what is happening? When
Ivan Ilyich was dying, in the Tolstoy story, everyone around him pre-
tended it wasn't happening and he felt so alone. That story haunts
me—have I abandoned her to a loneliness worse than death? Is it I
who impose this reticence, or she?

"I thought we'd talk," I tell Bob.

"About *death*? What is there to say?"

"What is there to say?" How can I begin to say, long-distance to
France...there's volumes to say, volumes that have been said, death
has been written about, sung about, deplored, implored, since language began, there are dirges, laments, poems, plays, epics about
death, death the definer, death that marks us as mortals—where
would we be without death, *what* would we be? Death, *the mother
of all beauty*, the mother of all art. I think all art is funerary art, carv-
ings on cave walls that say, *I was here, I passed this way*; what else are
the pyramids, temples, tombs, steles, standing stones, gravestones,
markers that say, *we were here, we passed this way*, commemorations
of our selves and the people we love so much we cannot leave them
for dead, we make scratchings on stone.

But between Mother and me, there are only frettings and reassurances. I who talk for a living, whose tools and trade are words, am
at a loss for words.

Toward the end, her speech becomes fragments, parts of sentences, nonsense syllables—*meow, meow, rio rio*. She turns her face to
the wall, scalp pink through wisps of white hair—*Mommy Mommy*,
she cries, I want to cry it too, I want to cry with her the way we cried
for Bill, the two of us together, I want to cry as I cried as a child,
Mommy, Mommy, this hurts too much, make it go away.

School time is ended, now there is only this time. I sit in her room, reading exams, I walk to the Rancho shopping center and drop the grade sheet in the mail, sorry to be finished—that's bad, when you wish you were grading; I wish there were someone to tell this to, it's almost funny.

I fidget, pace, wander out to the garage to her file cabinet, empty the drawers into shopping bags, upend the bags onto the long black table in the living room, where I used to work. Jenny is watching a sitcom, I ask her to turn it down—she huffs off to her bedroom and turns on her radio. The strains of a spiritual waft down the hall, *amazing grace, so sweet it is,* I hum along, how sweet it would be.

I turn to the file marked "Funeral." Mother has listed Paddy and my father as "next of kin," not imagining that she will outlive them both. Her directions are just like Paddy's, "simple cremation, no embalming," but where Paddy wrote, "no memorial," she has typed, *choice of family.* Ohno, that means she wants one—yes, of course, I rally, we'll have a memorial. In the blank left for "Minister," she has typed, "someone of liberal, humanist philosophy. Preferably not a Christian minister." No flowers, memorial donations to American Civil Liberties Union. *Way to go, Ma.* Ashes to be scattered off the Monterey peninsula, same as Paddy—I wonder, did they confer about such things or just coincidentally arrive at the same decisions.

Here are folders marked "Bank of America," "Great Western," thick, bulky files, bursting with papers—I swear, she's saved every scrap of paper for the past forty years. I am suddenly furious at her for this mess, furious at her for dying—how can she do this to me?

I look again and I realize these files are not a mess, they're far better organized than mine, for that matter, with notes to herself, or to someone, specifying a CD here, $12,000, a CD there, $13,500, squirreled away in different banks in case one failed. By the time I read through the papers I have a fair idea what there is. Her habits of thrift, which I tried to talk her out of, have left me something. If she'd spent on herself as I urged her to, she'd have ripped right through these small sums, but she tucked them away and left them for me—same as Paddy. My face goes hot—oh, Ma, oh Paddy, that's *why* you were so frugal, isn't it?

Next morning, I open the curtains—"look, Ma, the cherry tree!" She turns toward my voice, I don't think she sees me or the tree. It's Mother's Day. We've brought her a big bouquet, I don't think she sees it, I don't think she knows I'm here, or cares—this is her business, her dying, hers alone.

She screams when we change her. When I tell her Paddy is resting, she calls me a liar. She asks us to leave and as we file out, she says, "thank you very much," every bit the lady.

I hate it that it's spring, it ought to be winter, not this obscene riot of regrowth, the cherry tree in bloom, the merry month of May. In eleven days is her birthday.

I drive up to Berkeley for a root canal and dinner with Janet, the only friend I'm in touch with, and I stay the night. In the morning, Jenny calls and tells me Mother has been moaning so loud it set Nellie howling—"Get down here, girl."

If you think she's suffering, you know what to do—Nurse Allison's words are on my mind as I drive back. Christ, how do they do it, the professionals, turn their hearts to stone? they don't, I know, but I may have to. I get home midday, she is sleeping. She is quiet the rest of the day and night and the next day, but that evening, she begins to moan and thrash, and I see that Jenny wasn't kidding—this is another order of agony, it can't go on. "Where is it?" I say, riffling through the drawers, no doubt what to do.

"Here," says Jenny, handing me the morphine patch.

I want so much for Jenny to do it, but I know it should be me. I put on rubber gloves, clean a space of skin on her chest, fix the patch on firm. After a few hours, she is still moaning. I apply another. The bag on the side of the bed is turning dark.

The second patch doesn't send her over, either—she comes to, looks frightened. But I can still put a half a piece of chocolate in her mouth and quiet her down. Then her jaws lock, refusing the candy.

("I knew it was over the day you refused a chocolate," forms the sentence; "yes," she'll say, "that would be serious." I can't believe we won't be saying this someday.)

I sit, then stand by the bed, holding her hand, singing *Lullaby, and good night, may the angels now take thee*, I sing it over and over, it's the only lullaby I know. Around 4:00 AM I fall into bed, helping myself to the Ativan prescribed for her.

Next morning, or is it afternoon, I wake to a voice, sharp and critical—"You here alone?" breaks through my drugged sleep. Someone at the door. "No, the daughter here too," says Jenny. I grope for my bathrobe and stumble out: "I'm here."

The woman comes in, examines Mother, makes sure we're doing all we can, hands me a pamphlet, *Gone from My Sight: The Dying Experience*. I stare at the words. Gone. Sight. Dying. The words are inert black marks, saying nothing. Maybe Bob was right—what is there to say? "Thank you," I say, tossing the pamphlet on the table. Just then, Inge drives up and she and Jenny go in to sit with Mother, get her to take some Christmas juice. "You have a good team here," says the hospice woman. I want to go in and tell Mother, wake her up and tell her, look Ma, a good team.

That night, or was it the next, I'm in the kitchen when I hear Jenny say, "Agnes, Agnes," trying to bring her round. Oh no, I clench, she should not be doing this…I hear Mother say, "*Whaat?*" like, what are you bothering me with. I think I hear her say, "*this is something you know nothing about.*" But Jenny said she said, "*There is nothing you can do.*" Maybe she heard right, she was there in the room, but I think I heard right. I think Mother was saying, *let me alone, let me get on with it.*

Why, I ask myself now, as I've asked before, have I written this, and, in writing it, revising it, relived it, over and over, these worst days of my life—what is this impulse to tell? To bear witness, I suppose—but to what end? will it come clear in the end, in the writing, can I figure it out?

I have read about the rattle in the throat, the fluids accumulate, the heart no longer able to pump the lungs clear. What I do not know is how long it will go on. Three days and three nights. She doesn't seem to be suffering, she seems in a deep sleep, but what if she's not—should I put on another patch? I hold back. So strong, the desire to keep her here.

So hot, these last days, impossible to get air into the little room.

Wednesday, we know is the last day and we don't leave her side. Jenny sits, I stand, Jenny stands, I sit, we hold her hands, stroke her forehead.

"She be crossing over now. She be too far for us to call her back." Jenny is narrating her journey. "She be meeting Paddy, she be meeting her mommy and daddy."

"Think so, Jenny?"

"Oh, yeah, for sure."

Can she really believe in this fantastic voyage, or is she just saying these things to cheer me up?

"What's happening now, Jenny?"

"They be together now." I hang on her words, amazed at the strength of my desire to believe.

We sit, then stand by the bed, through evening and nightfall. Her arms and hands are swollen, her feet are cold, her breath comes slower; then, suddenly, toward midnight, stops.

Amazing how absolute it is, I'd have thought these days of waiting would have made it easier, but I feel it like a blow. Jenny flings back as though struck, rushes out of the room. I am shocked at what I think is her insensitivity, then I remember her beliefs about the spirit world and hear her sobbing in the other room. "When she die, you want to be out'a there," she'd said. Not me, I don't want to leave her side, I'm glad to be alone with her. I am patting her arms, stroking her face, cradling her head in my hand, feeling the warmth at the base of her skull. The tears come now that would not come before. I pull the sheet over her mouth, open from the long struggle for breath, smooth back her hair, drinking her in, and suddenly I see the young, proud beauty emerge through the crust of years—her face unlined, her brow, marmoreal, she looks poised for flight. I am filled suddenly with desire that she be out of here. "*Go for it, Ma,* flee this place, go to where you can be who you truly are—do it right this time, sweetheart."

I would have sat there all night, cradling her head, talking to her, but Jenny says we should call hospice. Hospice sends a nurse, Josh, a small bearded fellow who radiates kindness. He walks into the bedroom, notices the photo on the wall, the young dark beauty with the expectant smile. He shakes his head, takes out a stethoscope, holds it to her heart. There is paperwork, we go to the kitchen, he takes a sheaf of papers out of his briefcase, spreads it on the table. Nellie does this thing she does when she's just had a long, slurpy drink, looks around for a lap to thrust her dripping muzzle into. Jenny and I see it coming, exchange helpless glances as she heads for the stranger and sticks her dribbling beard into his lap, wetting his pants. He looks up, surprised, reaches out and pats her head, grinning—"you gotta love a dog like this!" As he fills out the death certificate, he notices—"two days more, she'd have been ninety." He hands it to me to sign. It will still need a physician's signature, but this way, no physician need come to the house, wouldn't want to trouble a doctor, would we. He calls the mortuary where I've made the arrangements.

Too soon, there's a knock at the door, a man in a black leather jacket and a black cap, strangely dapper, stands at the door. He makes sure he has the right house, goes back to his van to get a gurney, wheels it in through the door, sharp turn into the hall, another turn into the bedroom. I sidle out into the hall to make room for the gurney; he takes a large plastic bag from a kit.

"If there's anything you want to send along with her, flowers or a card or anything, you can," he says. I've never heard of this, I have nothing, there must be something—the blue bathrobe, where is it? I slip into the room as he maneuvers Mother into the plastic bag and onto the gurney. I search through the laundry basket, through the drawers—no bathrobe.

"Jenny," I call to her in the kitchen, "the blue bathrobe—where is it?"

"It in there somewhere," she answers, still reluctant to come back.

"I can't find it."

She finally appears, scoots in past the gurney, looks in all the same places I've looked, then ducks into the closet and emerges, clutching the robe.

By this time the guy has zipped up the plastic bag and wheeled the gurney into the hall. I appear, waving the blue bathrobe—"This goes with her." He looks annoyed, unzips the bag, has to raise her up to get the robe around her and it seems for a moment she might topple over; she looks cross, bewildered—I don't want that final image, I want that calm stately profile. He zips up the sack again, lays her back down on the gurney, opens the front door and wheels her out—out the same door she and I walked in together forty-four years before.

Too cruel, I want to shout, carting her out like a sack of garbage, this can't be right—even the hospital did better than this with Paddy, composed her face, tidied her up before hauling her off to the fire. I've been numb in the head to let it happen like this, to go about death as though it were a logistical problem—this is final, this is *forever*. It's not *malarkey*, Mother, there needs to be some ceremony, some cleansing, bathing, seasoning, Mitford was wrong, we were wrong. Now it comes back, imagination, bludgeoned by months of getting through, by *years* of rushing through, stirs like the tingling of a limb long numb, stings like nettles beneath the skin, now comes feeling, flooding back.

I don't want this feeling, I want sleep.

We follow the guy out into the driveway, watch him slide the gurney into the back of his van, a beat-up old van like a plumber might drive, someone come to fix the furnace, the door clicks shut. *"Be seein' you,"* he says, touching his cap as he walks around to the driver's seat. Funny. A joke. How many more stiffs on his route tonight?

Jenny and I stand, dumb, as the van disappears down Clinton Road, Mother in the back. *Too soon, too soon*, I want to cry, I am crying—she's still *warm!*

I shouldn't have listened to Jenny, I shouldn't have called so soon, I didn't think he'd get here so fast. I had a horror of morning, kids on their way to school, neighbors jogging down the block, I'd hoped it would happen under cover of dark, I know she'd want that too—but there are hours of darkness left, I could have sat with her, I didn't think he'd come so soon.

I am shocked to find myself outside—just stepping out the front door, I see there is an outside, the world hasn't shrunk to that room, there are houses, hedges, lawns drenched in moonlight, a moon so bright the trees cast shadows. We go back in and sit awhile, silent. But I need to move.

I grab Nellie's leash, "C'mon, Jenny, let's walk," and we set off to the park. Keith's light is on, Mother's Cadillac's in his driveway, he opens the door and his dogs leap out, Nellie joins them, charging, butting, herding. Keith gives me a hug, a bear hug, a bear of a man, we find a bench and sit, breathing the cool, sharp scent of the redwoods that ring the park, tall, spectral presences silvered by the moon. *Clair de Lune*, Mother played that, I hear it in my head.

The silent time of night, the still before dawn, I could sit here forever, watching the dogs, but too soon, the scent of morning— I don't want light, I need the dark, unholy spirit scuttling for cover.

We hurry back to the house, but Nellie won't come in, she hovers at the edge of the yard, I have to put on her leash, coax her in—she's never been like this. Jenny sticks by my side, for her sake or mine, I don't know, it's not what I want. I think about calling Bob, I might reach him with the time difference in France, but I don't want to talk on the phone, I don't want to talk at all. Jenny brings her blankets and pillow to the front room, settles down on the couch.

I should have sat with her longer, I should have taken the term off, I should have given her the morphine sooner, I shouldn't have called the guy so soon, I should have, I shouldn't have, I shouldn't have…

Before the sleeping pill takes hold, it's on me like a wolf on a bone.

MISSING PERSONS

They have their whole lives before them;
but also they are dead.

—ROLAND BARTHES, *Camera Lucida*

FOR A DAY OR SO, YOU GO ON AS USUAL. Like the cartoon character flung out over a precipice, not noticing the ground's gone out from under him, limbs flail on, assuming traction, I flail on.

I tackle her room. I need Jenny to help with this and she is leaving soon, so we do it now. Into the garbage go the medicines, baby wipes, nappies. I turn to the drawers, they are full, forty-four years full—what a jumble, what a snarl, scarves, beads, wigs, elastic doodads off a girdle, tangled in a ball. I am afraid of these intimate places, have always been afraid of them, fearful of secrets lurking there. But there are no secrets, only evidence that things had got away from her. On a shelf in her closet, shoved high out of reach, a jumbo package of toilet paper—so *that's* where you put it, Ma. You swore you'd bought toilet paper, you never could find it. "This house is too much for me," you'd mutter; I see it's true.

We pack bag after bag, taking Lysol to the floor where the catheter pouch dripped, to eradicate the stain. We move the bureau on the left over to the right, haul the nightstand to the garage. But I leave the bed so it looks out on the cherry tree, leave the chair by the bed.

Tomorrow is her birthday. I have an uneasy feeling she's not yet cremated. I don't like to think of her hanging around in her present form, I want her released. I call the mortuary. They haven't received the death certificate. It sits, unsigned, on Goldstein's desk.

She is cremated May 23. The day after she'd have turned ninety.

The day Jenny leaves. I stand at the front door, watch her walk across the lawn to the waiting car, ducking to avoid a cherry branch; she turns, blows me a kiss—"I'll call you, girl!" I wave as she disappears down the block, as Mother used to wave at me driving away, how many times, I wonder, wondering if she felt as desolate as I feel now. I go back in the house, sink into the chair beside the phone. I should call someone. I pick up the phone. I put it down.

I am alone. Alone in this house for the first time ever.

Not quite alone. Sammy and Joey leave a sandwich on the kitchen table. Janet drives down from Berkeley with food to last the week. My friend Kay drives down with dinner. I accept these offerings gratefully, humbly, wondering at the world of efficiency where people organize meals, drive cars, find their way from Berkeley.

Janet says it looks like I've devised a way of sitting shiva, staying in the house and letting people bring me food. Janet has always harbored a secret belief that I'm at heart really Jewish, a notion I suspect says more about her than me, but I leap at it now—shiva, yes. Kay tells me the Navajos believe the spirit sticks around for seven days and I grasp at this too.

"When are you coming home?" she asks.

Home...

It's not over between Mother and me, and whatever's left of her is here.

The fog wisps in. It clings to the branches of the redwood tree, hangs around all day. It's as chilly now as it was hot before, one of those damp, gray springs we sometimes get, feels a long way from summer.

I curl up on the bed. It makes no sense to be sleeping in the front room now that Jenny's gone, but I stay. I survived death here, I know this is a place I can survive. I am afraid to go back to that room where I slept as a child. I keep the arrangement, Mother's tall shoji screen around the bed, Paddy's lamp on the night table, I like the way it shines through the screen, the small, lit space.

I pull aside the heavy living room drape, gaze out at the redwood tree, trace the scarlet trumpet vine to the top. The sunflowers nod and wink, the purple lilies of the Nile bob on long, uncertain stems, the blue-green Buddha sits in the bamboo. I'd like to lie here forever, curled up in a ball.

Then I realize I could. I could stay on in this house and Sammy and Joey could stay too. It could all go on, just like before, me here instead of Mother.

The thought terrifies me. I leap out of bed.

I clear the papers off the kitchen table. For the first time in living memory, there are no papers on the kitchen table. I sit where she sat, staring out on the cherry tree.

What now?

Around midnight, I walk Nellie to the park. I stop by Keith's, sink heavily into his lumpy, dog-fuzzed couch. High-tech equipment lines his walls, computer terminals, monitors, audio and video devices, digital and electronic gizmos, exotic as a spacecraft, yet comforting for the mastery they suggest. Keith radiates competence, there is nothing he can't fix or make, though he's been put out of work by changes in the valley. Now he sets about fixing me, says I'm too thin, produces cheese and crackers, insists I eat.

"How ya doin'?" he booms.

How I am doin' seems so beyond saying, I don't even try. I sit and watch the dogs. Keith's white poodle puppy stands tall as Nellie— Nellie is besotted with this leggy, dancing creature, they cavort like puppies, though Nellie is no puppy. Keith gives up on talk, gets up to put on music, his sound system's like the instrument panel of a jet plane. Pink Floyd fills the room, pulsing, twanging, throbbing. Keith turns it up. Why did he put on The Wall? The lyrics are messages just for me, is there anyone out there, anybody home, any way home? The sound surrounds me, we listen through to the end, the walls come crashing down. How his wife Margaret sleeps through this, I don't know; a good sleeper, and, lucky for them, steadily employed. The music stops, the silence is stunning after so much sound, only the *grrr* of the dogs tussling, scuffling, gnawing each others' ruffs and ears.

"I'd like to be a dog." I find my voice and this croaks out. Keith's eyebrows shoot up, bushy and gray. "I mean, wouldn't you?" Now it's his turn to be silent.

He walks me back up the block, we stand in the front yard, saying good night. Mother's window is open; where there was a glow through gold drape is a hole, gaping to the night.

"You know," he says, hugging me good night, his bulk, reassuring, Bob was so wraithlike, I can barely bring him to mind, "you know, when my mother died, I said, *heigh ho, the witch is dead*. You're lucky—you had a mom to mourn."

A mom to mourn.

I fumble with my keys, let myself in. "Is that you, Gayley?" comes her voice.

"Sorry, Mom, did I wake you?"

"No, dear, that's all right."

There's a white unicorn on your pillow. With my glasses off, my eyes half shut, the unicorn is your snow-white head. I talk to it, talk to you.

I know I'm behaving like a crazy person. But it's not me that's crazy, it's death, mad beyond measure, beyond all bounds.

Now that you are gone, you are everywhere. The dying body that took your place is no more, but you are back, my mother.

You stand in the kitchen, wearing your old white cardigan, fuzz-balled and out-at-elbows. You bend down, take a pan from a cabinet, fill it at the sink. You open the refrigerator, take out an egg. You move slowly, deliberately, making your way from counter to stove to sink. A little crone-like figure, hairs sprouting indecorously from your chin, chest sunk in, stomach distended, you shuffle about on swollen legs—such a bag of bones, my dear little mother. You put the egg on to boil, slip a slice of bread in the toaster, wait for it to brown. Your eyes focus on nothing in particular. Perhaps you are lost in thought, or it may be that these movements require all your concentration.

You sit at the kitchen table, pull the curtain aside. You munch on your toast and egg, look out on the day.

Where am I? Probably I'm still in bed. Maybe I'm in the living room, head in a book. Maybe, I like to think, I sit with you at the table, and we chat.

Your cane hangs on the kitchen doorknob. Your purse hangs on the bedroom knob, red and black beaded hippie bag. These things have no purpose now, they are simply there.

So many things in this house. There always were too many things, now there are even more. Paddy's things in the garage, my father's things, your father's, your mother's, my brother's, all here, too. As they died, their things landed here.

I am going to have to deal with every single thing in this house.

Next day, I open the storage shed. The door scrapes, heavy on its hinges, reluctant to be entered, cobwebs clutch at my face and hair, reek of things long unexhumed. There in the recesses of the shed sits my father's steamer trunk. I drag it to the garage, take a hammer to the rusted lock—I've locked him out of mind so long, I need to know what's here. Here are packets of letters from my mother, neatly twined, dozens of letters, so many weeks, months, years, the war kept them apart. He has carried these letters his every move, his many moves, since World War II. And photos, hundreds of photos, of us, of her, the places he has seen. The things he cared enough to save.

I lug the trunk into the living room. So *this* is why people have children, I get it, so someone will share this. Another of those things everybody got but me, like writing *Thank You* notes. Someone will care about your ancestors if they happen to be *their* ancestors—otherwise, forget it, forget them, they might as well never have been.

Are you kidding? says another voice. Have a kid so they'll honor the ancestors—what world is that? I knew only one of my grandparents, he is a fond memory, but distant, *Grandfather Gruff*—and what difference can it make to him if I remember or forget? I knew none of the others, nor did I inquire, I barely know their names.

Yes, but, says another voice, something to pass down, something of my own. *Bone of my bone, flesh of my flesh,* whatever that means. Whatever it means, the words won't go from my mind.

I walk to the Rancho camera store and buy every photo album they have. I spread the photos out on the long black table where I used to work.

You and Paddy sit astride a horse—*Two Little Indians, Lake County,* says the back, Paddy's writing. You and Paddy walking down a country road—*Two Little Maids,* Paddy's writing again. Paddy, the keeper of the archives. She sang that song—*Three Little Maids from school are we.*

Who took these photos? There are photographs here for a dynasty. Why should such people leave photos for a dynasty?

They were not breeders, not ones to set down roots. Bolters on both sides, they cut loose from the past, broke with family and faith, severed the ties that bind, leaving it all behind. Restless people, rootless people, they headed west.

My grandfather, Edward Paterson, Scottish on one side, Irish on the other, ran off with his boss's wife. Christine Heuser had been a dancer in a chorus line. She'd married a rich man, then fell in love with the dashing young man who worked on his yacht. She and Grampa arrived in San Francisco, 1906, the city a ruin, or soon to be a ruin—was this before or after the earthquake? I never asked. She brought her baby, my Uncle Ted, *Teddy Bear* (the fond names, the family names), and the Morris chair. That prized family heirloom, crafted in the studios of William Morris, its rich, dark oak carved into lions with flaring nostrils and flowing manes—that chair now sits in my front room in Berkeley, the house Ted left me. The lions came out to prowl the room at night, or so I imagined.

But wait—why would a woman in flight from an outraged husband haul a chair like that across the country? She ran off with his son, and the furniture, too? The stories don't add up.

My poor dear mother, you'd say, the mere mention of her name brought tears to your eyes. Such sadness, so many secrets, one of which popped out not long ago. You and Paddy and I were at the kitchen table, you were sorting through some old jewelry, you handed me a slim gold band—"Here, your grandmother's wedding ring—you can wear it. You're not married, but neither was she."

"We don't know that," spluttered Paddy, shocked to hear you say it.

"Of course we know. She was never divorced—he said he'd kill her if he found her." Or was it Paddy who let the secret out and you

Two Little Maids.

who were shocked? I can't remember. I remember only that I was amused you thought it worth keeping secret, when it made perfect sense—*illegitimacy*, bred in the bone, bred in our bones.

Never trust the outside world, Grampa said, and that other thing he used to say, *man was made to mourn*—you'd quote this to me and I'd glare, dead set against you. It was so hopeless, so like your life, stopped short and stuck in the past.

Now here I am, heir to your belongings, to your terrible lack of belonging. *Never trust the outside world*. But Mother—that's all that's left now, the outside world.

My father, too, that unbelonging. In his steamer trunk, I find a photo of him as a boy, the only photo I've ever seen of him as a boy (there are hundreds of the Patersons); he never showed me, I find it, buried in the trunk. They stand, unsmiling, father, mother, four boys and a girl, a dour-looking lot, the Greenbergs, 1910. The immigrants, Russian Jews landed on the Lower East Side, rural people cast on urban shores. My father Jacob, the first of his siblings to be born in the new land, three years old in this photo, and even then, those sad, dark eyes he had always, as though he knew that soon he would lose mother, father, and the brother he loved most, William, dead by his own hand. *Why* did he give his son that name? The family sadness, the family doom. Only once did I hear him say his mother's name, and that was because I asked: "What was your mother's name?" *Anna*, he said, seeming to dredge the word up from a deep, closed place. It was all he said, *Anna*, not a word more.

He fled at the first chance. He'd seen a valley on a produce crate, an orchard of blossoms with rolling hills beyond. It looked like paradise, he said. He set out to find that valley.

So they landed here, restless people, romantic people, drawn west by the promise of new beginnings.

Beginnings that all end here with me.

The Greenbergs, 1910.

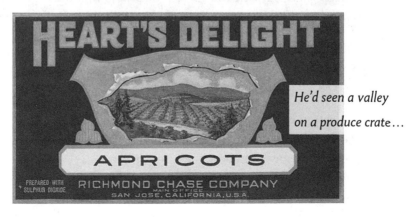

*He'd seen a valley
on a produce crate…*

Sepia, the color of your childhood, the color of memory. A swimming hole, a deep dark pool set in tall, pale boulders and arching oaks that filter the sun so it dapples the water and lights you children with a magic glow. *Siegler Springs*, says the photo, *Lake County*. Lake County, how you loved it. You'd speak of it and I'd see a land of lakes, rivers, streams cascading over rocks that glisten in the sun. Lake County, where I have never been, which I have only known filtered through the haze of your nostalgia.

Paterson homestead, says the writing on the back. I remember, you told me Grampa homesteaded land in Lake County. But where is he? He's not in the pictures, maybe he's taking the pictures—somebody is. But you said he kept his job in the city. San Francisco is a hundred miles away, a long way on country roads. "She was a brave woman, my mother," Paddy said, "living winters all the way up there, alone with us." No plumbing in that shack, no electricity, that's sure—how did she cook for you, keep you warm? Winters up there are *cold!*

My grandmother, Christine Heuser, is no longer a shapely chorus girl but a sturdy, stocky *Frau*. She stands, feet planted firm, holding the reins of the horse you and Paddy sit on, such a big horse, such little girls; she looks proud of her two girls. Paddy sits behind you, clinging to her big sister, peering at the camera as though from a hidden place. You were the bolder, you always said, and I see it here, though not as bold as you pretend. I see the bravado, I know it for my own.

There is a dog, there is always a dog—this one's a scruffy mutt. On the back is written, *Jack*.

Jack? You will both marry men named Jack.

You and Paddy dancing the hula, *Palolo Hill*, says the writing on the back, off in the distance, I see Diamond Head. Why did you leave Lake County for Honolulu? Why leave Alameda for Lake County? Alameda, where you were born, where you were bounced on Jack London's knee. One of the great family legends—he and Grampa ran for office together, drank together, quite a lot, you recalled. Why all this moving around?

Grampa the nomad who dragged his family from Alameda to Lake County to Honolulu and back to San Francisco, Grampa the homesteader, Grampa the union organizer who kept a steady job through the Depression, Grampa the Socialist who warned, *never trust the outside world*. Words you use for him are *prima donna* and *paranoiac*.

There are a lot of stories, and they don't add up.

I clear a space for the photos my father took of you, dozens of these. You look like a 1940s movie star, suits cut long and smart, hats with a flair. You have on those ambers you brought back from the Soviet Union, you said the pawnshops in Leningrad were full of amazing things in 1937, I bet they were. You didn't go there to shop, you went in search of a socialist paradise, yet you did shop. I loved those beads, they held the warmth of your body. You showed me the fly in the big bead, trapped in time.

No wedding photos, no wedding, you honeymooned in Europe for six months. You on the steps of the Parthenon, you in profile in a field of tall grass, you on a bicycle on a country lane, you, you, you—where is he? He is there, of course, taking the photos, there and not there, as he always was, shaping our lives from behind the scenes. Even in these photos you are gazing in the distance, tuned to a distant drummer, or are you just posing, knowing you're being photographed by a man who loves you? He must have loved you, he took all these photos, or maybe it was your looks he loved. He's not bad-looking himself, in the few pictures you take of him, dark, intense, a lot going on in that face, a complicated look, a look women like.

Then there's this baby: baby in a high chair, wielding a spoon; baby in a bathtub, eyes wide with glee; baby crawling in the sands at

Honeymoon, 1937.

Santa Cruz, reaching for your hand. Many many photos of this baby. *The Little Rascal, Caught in the Act!*—captions you've written on the photos you sent him while he was away at war.

Then he's back. *"Go way!"* my first words to this man in uniform come to boss me around—*"Go way far way!"* He hoists me up, delight in his eyes.

The photos go color when he gets back. A girl in ringlets peers coyly through the blossoms of a cherry tree: *Los Gatos, 1948,* says the back. A girl in organdy on a split-rail fence: *Big Sur, 1949.* The girl has a heart-shaped face like yours and your high, broad brow. For a while, she is beautiful, you are beautiful, and there are lots of photos. So *that's* what the valley looked like those days, Campbell, Saratoga, San Jose, poppies and mustard splash down the hillsides, gold and yellow streaks on slopes green from winter rain. Long gone, those fields and flowers, now there's no one left to ask—was he there when I was born, were you happy together?

He hoists me up, delight in his eyes.

Rap rap rap on the window jolts me back to now, where I do not wish to be. Sammy and Joey peer in—do I need anything from the store? No, nothing from the store. Only I need to know who these people are…

I eke out a chronology, beginning an album for your early years and another for your middle years. I begin an album for Paddy and an album for my father, and here are photos of Uncle Ted and a Liberty ship he helped build, war work that paid for the house he left me, and Ted's wife Mabel, and Mabel's sisters, who I never knew, and—oh dear, this is getting complicated. And Bill, Billy Boy, brother Bill, no, can't look at these, I shove them to the side.

I do this sitting at the long black table by the window where I used to write. I work all day and through the night, and the next day and the next night. Crazy, what am I doing, who the hell cares if the photos are organized now?

Sammy and Joey peer in as they walk by, curious, concerned.

Oakland, 1948. I am five. I sit on the couch, a book in one hand, the cat in the other, clutching the cat so it can't get away. I am reading to

So that's what the valley looked like those days...

the cat. You said it was so cute, the way I read to the cat. I didn't know how to read but I'd read to the cat.

Me as a fire-breathing dragon, Cookie as a princess in a long white gown, Cookie is my best friend, we go trick or treat.

This is where memory begins for me. Or do I only think I remember because there are photos? *Snapshot*, a moment *shot, snapped, snapped up* from time, wrested from the flux of minutes, days, years. Time stopped, time arrested. This then fixes memory, *becomes* memory. But is it *real* memory, or *photo-memory*—is it only the photos I remember? I remember so little...

Can I remember without the photos?

I remember, Cookie and I swing on the schoolyard bars, we whirl round and round. I don't want to come home, you can't get me to come home. Home is a dark place, shadows in the hall, voices raised. I don't think he ever hit you but there was anger in that place. I wish I could remember something about him besides the anger.

I remember, he fixed my wrist. I fell down, he took me to the hospital, put a splint on my wrist. *Slow down*, he'd say. But maybe that wasn't anger in his voice, maybe it was concern. *You're going to really hurt yourself if you don't slow down.*

I remember, we drove back from San Francisco, across the bridge. I didn't get to sit up front, you had a baby in your lap. *I don't want a baby, I want a dog*, I said, one of those funny things you said I said, you'd repeat them to people, repeat them to me. Not so funny anymore.

Back to the photos.

Billy and I are playing in the sand, *Lake Tahoe, 1949*, says the back. I am not really playing with my brother, I am playing for the camera, for my father who is the camera. *Billy Boy, Charming Billy, Sweet William*. Now I see the waif in him, the shy, sad grin, now I know the end of the story.

Billy has on a suit, I have on a wool plaid dress, we are dressed up to look grown-up, we are seeing Daddy off—he is going to be the ship's doctor, the doctor of the ship. *Way far away*. We have moved again. No photos of this house, no Daddy there to take them, a cabin in the Santa Cruz Mountains with a patio and garden wall made of stone, redwoods all around, swish and scent of trees, lights in the trees even though it wasn't Christmas. I'd skip down the hill to school, a two-room schoolhouse, the neighbor's collie at my heels. Was it the trees or the collie that made this a happy place, or did you breathe easier with him gone?

Then he's back, we move back to the valley. *Campbell, 1949*. A small house, a street fresh hacked from an orchard, the tar stings my nose, sears my feet, sticks black and gummy to shoes and tires. Dirt in the front yard, dirt in the back, you tried to grow grass but the birds ate the seeds. No trees. Tractors, bulldozers, backhoes, grinding, devouring, they eat trees. The drone of big machines, crunch of metal against bark, thunk of branches hitting ground, trunks ripped from the earth, dirt clings to the roots, smoke rises from the pyres, wood frames shoot up, skeletal against the sky.

Sundays we drive around, follow the colored flags and signs that say LOW INTEREST, NOTHING DOWN, TERMS TO VETS, words I can read but do not understand. Nor do I know that the names *Oak Grove, Apricot Acres, Brook Haven* refer to the brooks, oaks, and groves that are no more. Chop it down, pluck it up, hack it up, pave it over, parcel it out—everywhere in the valley, the whir of buzz saws, *rat-a-tat-tat* of hammers, those unsettling sounds, you and my father still looking for a place you restless pair might rest.

We move in with Paddy and Grampa in San Jose, a tumbledown house on a street with tall trees, huge, after Campbell, cavernous closets where I play with Whissy Bow-Wow and hide from the shouting. Whissy Bow-Wow is white like Grampa's dog Rags, I take him everywhere. *Whissy* is a word I've made up, it means soft and nice to touch—I make up lots of words, you tell people proudly. *Whissy* is a word for people, too—Paddy is whissy, Mommy's whissy too, sometimes.

Grandfather Gruff is not whissy, his whiskers scratch, his pipe stings my eyes. Grampa has white hair and a black silk vest and a watch with a gold chain, he teaches me how to tell the time. *Tell the time*, he says. *Tell it what?* I say. *No, tell what time it is*, he corrects, *what is the time?* And, giggling, I say it over again, *tell it what?* Set in his ways, you say he is, he has to have porridge with raisins every morning, exact same time. I fasten on him like a barnacle on a rock, tag along with him through the yard and garage. He shows me how to make Rags do tricks, and after dinner, I crawl up on his scratchy army blanket and we hear *a fiery horse with the speed of light, a cloud of dust and a hearty Hi-Yo Silver*, a clatter of hooves and *the Lo-o-o-ne Ranger*, then comes a creaky door and spooky laughter and the *In-n-n-er Sanctum*. And sometimes, surprisingly, Grampa bursts into song, right there at the kitchen table with the red-and-white checked oil-cloth, *you'll have pie in the sky when you die*. Why *pie in the sky?* I ask. *Joe Hill*, he says. I see a hill. "That same fine voice that made him popular in taverns," says Paddy. "Too popular by half," says my mother; "he's in his cups." I see my grampa in a cup, sailing off with the owl and the pussycat on a pea-green sea.

Then he and Paddy move out. Then we move out too.

He shows me how to make Rags do tricks.

C'mon! she says. She has come to school to get me, this is no ordinary outing.

Whereto?

She told me later she'd ransacked the joint bank account, left a note on the kitchen table. Bold, she was, leaving like that, with a two-year-old and a seven-year-old in tow, and only the man she was leaving for support.

All those moves, I remember the rooms, the feel of the rooms, but not what it felt like to leave them. If there was pain at leaving, I don't remember—it felt like adventure. Trains those days went on forever, you could barely walk one end to the other, and the journey, too, went on forever, the Silver Comet to Miami, clickety-clack, telephone poles whisk by, it is dusk, it is dawn, hills in the desert glow purple and pink, it is hot, it is Texas, it is still Texas, days of Texas, brown and flat, clickety-clack.

We move in with Grampa and Paddy. Then they move out again.

Miami is paradise, long white beaches with swishing palms and balmy air, the paradise the sisters seemed always to be seeking. She takes me out in the waves, the water's warm, not like Santa Cruz, we bob up and down, she lets me go—*swim!* she says. The water buoys me up, sweeps me along—I can *swim*!

We go to the beach a lot. She likes it here, she has friends, they play music. But what were those years really like for her, I wonder now, what was going on between her and my father—did she want him back?

He wants us back, or thinks he does. He comes to Miami, picks up Billy and me, takes us to the beach. A woman walks up, says hello, how are you, sits down on our blanket, stays the day. On the way home he says, "don't say anything to Mother about Serafina..."

We go back, the long train ride back to San Jose, I am ten, Billy's five. We move in with my father in a small apartment near the hospital, rooms cramped and thick with anger and the smoke of charred dinners, and the shouting again. He stays out all night, he gets to stay out, he's The Doctor. But one night, the phone rings and it's the hospital saying, *where's The Doctor, where's The Doctor?* But the hospital was where he was supposed to be.

She knows where he is, I don't know how she knows, but she knows. She gets dressed, I mean, dressed *up*, a dress-up suit with a Joan Crawford look, lips painted red, eyebrows black.

Wait here, she says.

Billy and I wait. It is morning when she gets back, she is crying. She hurls a suitcase on the bed.

C'mon!

Whereto?

Can I be remembering right? It's like a scene from a movie. There is so much I'm not remembering—she and my father would have had to find a house, agree on a house, buy a house, I remember none of that, only this scene I remember, but maybe it's a movie I'm remembering.

And that is how we landed in Los Altos. Where the trap sprang shut, where she'd be a housewife but no longer a wife

The photos show a large girl, slouching to hide height and bust. Everything about me grows too fast, nothing stays put or in place, hair so flyaway that bobby pins fly out, hips all wrong for the pencil-slim skirts the girls wore then. My nose gets larger, more of my father in my features as there is less of him in our lives, and I wear glasses, like him, though never in the photos. But it's the expression that strikes me now, anxious, edgy, as though I'm trying to figure out how to get into the game, trying to figure out what the game is. I always have a crush on someone, someone always has a crush on me, though it's rarely the same someone.

Junior high school, hair straight and bristly, arms are too pudgy for the strapless prom dress I have on, the effect's all wrong. She is still trying for glamour, almost pulling it off, attractive in the turquoise silk jacket my father brought her from China, but there is strain in her face, her hair's a tad too dark, her middle thickening. It can't have been easy, losing those looks; it was all men cared about, she said, what fools.

High school, such a pack animal I am, such a fierce desire to belong. I hang out recesses in the bathroom, smoking with the *fast girls*, as they're called; I'm called that, too, though I'm not really, it's a part I play, waist cinched in, sweaters tight, hair dyed black. I hang out with guys in the Great Books Club and the Debate Society— *brains*, they're called, I'm called that, too, though I'm not really, not like them. They slip me my first serious novels, *Anna Karenina, Madame Bovary, The Brothers Karamazov, The Alexandria Quartet.*

Slumber parties, girls in PJs and curlers mugging for the camera, playing at smoking and drinking—they're playing, I really *do* smoke and drink.

I land at Sally's after school, Sally is my best friend.

"Hi, Mom. I'm at Sally's."

"Well, what else is new."

"They invited me to dinner."

"Okay. But get home early."

"They said I could spend the night."

"Oh, Gayley, not again. You get back here, you have homework to do." She disapproves of the Sorrensons, says they drink too much— they do, and so do I. "What'll it be?" Sally's mom, gravelly smoker's voice, bourbon tinkles over ice, goes down easy, laughter's easy, they have parties, friends, a pool. In my mother's voice I hear hurt and irritation, I hear, *get back where you belong*, she is so high and mighty, so alone.

We are fourteen, Sally and I go riding in the hills. In summer, the grass grows tall as the horses' heads, scent of sage and something tangier than sage, *tarweed*. In winter, mud sucks at the horses' hooves, the trails turn to bogs, creeks flood their banks. We are singing, *mud, mud, glorious mud,* then in a fit of giggles, we leap off the horses and roll around in the mud—it's *cold*, our breaths steam. Cold in the winter, hot in the summer, enough of each season to make us long for the other.

We are sixteen, I put down the top of the little Lancia my father loans me, Sally and I speed over the twisty roads to the coast, winding up the mountain, through conifer forests, hair tangling in the wind, faces pinking, ears popping as we near the summit, then un-popping as we weave down to the fishing villages Half Moon Bay and Pescadero. We zoom up the coast highway past artichoke fields and pumpkin patches to San Francisco, we hang out in North Beach coffee houses, we have on black tights and turtlenecks, playing at being beatniks, playing at picking up beatniks. *I have seen the best minds of my generation dragging themselves through the streets,* I shout into the wind, driving fast, *starving, mad, howling for a fix.* I have never actually seen these things, but I can imagine; Ginsberg's words make me imagine.

I look tough, tight sweaters and painted mouth, I look like I'm aspiring to be the star of a grade-B movie, bold and brassy as Elizabeth Taylor in *Butterfield Eight*, a call girl who breakfasts on bourbon and crashes her sports car, tragically, just as she finds True Love. If I can *look* bold, sexy, self-assured, maybe I can *feel* bold. But it's a part I play. Somewhere in there, guarded and out of sight, is me.

Who do you think you are? That question gets thrown at me more than once, by my mother, by my father—*Who the hell do you think you are? Where do you think you are going?* hurled at my backside as I disappear out the door.

I could not for the life of me have told you who or what or where.

You, my dear mother, never try to pass, never play the game. There is no small talk in you, no conversation about cooking or clothes or bringing up baby—on such matters, you are mute, though when it comes to the Rosenbergs, the arms race, your voice gets high and excited, the room goes quiet, glances get exchanged. "Well, I guess some people don't *care* if the human race survives," you huff. You scoff at the churchgoing ladies in white gloves and pillbox hats, at the *holier than thou* across the street who snubs you still—*so conventional*, your worst term of disapprobation, though I know your huffs hide hurt. When I tell you I intend to go to church, you are horrified, but you have to let me, according to your lights. You needn't have worried, I lasted two weeks. Under our Christmas tree, we make a crèche of Billy's plastic dinosaurs, the long-necked lizards with their horns, crests, and tusks, the T. rex with its toothy grin. "A more informed account of origins," you say.

You are hungry for conversation, you corral the unsuspecting passerby, the guy come to fix the refrigerator—doesn't he agree, we're naked apes made crazy from overcrowding? (you'd read Desmond Morris). Doesn't it seem like the planet is shrinking and everything's speeding up? (you'd read Paul Ehrlich and Alvin Toffler). Nobody wants to talk about these things, not in Los Altos, nor do they want to hear about *The Lonely Crowd, The Organization Man, The Power Elite*, let alone psycho-cybernetics or Zen Buddhism. You come on strong.

I cringe, wanting to disown the weirdness of you, knowing it for my own.

You are pacifists, you and Paddy, in a valley given over to war. Defense contracts are pulling money and population into the state; people on the block, parents of my friends work at Lockheed Missiles, Varian, Moffett Field. You talk about *blacklists, witch hunts*, the *Cold War*, I don't know what these words mean, but I hear their menace, friends of yours lose jobs—*never trust the outside world*. You march up and down the street with petitions, you warn about the *military-industrial complex* before anybody knows what that even means.

I have nightmares about nuclear holocaust, I write poems about nuclear holocaust.

Then, in a strange twist of events, the Younger Woman starts calling you. Maria, a black-haired, blue-eyed beauty who looks a lot like you, or what you'd looked like twenty-four years before (she's that much younger), is on the phone to you a lot, crying, my father is having an affair. Such scenes, she describes, middle-of-the-night stormings out, déjà vu—only he's not so young anymore, he puts in long days at the office after nights like these. What she wants you to do, I don't know. "Talks your ear off, that woman," you sigh, as you get off the phone; Billy and I roll our eyes, but there is worry in your voice, along with satisfaction. Now you and the Younger Woman are allies against another Younger Woman.

There is no footing in these shifting sands. Secretly, I envy the *Father-Knows-Best, Leave-It-to-Beaver* families, *so conventional*, you'd snort, but there is no safety where we are, out on the edges, making it up as we go along. It's a mined field, bombs can go off, bullets zing by, sinkholes open up, ground falls away, I have no equipment to navigate this treacherous terrain, brash on the outside, unbaked on the inside, and a desperate desire to belong.

Later, when *alienation* becomes cool and *rebellion* is all the rage, I can't even pull that off, since you've already overthrown pretty much everything there is to overthrow, religion, capitalism, imperialism, marriage, the family; there's not a lot left.

It strikes me now, how many of these photos are taken in this house or yard, how much of your life you lived in this narrow space.

But you make the best of it. You stand barefoot in the backyard, holding a zucchini fresh picked from the garden, a giant zucchini, a giant grin, a towel wrapped around you—you've been skinny-dipping. The pool we always wanted, you finally had put in, *the smiling pool*, you call it.

Once you stop trying for glamour, you find the look that becomes you, you and Paddy both, v-necked or scoop-necked blouses set off by a brooch or beads. Not for you, the high necks and prissy collars of the age, of the aged—you're not afraid to show skin. If a blouse or a sweater doesn't come with a v-neck, you cut a V and hide the ragged edge with a pin. You don't care that nobody else is wearing it—*don't be a slave to fashion.* The garage sales have blouses, pants, jackets galore, to combine in artful ways; you're into color in a big way.

I, of course, become a total clothes snob.

The two of us stand in the backyard, you are plump, blond, wearing a purple sleeveless, v-neck blouse, I have on a miniskirt, 1970s *haute couture*, hair long and straight, a Gloria Steinem look. I am grinning, but you are *really* cracking up—what *is* so funny? something I said? something Bill said? he took the photo.

I see that these photos tell a different story from what I remember. I remember a woman who wept and railed from Sunday through Tuesday, the photos show a woman full of fun. Maybe you're just smiling for the camera. Or maybe I need to remember...

Re-remember.

Summertime, the trees out back are puddled with rotting apricots. I pick up an apricot, throw it at Bill—I get him, splat, in the bum, he hurls one at me, then we're on each other, mashing the thick, orange goo in each other's hair and clothes, then we turn on our poodle Sue, working apricot mush into her fur. You hear us squealing and come out to investigate. "A couple of idiots," you mutter, trying for disdain, but your eyes betray you, you're amused.

The day you come home a blond, it's on the wires before you walk in the door. Sally called, swore she saw you downtown—it was *you*, all right, only you were *blond!* Billy and I greet you at the door, leaping about, yipping like puppies—you look so-o-o-o funny, so fine.

The night the french fry fat catches fire, smoke pours out the kitchen window, the neighbors call the fire department, black grime coats the walls and ceiling for months, so thick we can write in it.

Billy scrawls, "Help, help, I'm a prisoner in a dirty kitchen." My friend Suzy writes, "Dear Julie, if you read this before I see you.."

When Julie ran away from home, she hid out at our house and you let her stay. Her stepmother called, furious, but you made her promise never to lay a hand on her again. *Way to go, Ma,* my friends said you were cool.

One night my boyfriend and I were out parking in the hills, his car got stuck in the mud, I got in at dawn. Other mothers would have called the police, grounded me, you were just thankful I was safe. You trusted me. You were right to, actually. I wasn't going to go losing my virginity in the back seat of a car, I was cannier than that, surprisingly—girls like me, large-bosomed girls who needed to be liked, often got "in trouble," that was the term. I had friends who got knocked up and ended up in small, cramped apartments down on the highway, married to guys who looked like Elvis, heavy-lidded, wavy-haired—no way I was going to let that happen to me. I knew about small, cramped apartments, we'd lived in a few.

The woman who came home a blond, who set the fat on fire, who hauled in Buddhas and boulders and a giant clam shell, who planted birds of paradise and lilies of the Nile and made a pool for her body and a music room for her soul, who pushed out her prison walls and let in the light, until our dumpy little ranch style took on character, *her* character, who took out a Universal Life Church license so she could do weddings in the backyard, who went skinny-dipping until the summer before she died—how can I square this with the mother of my memories, trapped in a house, pining for her unlived life?

A photo of me in this very room, reading. I am twenty, I have long, straggly hair, I am wearing a bathrobe and glasses with square black frames. Strange to see a photo of me with glasses, I usually take them off for the camera, but I don't seem to be aware I'm being photographed—of course I'm not, I'm reading. Bill took this photo. He sure got that about his big sister, *head in a book*. He would have been fifteen in 1963, only fifteen, but he got that right.

It was what I did, what I mainly did, not serious books like Mother's, only novels. Before love came adventure, then love and more love: *Peyton Place, Forever Amber, Gone with the Wind*, the *Alexandria Quartet*, the bigger the book, the heavier the hit. And when a novel ended, as novels must, I'd come to, dazed to find myself in Los Altos, when I'd been to New York, London, Paris, Moscow, St. Petersburg, Alexandria. I'd go there someday, where Real Life was, *real*, as read in novels, more real to me than flesh and blood.

Novels are where I'm at home because they're a way of *not* being at home, not being in my own skin, a way of disappearing into the words and worlds of others, taking on the shapes of other

He sure got that about his big sister, head in a book.

lives. I love words the way Mother loves music, the sounds, shapes, patterns of words, they send shivers like those great rolling chords, only they're sounds that make sense, they satisfy the senses and the sense. I keep lists of books I've read, books I want to read, I want to read every book there is. The lists make order, writing makes order, words are a mastery, a footing in shifting sands. "You scribble away as though your life depended on it," she'd say; I think it did. A bump appears on my middle finger, sore at first, then it turns hard and doesn't hurt anymore—she says it's a *writer's bump*, it will go away; it never did.

But they give me some strange notions of life, those doomed, desperate heroines at the end of their tethers, doomed Anna, Emma, Justine; they give me a sense of myself as interestingly, dramatically doomed. Someone savvier than I might have cast her lot with the good woman, the woman who gets the man and lives happily ever after, but not me—I go with the shady ladies, the way that wasn't a wife. Disastrous blueprints for a life, but there weren't a lot of choices for women those days: marry or die. Truth is, there was no future I could imagine, let alone a future I could imagine bringing about.

As I get older, the scenes start spilling over into life, it gets harder to tell which is which. I stand in a long, black, backless dress, smoke curling from a cigarette, I am scowling, or is it weeping—there's no photo of this but it's engraved in my memory, I've seen it in the movies a million times before and since, but this was my scene, it may have been my last scene with David Packard. The thrill of a relationship was its potential for drama. *Fasten your seat belts, we're in for a bumpy ride.*

Then the scenes begin to repeat themselves—though this takes years for me to see—the scenario falls into a rut: there are guys I want desperately who don't want me, not long-term, anyway, and there are guys who want me for real and forever, but I feel walls closing in. No mystery, that fear of walls, that fascination with the halfway-out-the-door kind of guy—David did that part well, as did others. At first I thought it was bad luck that I fell for guys like this; then I began to see it wasn't luck, it was choice: there was safety in the guy who was halfway-out-the-door, and isn't that what a man is, anyway, halfway way out the door, gravel flinging from car wheels as he speeds off in the night.

But this is not the story I want to tell, this has taken too much of my life, all that breaking up, making up, starting over, as though the shape and end of the story was always the man. *Who did I think I was?* And now, *who do I think I am?* That is the story I want to find out here.

The Stones, the Doors, Janice Joplin, Ray Charles, Jefferson Airplane, that beat besieged reason, that sound savaged sense. The strobe light of memory lights those years, post-pill, post-sexual revolution, AIDS, I was a wild thing loose in the city. There are hardly any photos from my years in New York, except this: me in a miniskirt in Riverside Park. Did I really wear a skirt that short and ride the subway and live to tell the tale? But this is another story I'm not telling here.

Except to ask, why New York? Go east, if you're west, I guess, same restless energy that drove my ancestors. New York was where Real Life would begin, real as read in novels, *Breakfast at Tiffany's*, *Marjorie Morningstar*, *The Best of Everything*, where I, too, might get real, turn into something more plausible than I felt myself to be. I'd sashay down Park Avenue to a job on Mad Avenue and Forty-Fifth Street, high heels smartly tapping. Think *Mad Men*—it was publishing, not advertising, but the look, the dress, the feel of the office were the same. A lot of effort went into that image, I spent my lunch hours and salary in Bloomingdale's, Lord and Taylor, Saks, polishing that image—though what I *felt*, as I stood in those dressing rooms, trying to glimpse, in those three-way mirrors, my back side, my side side, trying to see what I was by the image in the mirror, was confused: is *this* what I've come to, is *this* what my life is about? And the men, the string of men, like the outfits, a trying on of selves I wore for a day to find out they didn't fit.

Luckily I got fired from that job and found a job teaching, where I opened my mouth in class for the first time and discovered, to my surprise, that I had something to say. Literature had saved me, it could save others, and though the particulars of the process were a little vague, I took to teaching as to a vocation. And that made other things fall in place: Anglo-Saxon, History of the English Language, Latin—Columbia had some pretty arcane requirements those days, but after that MadAve job, bring 'em on! I found a rent-controlled, run-down apartment on the Upper West Side, where I could see the river and read. I sat by the window and read my way through *Gawain and the Green Knight*, *Middlemarch*, Milton, the Metaphysicals, and wrote my way to a job.

If I'd had more nerve or talent, I might have tried for the stage. I did the next best thing—I got a job teaching Shakespeare. Channeled the drama into a living wage.

If I were telling this to a student, as I have at times, I'd say, sometimes you have to find out who you are by finding out who you are not. How smart hindsight is, how smug, what a crock—no wonder kids never listen to us. The feeling of those days was confusion and fear, the job market crashed as I was halfway through the PhD, and when a job turned up, as I was sure it never would, it was sheer dumb luck: I met someone who knew someone who knew someone who knew of a job; we clicked, I got the job. That's what we never tell the young, how much depends on luck; because there's no moral to be drawn from it.

But it wasn't entirely luck. I'd soldiered on through Anglo-Saxon, History of the English Language, Latin, I'd stayed the course, done the hoops and hurdles, no safety net would have caught me if I had not. There's a moral there, I suppose, about chance favoring the ready mind, only it never does any good to tell anybody anything, I mean, you can tell them but they have to learn it for themselves; but what kind of a thing is *that* for a teacher to feel?

All my New York friends wanted jobs in California, I did not, so I was the one who got one. When I flew out for an interview and saw that the main street of Claremont looked a lot like the main street of Los Altos, I knew that I'd get this job and that I'd stay a long time.

That was 1974.

I can tell the decade by the hair. Bill has a butt-length ponytail, his girlfriend has hair to the waist, his next girlfriend has hair to the shoulders, a pixie cut on the next. Billy Boy, barefoot boy with poncho, cutoff jeans, laughter in his eyes—women went for him, he went for women, only one at a time, unlike our father; but the ones he really fell for never fell that hard for him.

I can tell the decade by the dogs: a small black poodle, a large gray poodle, a yellow spaniel, a golden retriever, a German shepherd, a brown-and-white short-haired pointer, a doberman, a little white poodle, a black-and-white puppy growing larger, shaggier, Nellie.

Dad's in a lot of these photos, grayer, stouter, bent. He drives up from San Jose, takes Mother out to lunch, helps her in and out of the car, hands her her cane, the two of them strolling arm in arm, looking, for all the world, like anybody's aging parents, kinder to each other in their old age than they were in their youth. Maria's here too, the Younger Woman, not so young anymore. She's made a go of it with my father; she has old-world skills my mother lacked, cooking, cleaning, patience, expecting less.

What a change from the days when everyone was shouting!

The neighbors, too, are in the photos. Linda from across the street, her daughters playing in the pool; Linda giving Mother a hug, Mother looking pleased. That photo gives me a pang—there are no photos of me giving her a hug. I wish it had been me, giving her that hug.

Imagine, Clinton Road a friend.

Each time I come back, I hear more about the neighbors, they're a bigger part of her life. Sammy makes sure that anything that happens anywhere on the block is known everywhere on the block, and from her place at the kitchen window, she looks out and sees neighbors walking dogs, kids playing ball, shooting hoops, jumping rope. The park at the end of the street nourishes neighborliness, makes the block a little ecosystem where delicate life forms survive and thrive, the trees grow full and fragrant, magnolias, cypress, pines, redwoods, and something that gives off a sweet gingery fragrance on a summer night, I never knew what tree or bush it was.

And Mother and I become like…mother and daughter. And I begin to feel, not all at once, not in a year but two or three, the rightness of my coming back to California. "It really *is* paradise," said a friend, visiting from New York; "I've died and gone to heaven."

How could I ever have wanted to live anywhere else? *California*, the name meant *paradise*, a mythical paradise west of the Indies where the Amazons once ruled.

I know, I know, the tricks memory plays. If you sliced down into a day back then, dropped into a conversation between Bill and me, those years just before he died, you'd have heard us talking about how our lives felt jerry-rigged and patched together, how always he fell for the wrong woman and I for the wrong man, how I drowned myself in work and couldn't sleep and he had those depressions. We said we'd do it differently, we'd watch how others did it, imitate their moves, help each other through; only he understood this about me, only he in all the world.

One night, not long ago, I found myself telling Keith and Margaret about the years I spent in therapy. They were astounded—"Why, what was unhappy about *your* childhood, Gayle?" They knew nothing of the dish-throwing mother of our youth, the mother they knew was genial and self-assured, friend to a daughter who was friend to her. They had no idea how Billy died—she'd passed it off as an accident.

So I shut up about Bill and let them take us for what they see. And who knows, maybe it *is* what we are, since it is what we have become.

But I can't shut up about Bill, can't take my eyes off his photos. Barefoot boy with poncho, ponytail, and dog.

It was evening when she phoned. Friday, April 6, 1979. I was in Claremont, he was here at the house with her, she was worried—he'd driven to Half Moon Bay that morning, he'd been gone all day, that twisty road to the coast. I was worried, too. "Don't you see it's no good his hiding out with you? He's been there too long, he needs to get back to Pasadena, put his life back together." She knew I was right but she wouldn't admit it, she liked having him around.

"Well, Gayley, I don't know what to do."

I tried to get her to own up to it, he was in bad shape, he needed to get back to Pasadena, face his life. But I was in a hurry to get off the phone—I was having people over, I wanted to impress. He was dead as we spoke.

Later that night (she later told me), there was a knock at the door, a policeman stood there with Reggie, he'd gone next door to get a neighbor to help him break the news. She didn't call me till morning—I thank her forever for that kindness, for leaving me one more night not knowing, I don't know how I'd have got through that night, unable to get a plane till the next day. Only now do I feel how that night must have felt for her.

I knew it the instant I heard her say, "well, Gayle, I have something terrible to tell you." "No!" I shouted, as though I could stop it by stopping the words, I was screaming *no no no no no…*

We sat in this house all that week, she and my father and I, going over the things we should have done, the things we failed to do, I thought I would die of that pain, a vice clamped round my chest, I can feel it now, I thought I would never be without that pain, there would never again be room in me for anything but that pain—he'd proved they were right, the family sadness, the family doom, it had been the two of us against the two of them, now it was just me. I kept looking at the phone, willing it to ring—please, somebody, wake me out of this nightmare—just like now, can't catch my breath, drowning, you've won, you've got me back.

This is not a story I can tell, it was years ago, I can't open it up. But it is opening itself, ripping itself open, as though each death leads back to every other death and all deaths lead back to Bill. I shove his photos to the side.

I heard you say to Paddy—you were in your bedroom, talking on the phone—"I would never tell her, but I think this might not have happened if she'd come back to be with him." But Mother, you *were* telling me, you left the door open, you were telling me what you dared not say to my face, I felt it like a body blow though I knew it already, *not my brother's keeper*, forever.

I went to pieces in the strangest way, a long crazy time, got beat up and knocked up the same summer, not by the same man—if I wanted drama, I got drama, only I did not want it anymore, not like that. What I wanted was to follow Bill over that cliff, just have it happen, not make it happen, just cease to be. The way I'm feeling now.

Back in the boxes go his photos, his girlfriends, his dogs, the Baskin-Robbins bunny, the Rose Bowl parade.

I go back to the albums, you and Paddy and my father. I work all day and all night and the next day and the next night. It is strangely soothing, fitting the pieces together, weaving the threads, finding the patterns in our ragtag lives. I work the whole weekend, a long, three-day weekend—*Memorial Day*, says the calendar, only this is not calendar time, this is time out of time. I go out late to walk Nellie, not even stopping by to see Keith, it is dawn when I crawl into bed, I close my eyes and there you all are dancing on the inside of my eyelids, Billy Boy, Paddy and the poodles, you in your many incarnations, young and dark and slim, older and plump, old and thin, spectrally thin.

But on the third night, as I am fixing the last of the photos into their places, I come to. I look up, look around, amazed to find myself alone in the big front room—where *is* everybody? where has everybody gone? A cry wells up, a wail—*where have you all gone?* A high keening sound, I don't even care if Sammy and Joey can hear through the walls—*how could you leave me like this, how could you go and leave me all alone?*

MAKESHIFT MOURNING

Once, ritual lament would have been chanted...

—Rainer Maria Rilke, "Requiem for a Friend"

I FUMBLE AROUND like I've never been here, can't find the light switches, tooth throbbing, novocaine wearing off. The air is stale, whiff of rats from the basement, my house has been shut up too long—how many ages have I been away? I wouldn't be back now, except I needed a root canal. Another tooth bit the dust—by the time I feel them, I've lost them, seems the sad story of my life.

The bed feels too big, too high off the floor. I wake up, not sure which side to get up on. So I don't get up, I pull the covers over my head. But I have to get going, I have to get to Colma, City of the Dead. Before they close.

I get a late start, the Bay Bridge is clogged, we grind to a halt—*rush* hour, they call this, no rushing here, five lanes of traffic ground to a halt. We inch along, I get off at what I think is the right exit, but I'm lost, also I'm nearly out of gas—I'm frantic that they'll close and I'll have to do this all over again. I stumble onto El Camino, not sure I'm headed the right direction, I slow down to read the signs. But then I see a cemetery beside an auto dealership, stone angels and plaster virgins alongside yellow arches and fried chicken buckets, and I know it can't be far. Colma, population 1500 above ground, 1.5 million underground.

A great Gothic structure looms on my right—*Can't miss it*, like the guy said.

It's 4:30, they close at 4:30, he's not happy to see me. He looks down a long list of names. No Agnes Greenberg.

"You mean you don't have my mother?"

He assures me human remains are not so easily misplaced. He picks up the phone, makes a few calls, tells me she's been kept at the crematorium, marked *delivery to family*. Only they didn't know where *family* was.

"I'm it."

"Wait here."

After a while, a black van drives up, a girl gets out, spiky hair, black leather jacket, black leather miniskirt, long black boots. She strides over, snapping gum, hands me a box like a shoebox, only heftier, plain brown wrapper, same as Paddy's.

"So, that's…it?" What I mean is, there's nothing more for me to sign or pay, I can go now, but her eyes meet mine, a flicker of curiosity, and I hear the resonances to what I've said—that's it, then, that's my mother in the box.

Holding the ashes makes me start to cry, and since I have no idea how I got here, I have no idea how to get back. I drive till I find a gas station, find a freeway and get on, hoping I'm headed the right direction, really sobbing now. An old song comes on the radio—*This ole house once rang with laughter, this old house heard many shouts*—I turn it up and the years fall away and we are kids again, Billy and I singing and bobbing to the Hit Parade, *Silly Billy*. I sing along now, getting into its rollicking, let-it-all-go rhythm—*Ain't a'gonna need this house no longer, ain't a'gonna need this house no more, ain't got time to mend the windows, ain't got time to mend the floors.* I love this swaggering spirit, this upbeat, polka beat, *'cause I see an angel peeking through a broken window pane*—the angel, that's a comfort, too, not that I believe in angels but I'm glad someone does.

I get back to Mother's, take the box of ashes to her room, put it on her cherrywood chest. I take Paddy out of the closet, place the boxes side by side.

Here are the ashes, here is the house. It was your house, now it's my house. It's a husk filled with things.

There's a hole in the world, the world takes no note.

There should be a sign, a ceremony, something that says, look here, mark this life, this death. I get it now, the mourning rites, the mourning weeds, I understand the wailing women, women who rend their garments, tear their hair, smear their face with ashes—I'd do it, too, rage and wail and keen my sorrow to the skies, raise my fist against the heavens. I'd put on a veil, drape myself in black, I'd have it known, have it heard, not this crawling away and crying alone.

Yeah, and I'd look like a lunatic.

Once, ritual lament would have been chanted;
women would have been paid to beat their breasts
and howl for you all night…
Where can we find such customs now?

We believed in nothing, we belonged to nothing, nothing to sanction ceremonies such as these. But I need to do something, to perform, enact, accomplish *something*.

Wing it, then, make it up on my own.

"Things, things, how they outlive us," she'd say, said it that day she gave me her mother's wedding band. "Just think," she said, slipping the ring on her finger, "Mother wore this. Imagine, this ring on her hand!" I looked at the ring, tried to imagine it on my grandmother's hand, that hand gone to dust, the ring going on. I put the ring on my finger, tried to imagine my hand gone too, the ring going on. Failed to imagine any of it.

"So now what do I do with this stuff?" I say to Janet, come from Berkeley, again, bearing food. She's like that, my friend Janet, busy as she is, she makes time. We're all so damn busy, it's the way we live, but Janet's the busiest, two kids, an ailing husband, chairs a complicated

UC department; yet she finds time. But when did her hair turn so white? she looks pale and stout as my grandmother in the photos, and those lines in her face, were they there before—no, this can't be, she's not so old, hardly older than…I am. Oh, lord, we're next in line.

Janet studies the posters on the kitchen wall, Earthrise from the moon, Saturn and its rings, Koko the gorilla cradling the kitten in his paws, a white seagull soaring off into the sky. "What should I do? Get someone in, strip it down, paint it over?"

"Nah, leave it. There's a lot of her still here." I'm glad she says this. I don't want to touch a thing.

"What about these?" I point to the afghans I found in the store-room. I thought they were rag bags, I opened one up, and there was this wild weave of turquoise, teal, sapphire blue. Another bag, another afghan, diamond zigzags of violet, burgundy, rose; and another, swirls of orange, brown, and olive. Stashed deep in the storeroom, wrapped in plastic, the colors bright as new. And the zaniest, a weave of red, yellow, purple, green—scrap afghans, she called these, stitched together from remnants in her yarn basket. I've been pulling them out, piling them on the couch, wondering, what will I do with them. Now they sit beside us, two stacks of afghans, columns of color tall as we are.

"Wow," breathes Janet. She reaches out a hand, strokes the wool, her eyes meeting mine. "Wow," soft as a sigh. A few days later she sends me the beginning of a poem.

> *You sit in your mother's house,*
> *wrapping yourself in your mother's presence,*
> *wearing it*
> *Like an afghan she has made for you alone,*
> *Not quite the right colors, and where could you put it?*
> *Thinking: I could paint it, move this, change that,*
> *wanting to keep her with you*
> *Without taking on the shape of her life,*
> *its texture and color.*

…She has moved on,
willing you this place, letting it go,
bequeathing it to you…

She has moved on. In her things, on her things, I find birds—purple peacocks on a gray-green rug, black birds on a gold Japanese screen, and, on a dark Chinese screen, songbirds with wings of delicately imbricated mother of pearl, hued like the sea at dawn.

I bid her fly away, and lo, *there are birds.*

"Call Cambridge Auction," says Keith. "Just call someone—tell them to come and haul it all away." This idea horrifies me. These are their things, hers and Paddy's. I am the only one who knows what any of them mean.

I stand in the garage, knee-deep in Paddy's things. How can there be so many things? Paddy was a moving woman, so many moves to Miami and back to California, so many shacks in the orchards, apartments, rooms—and still all these things?

In a box full of papers, I find…a story? a story I sent her? No, it's not my story, it's *her* story—it's the poodles' story, actually, told from the point of view of the poodles on a day when Billy comes to Poodle Rancho. The dogs greet Billy and take their places in a baseball game, the spirit of fun leaps off the page. Billy and Paddy, that closeness they had, I'd forgot.

A small brown leather suitcase, full of…ducks? Pink ducks and blue ducks, gray, white, and brown ducks, wrapped carefully in crinkly tissue. Ceramic imprints she took of Bill's hand, of my hand, age one, three, and five—here we are, immortalized in clay. Her own little bit of immortality, she said, would be the theater program my brother came across on a high school field trip to the Palo Alto Little Theater: there in a display case, he saw a 1936 program for *Iolanthe*, *Lydia Paterson* in the lead. "Look, there's my Aunt Paddy!" he beckoned his friends over to see. "Imagine!" she said, each time she told me (she never tired of telling me), "that program will be my little bit of immortality. That, and the dedication of your book." "To Agnes, Paddy, and Jack," I'd written, "who gave me a place to stand." I hadn't the heart to tell her, that book was headed for the remainder bin, not the company of the immortals.

In a yellow-flowered plastic shopping bag, I find scrapbooks from her Gilbert and Sullivan days. I see how carefully she's kept the programs, the photos, the clippings, the congratulations, the reviews. "Lydia Paterson as Patience, the leading lady, from the moment of her entrance captivated the audience with her beautiful voice and

"Lydia Paterson as Patience, the leading lady... captivated the audience."

dainty appearance" (*Palo Alto Times*, May 18, 1935). A cast photo, the cast is on stage, decked out in nineteenth-century finery and fairy costumes, the faces are tiny, hard to make out, but I find Paddy by her plump cheeks and curly hair. "A moment of beauty was Iolanthe's scene with the Lord Chancellor in the second act when Lydia Paterson rose above personality and sang so simply the beautiful strains that there was that complete silence in the audience which is desired by all singers" (*Mayfield News*, February 7, 1936). A fine moment, that must have been. If a life, or a person, could be crystallized into a single moment when they shine, simply and splendidly shine their best, this might be Paddy's.

Out of a scrapbook falls an old 45 rpm record, Paddy's writing on the sleeve: *Alice Blue Gown, 1941.* I am thrilled; but when I try to take it out of its sleeve, it sticks. Sixty Florida and California summers have melded it with the paper, I can't pry it loose. Now I will never hear my young aunt sing.

But I think I understand the blue bathrobe, the robe Mother clutched to her those last days. *Alice Blue Gown.* "This has nothing to do with you," she said. I knew it was about Paddy, her way of holding her sister with her to the end.

I put the scrapbooks back in the flowered shopping bag, I leave Paddy's white wicker shelves where they landed, draped with shawls, scarves, and beads. Later for the garage.

Try the kitchen. I open the oven, out clatters a pot. No pot or pan ever had a lid that fit, no two pieces went together. Mother's mismatched dishware, plastic cups, china saucers, Mexican plates, bowls marked *Gumps*. *Anyone can have an electric kitchen—I have an eclectic kitchen*, she'd say.

To the left of the stove is a cabinet with recipes, some neatly typed on three-by-five cards, most scrawled on the backs of envelopes. For all she complained about it, she did it, and did it well, when the spirit moved her (way better than I do; my sole culinary skill has been finding men who cook). I riffle through the recipes, finding none for the dishes I loved best, apricot cobbler, cherry pie, nor for her amazing cookies, crunchy with walnuts, hoary with coconut, dark as molasses, no two batches alike, concocted from what was at hand—you could sink your teeth into those cookies, they bit back, put me off supermarket cookies forever.

Later for the kitchen.

I wander out to the living room. How lonely this house is, I feel it now, her years here alone. Behind the kitchen door, there's a black cabinet with brass dragon knobs; I forgot it was there, *out of sight, out of mind*. It is filled with sheet music, a metronome, flash cards, things she used teaching. There are tapes here, too. Some have labels, Beethoven symphony number 7 in A major, op 92. Mozart piano concerto number 23 in A major; most are unlabeled. I take out an unmarked tape, it's covered with grime, a bug carcass flakes off, something flutters and flies away—Christ, she was right, there *are* bugs in this house!

I dust it off and find my walkman, not at all sure I should be doing this. I slip in the tape—and there she is. I don't know what she's playing but it's familiar, I close my eyes and sink into the sound, I remember trying to shut this out, slamming doors against it, now I drink it in. I see her, plump, blond, leaning into the keyboard, concentrating but self-conscious too, enjoying herself playing, enjoying herself performing. I lie back, letting the music envelop me, wash through me, there's a vice around my chest, *heartache*, all the old, worn words are true, my heart *hurts*. "Cry it out," people say, but it doesn't work that way, I cry and it makes more tears, my eyes are so swollen, the face in my mirror looks like a stranger's—what if I can't stop, what if I never stop?

I put in another tape. I don't know the name of the piece, though it's as familiar as her voice. Liszt, I think, *Un Sospiro*, a sigh, so full of yearning. Finally, the pain begins to ease, the sobs get less wrenching, my mind begins to wander—thank god for my short attention span, it's probably our short attention spans that keep us all from dying of grief.

I am not getting anywhere with this.

The next night, I make my way through more tapes. The names come back, the *Moonlight*, the *Appassionata*, I see her fingers racing over the keys, a strong touch, a sure touch—well, not entirely sure, best on the great chords, which she rolls out magisterially, some fudging on the finer finger work, she'll trip on a passage then speed away or come down hard on the next, her staccato too strong. How distinctive, her playing, how like her, so graceful, so gauche, so full of longing. *Clair de Lune* is my mother, I play it again and again.

Then there's another zinger—their voices! Mom and Paddy and someone it takes me a moment to identify—Louise. This is a good friend, this is the friend who made it to both their bedsides the week

How distinctive, her playing, how like her...

Paddy was dying, and not easily: she lives the far side of the Santa Cruz Mountains, and she's wheelchair-bound. Louise is asking them questions, sort of interviewing them. I always meant to do this, never got around to it—but Louise has done it, and recently, too. Paddy's question about my father's angiogram tells me when this was, five years ago.

"Well, he's better," says Mother.

"Humph," says Paddy. "We don't get better. We just get older."

"There's Gayley!" A photo? they seem to be looking through albums. My heart stops—oh no, here it comes. Mother, be careful what you say, I am listening to you here beyond the grave, be very careful. I know what you say will be true, irrevocably true, every word, a truth for all time. "The little rascal," she chuckles—good, it gives her pleasure to remember—"she was such…an…*interesting* child." She sighs. Silence, I hold my breath. Finally, she says, "I wish I could live those years over again. I think I'd have appreciated her more."

Mother, how could you, how could you say exactly the words *I'd* say?—such an *interesting* mother, *wish I could live those years over*. We both did it, lived it and missed it—though I must say, I might say, you did it first, but I'm in no mood for recriminations.

Cindy and Alfred and I sit, silent in a motel room in Monterey. Not a comfortable silence. I haven't seen them since the weekend they helped me move Paddy, two months before; I don't know them well enough for silence to be comfortable. I am thankful they are here, that they care enough to help me with the ashes, but I'm out of talk. I used up all my talk on the drive down.

I pass them an album, ask them which photos they'd like copies of. They pick out the photo of Grampa's old car parked in the hollow of a redwood tree—*Wawona*, says the sign, Yosemite, *diameter 26 feet, height 227 feet, roadway cut in 1875*. Grampa stands by the Franklin,

Wawona, Yosemite, 1920s.

looking dapper in a white shirt and black vest, Paddy by his side. My grandmother, stout and white-haired, in an old-lady print dress and sturdy shoes, sits on a redwood burl. Agnes perches on a bumper, bold in a middy, bloomers, and a rakish hat. The sisters are in their twenties, the century's in its twenties.

"*Agnes* and *Lydia*, such old-fashioned names. *Agnes* means lamb, doesn't it?" says Cindy.

"*Agnus Dei*, lamb of god..." I dredge this up from requiems I have heard.

"They sure didn't know who they were dealing with, when they named her that," comments Alfred, picking out another photo from the 1920s: Agnes sits at the piano, dark hair pulled back, wearing a fine, dark, figure-fitting gown; Lydia, standing, has on something white and ruffly, soft curls frame her face. The sisters gaze dreamily into the distance, into a future they imagine, perhaps, as full of music.

Agnes sits at the piano, Lydia stands.

We linger over these pictures a long time.

"So these two lovely ladies are no more," says Cindy. "Say, you know about human ashes, don't you?"

"Know what?"

"They're not fine like fireplace ashes—they have things in them, bits and pieces, they're, like, chunky." Then, suddenly solicitous— "You...okay?"

It's the word *chunky*. I was okay, but I hadn't really taken it in, what we're doing, what with the logistics of meeting Cindy and

Alfred at the airport, getting us down to Monterey, finding a motel that takes dogs, I hadn't really thought what this is about, disposing of *human remains*—is it even legal, what we're doing? I am suddenly not okay, as Cindy sees. "We don't have to do it now, you know, we can come back later this summer or next year." But there's no way I could take Mom and Paddy back to the coat closet where they've been, I want them released.

We set off the next morning. I take a wrong turn and get us tangled in traffic, Cannery Row, long, slow stoplights and souvenir shops with Steinbeck tee shirts, a honky-tonk feel. I used to know my way around here, but no more. We head for the Seventeen Mile Drive, a stretch of coast famous for wild, rocky promontories and witchy, wind-twisted trees, and we come to a toll booth—this is new, they charge admission to drive the coast? We pay the $7.50, and drive past the Lone Cypress, the Ghost Tree, magnificent, but tour buses swarm the sites.

We come to a place off the main road, China Rock, a granite outcrop that stands, solitary sentinel to a cove below, named for the Chinese who fished these waters, whose Chinatown, I recall, was burned to the ground by their Christian neighbors. We like it here, but decide to drive on.

We head south, hugging the shore, south to Nepenthe, where Big Sur artists and writers like Henry Miller and Robinson Jeffers once hung out. This used to be my favorite place in the world, but I've got used to the north coast, not so crowded. We find a seat on the terrace where we can see the view, gaze down the coast at the Big Sur cliffs, bluffs beyond bluffs that vanish into blue-gray mist; we watch as the fog thins and wisps away, revealing a bright blue-green sea, a turquoise of liquid light, no solid can hold light like that. The Pacific looks like its name today, *peaceful*, though I know it is not. The *staring unsleeping eye of the earth*, Jeffers called it; who knows but what he might have written those words on this very spot. *It is half the planet, and what it watches is not our wars.*

We drive back north to China Rock. A silver Mercedes is parked where we parked before, a woman at the wheel sits, staring out to sea. We pull up behind her and wait, a long while before she drives away. "She probably left someone here, too," says Cindy.

We make our way down to the cove, keeping to the path to avoid thistles, stepping lightly through the coastal scrub, a wind-tangled mantle of dune heathers, succulents, yellow California buttercups, purple seaside daisies. Alfred takes out his Swiss army knife and cuts through the cardboard to the plastic bag within. I hesitate, not sure how to do this—suddenly, I don't want to let them go, I wish we'd brought a plaque to fasten on a rock, some marker more lasting than memory. I reach in, not even sure whose box it is, I scoop out a handful of ashes and feed it to the sea, and another, a handful at a time.

Cindy was right—they are chunky, bits and pieces of bone and gold.

The water turns gray. We stand back while the waves swirl in, relieving the cove of its human load. What was it Mother said about my brother, quoting someone on someone—*now he belongs to the ages*. She and Paddy would have loved this place, so alive with the light and creatures—a sea lion pops up, nose in the air like an English lord, a pair of seagulls reels into view, dipping, diving, teasing, we wave as they soar away—"Good-bye, good-bye!"

We sit while the light fades. It feels right, like we've found a proper, ceremonial thing to do. But suddenly the air chills, the color begins to leach away, there's a sound in the sea I hadn't heard before, harsh, grating, scraping, waves roiling in from half a world away, beating, hammering, pummeling the shore, hissing, seething, baring the pebbles on the ocean floor, sucking, swelling, they slam down hard, then swell and slam again, grinding gravel, bone, teeth, rock, all to bits. *Make up all the meanings that you want*, whisper the waters, bellow the winds, *this is what it comes to in the end*.

Nothing that hasn't been thought and said before, wept and wailed and written a billion times before, people have cried it,

We sit while the light fades...

keened it, railed it as they've watched loved ones vanish into water earth fire air, they've sung it and sighed it and scratched it on stone, and where is the stone that says they passed this way, yet even the stone will be battered to bits, even China Rock, stalwart sentinel to the shore, pulverized to sand.

I know, we all know, but there is something about seeing your mother and aunt swallowed by the sea that makes you know it as never before, know it in your bones, your own soon-to-be charred and chunky bones.

I need some ceremony more to human scale.

We get back to the house late that night, to find it as I left it, dustballs and disarray—except there's a tall red vase in the front room that wasn't here before, an extraordinary arrangement of sprigs, flowers, birds of paradise, geraniums, rosemary, sage. "These are from Clinton Road," says the note. "Some are from cuttings your mother gave me. Your mother loved Clinton Road. Melissa." *My mother loved Clinton Road?* How *interesting* my mother would find that! I don't recall a Melissa, but the note says how she admired Mother, how grateful she was that she taught her daughters piano, that they had her as a model of an older woman living on her own.

The memorial is set for the next day, Sunday at 2:00, but people start showing up before. The couches and piano bench are full, there are people standing—who *are* these people? Mother has barely been out of the house in ten years and her closest friends are dead. Some are here for Paddy—this is her memorial, too, whether she wanted one or not.

I put the albums out on the tables. I wish I could let the photos do the talking. "These tell more than I know how," I say, passing them around. I say a few words about Lake County, Honolulu, about their music, their work for a better world, the League of Women Voters, Cesar Chavez (I skip the Communist Party). I tell a little about their deaths, the people who helped us through, then I say, "I believe our immortality is in the hearts and minds of those whose lives we touch—they believed that, too. Tell us what you remember."

Silence. I guess they thought I was going to do all the talking or that I'd arranged for people to make speeches—they didn't know they were the whole show. My hands go clammy, I feel like I feel in class sometimes, when the stunned silence tells me nobody's understood a word I've said, only the stakes are so much higher—*Please, somebody, say something. Tell me you knew them too.* I can't bear to be the sole repository of them.

Finally a voice, timid, Norma from down the block: "Agnes and Lydia were our best customers at garage sales." Laughter, relief.

Then a neighbor I've never seen before: "I miss seeing Agnes drive the Cadillac down the street."

And somebody else I don't know: "Yes, we called it the QE2—such a big car, such a little lady. I can still see her, propped up on cushions so she could see over the dashboard."

"There was music in this house," says Melissa, lady of the flowers, who I now know lives across the street. "I miss hearing the piano—she'd leave the front door open summer nights, I'd hear her play."

They're off, memories triggering other memories, stories taking off from stories—"that reminds me of the time..." "that was like the day she..." I settle back, enjoying this.

Linda, tall, trim Linda, also from across the street, tells a story: "When I was going through my divorce, Agnes said, 'you know, you don't really need a husband, you'd do just fine without one.' Then I met Rick, and he asked me to marry him. He proposed in the park, and we were walking back down the block, when we ran into Agnes—she was the first person we told. 'Good,' she said, 'he's a good man, intelligent, an engineer, good at fixing things [this draws a laugh]. But you don't need to have children—there are enough children in the world.' Then we had Lauren, and Agnes loved her, but she said, 'you know, one child is enough.' Then we had Katie, and she loved her most of all."

"That was *so* Agnes," says Alfred.

It was, too, those comical contradictions: the general principles, stern and uncompromising, the exceptions made for people she loved—*those precious children*, she called Linda's children. Katie must be five by now, *Little Katie*, Mother called her—where is she? sitting by Nellie, of course. I catch her eye and she comes in on cue: "When I came over, she gave me oatmeal cookies and showed me a music box that played *Swan Lake* with dancing swans." (Better find that music box, I think.)

"She was a spunky, original woman with strong convictions," says Melissa, lady of the flowers. "Both my girls love music because of Agnes. She could relate to the younger generation. A woman of the nineties, in her nineties."

"She was an original, the oldest and longest resident of the block," says Norma, who is the oldest now, whose long, straight, silvery hair, I remember a glossy brown.

"She was the conscience of the block," says a man from down the street—"she never let us get complacent."

"I didn't always agree with her," says Rick, Linda's husband, "but you had to admire her conviction."

"I never agreed with her," says another, "but I loved her spirit." I look around and see, she really is unusual for this block, even now, when two gay guys live in that house where the woman lived who wouldn't speak to a divorcee, snubbed her till the day she died, which was, thankfully, a long time ago.

"She could barely walk across the street," says one of the gay guys, "but she'd be at the door with something for me to sign, and I'd think, by god, if she can make it across the street, cane and all, I can sign it, whatever it is."

There's a warmth in their voices that tells me they knew her too, and as they speak, a picture begins to emerge, fuzzy at first, then taking on form and feature, *her* features, not all of them, of course, not the dish-throwing, door-slamming mother of my youth, but *their* portrait, a neighborhood portrait; it comes into focus like an old polaroid photo, touched up a little, perhaps, for the public occasion, a woman nearly ninety, living on her own, champion of just causes, feisty octogenarians, she and Paddy, both, the kind of little old ladies we all need to believe in, need to because we'll be old someday and need to believe somebody's done it right.

And so the block that snubbed her once has come to celebrate her now.

Felicia, Paddy's best friend at the retirement inn, speaks next. "I met Lydia only a few years ago, not a time I expected much good to come into my life." She reads a few lines from Browning: "*Never say the twilight years mean life is over. The best may be yet to come.* I never met anyone like your aunt. I'd never have made it through my husband's death without her. She read every one of your books and articles, Gayle," she says, turning to me—"and I did, too."

Then Norma says something surprising. "You know, your mother is why we have the park."

"The park at the end of the block?"

"Remember old man McKenzie?"

"Sure I do. He'd yell at us when we cut through his orchard on our way to school."

"When he died, the orchard was going to be sold to a developer, but your mother went up and down the block collecting signatures and took them to the city. That's how we got McKenzie Park."

An appreciative murmur ripples through the room—what a difference *that* would have made, Clinton Road run through to the expressway. It's the park at the end of the street that makes this block special, keeps it closed to through traffic, the park with its wide expanse of lawn and playground, swing sets, sandboxes, picnic tables— it's those July 4th picnics, Memorial Day picnics, that have brought this neighborhood together. And my mother made this happen, and I'd never have known it if not for this memorial. Imagine, the neighbors telling me something about my mother I hadn't known, something important.

"I was very fond of your mother and touched by her kindness and struck by her alertness to political issues," says Judy, a friend from San Jose. "That evening I asked her to play Chopin—do you remember?—and she did, and very well, even with her hands less agile than they'd been. I remember hearing her play that complex nocturne, and I thought even then how I would cherish those moments when she was gone." Judy speaks formally but feelingly, too, a trace of an English accent, a quaver in her voice that reminds me she lost her mother not long ago. "Your mother delighted in you and your work, Gayle. You know that Alice Walker essay, 'Our Mothers' Gardens'? 'In me the meaning of your life is still unfolding.' I will miss her, and will want to help you carry her story, valuing it even as you are changing it."

I'd have gladly sat there all day, listening to them go on about my mother and aunt, but I'm afraid of keeping them too long, so I bring it to a close. Too soon, it turns out, because a neighbor comes up afterwards and says, "I was going to talk about the time she…"

Memorial, Los Altos. Janet Adelman, Vicki Ratner, Judy Dunbar.

and another, "I would have told about..." I should have let it go on. Then dinner sort of magically appears on the redwood table, and we all drift outside.

Louise stays over that night. This is a good friend, this is the friend who taped that interview I found. Handsome, large-boned, a mane of black hair though she's seventy, a magnificent presence though she's been in a wheelchair fifty years. I seem to remember something about a Native American background.

We sit at the kitchen table, looking through the photos. "They were kindhearted ladies," she says, with a sigh. "Well, they're safe now. You gave them a great send-off."

"Yeah. I thought I was doing it for them, turns out it was for me." I ask her about her Native American background. She looks puzzled. "I'm WASP," she says, "through and through."

"But I had this whole history constructed for you. I guess I made it up. Or Mom and Paddy made it up."

"Well keep it!" she says, handing the album back to me.

It's the last family event this house will ever see, *our* family, anyway. I have to think differently about the house, pack it away. *This ole house.*

But the front room is full of flowers and photos. I want to stay in this room till the flowers die.

So I walk to the Rancho camera store and buy more albums. I spread Bill's photos out on the long black table, summoning the nerve to look…no, not now. I have brought photos down from Berkeley, photos of me tossed into bags and boxes through the years. I dump them out on the long black table where I used to work, photos of me with Mother, me with friends, me with students, a surprising lot with students, but mostly with men, Trond, Norman, Joe, we are smiling, we are happy, we look happy, Michael, Sol, Steve, George, Gerwin, David, Bob, on the beaches at Big Sur, Baja, Santa Cruz, San Simeon, Laguna, Mendocino, the Aegean, the Caribbean— what is it about seashores that call forth cameras? It's the places that strike me now, interesting places, so many more places than the house and yard that framed my mother's life: there I stand on the Pont du Gard, by a Stonehenge pillar, on the steps of the Parthenon, on the steps of a Roman theater, by a lion in Trafalgar Square, by a ruined castle on the Isle of Skye—good to remember this, now that everything seems so over.

I stay on, still sleeping in the big front room, fitting the photos into albums, falling into the old rhythm, going out late to walk Nellie, stopping by Keith's if I see a light. But after a few days and nights fiddling with the photos, the good feeling of the memorial drains away, the smiles in the photos seem like lies—that day at the Parthenon, I was weeping, reeling from an abortion, we trekked around the Greek islands trying to pretend it hadn't happened, I'd wake screaming from nightmares, ditched the guy the minute I got home, I was so good at leaving, and what do I have to show for it now, a dozen photo albums of ex-lovers…

Stop it, Gayle, you know better than this—you know this is no time to ask the meaning of your life, you tell that to students, "don't think about the big questions when you feel this bad, wait till you get to a stronger place." Like the time a student came to my office after her father died, crying that she ought to be doing something else with her life, ought to drop out of school, do something import-ant—"don't do this!" I said, "don't think about the big things when you feel down like this." But it's bogus, that advice, because when you feel better you don't want to think about the meaning of your life, you want to get on with your life, so it's useless, another of those things grown-ups say, maybe true but useless, so what good does it do to tell anyone anything...

And I'm down in the ditch again, and the front room that seemed alive with the flowers and voices that brought back my mother and aunt feels like a funeral parlor, the body left too long. I throw out the flowers, pack away the photos, I have to leave, I don't want to leave, but I have to get to the San Francisco Airport to meet Bob, back from France.

It's the first time I've seen him after long absence that I don't feel a rush of joy. I think, who is this stranger come back into my life and what am I going to do with him?

He says I seem far away, like I'm in a cave.

We sit in a circle at my house in Berkeley. A circle of women I have conjured for help. We are women of a certain age, Janet, Kay, Wendy, Barbara, Mimi, Elizabeth, Marilyn, Claire; we've known each other a long time, not all our lives but all our professional lives, which is a long time. I see that we've taken to dressing in similar ways, long dark skirts or slacks with bright blouses, scarves, or beads. Beyond this, we're aging differently: Janet, her long white hair pulled back in a clip, resolutely allowing the years to show; Mimi, gray curly hair puffs around her face like a halo; Wendy and Kay, not a gray hair in their heads; the rest of us, in various shades of touching up.

Another memorial, this one for me. I'm not sure how it will work—they did not know my mother, only Janet ever met her, they can salvage no missing pieces from the past. But they all have mothers or have had mothers, they are all at some stage of loss or letting go. I can say more what I feel here than I could in Los Altos, maybe even figure out what I feel.

The beginning is hers, the ending is mine. They all know this line, the end of Maxine Hong Kingston's memoir about her mother, *The Woman Warrior*, they know what I mean when I say her death leaves me needing to sort out me from her. As though it's as easy as sorting the things in the house, not that that's easy.

I pass around the albums. I say something I could not say in Los Altos: "I don't know how anyone that beautiful and bright could be that unhappy." Though I do know, in a way, we all know how it was for women in the 1950s. What I don't know is, what was the times and what was just us?

"What was her childhood like?" asks Mimi (who has just finished writing a book on Freud).

"Happy, I think." But then I remember, the mere mention of her mother brought tears to her eyes. "Well…relatively happy—there wasn't much support for her ambitions." I found an alphabet book in Paddy's things: *B is for Baby, C is for Cat, D is for Dog. A is for Agnes— Agnes is ambitious.*

"Not a lot of support for female ambition those days," says Elizabeth, whose mother is the age mine would be, only still going strong. "How old was she when they divorced?"

"Late forties. But they never divorced. She left him when I was seven, took us to Miami. They got back together when I was ten, lasted a summer, then split up for good. She would have been forty-six when we moved to Los Altos."

"Not an easy age to be left alone," says Claire.

"Not an easy decade to be left alone," says Janet. "The suburbs, the 1950s, a slow death. We'd have gone batty too if we'd stayed home like that."

"I know, Los Altos was full of unhappy women. Even women with live-in husbands couldn't stand their lives sober." It was a sort of joke—friends said they always knew where to find mom after school, Mac's "Tearoom," the bar downtown. Sally's mom died of drink decades ago; another friend's mother was doped up on drugs till they gave her a lobotomy, that caved-in look her forehead had, I couldn't take my eyes off it.

"It's why we became feminists, watching that," says Janet.

"All those women going nuts by themselves, all thinking, there's something wrong with me. That self-righteous bitch across the street—don't get me going, I teach courses on this stuff now... Mother was nearly sixty when the women's movement came along, I don't know who needed it more, her or me." I also don't know, that beat-up old paperback of *The Second Sex* I found in her bookcase, the pages falling out—I can't remember if she gave that to me or I gave it to her.

"We all needed it," murmurs Claire. I look around the circle. We sure did. It changed our lives, transformed our work; it's how we found each other, through our work as feminists.

"What saved her was the piano. I didn't appreciate it. I saw it as one of her enthusiasms, like Zen Buddhism. But she was serious about it, and very good."

All eyes turn to the piano, which looms large in my front room. It arrived this morning. I couldn't imagine how it was going to fit, but Bob rearranged the furniture and it fits. He was like a kid with a new toy, admiring its lines, its tones, says it's one of the finest pianos he's played.

"So here it now stands," comments Janet, who knows that I slammed doors against it. I shoot her a look—there's no way I would let this piano go. Though it does fill this small room.

"I didn't know you...played," ventures Barbara.

"I don't. Bob does. They have that in common"—and other things, too, I am realizing, his rants against the logging off of old-growth forests, against the fishing nets that snare dolphins, the Navy sonar beams that deafen the whales—"you sound just like my mother!" I'd love to ask these women what they think this means, these similarities, they'd have theories, I know, they're academics; but I have summoned them here to talk about Mother, not Bob.

"You and she were very close," says Elizabeth, holding out a photo—"Look, you can see it here." Mother has her arm around me, I am five, feisty, maybe she's just trying to hold me still for the camera, but it's true, some part of me is often, in the old photos, touching some part of her. "I never had that kind of closeness with my mother," says Barbara, whose mother, I recall, is in a home with Alzheimer's, hasn't known her for years.

"Nor did I," says Claire.

"Nor I," says Mimi. "You were lucky."

Lucky, again. *A mom to mourn*. I wish I felt lucky. "But you know, now it just hurts, something else I was too dumb to appreciate."

"But there's something reassuring about that primal stab of loss," says Wendy. Wendy, whose mother died a few months ago, is a look-on-the-bright-side kind of person. But her mother was whisked off to an institution where she was cared for by others and slipped quietly away, nothing like our down-and-dirty grappling. Wendy, her black hair striking against the dark red of the Morris chair, finds reassurance in pain.

"You mean, pain's good because it shows you're alive?"

"Something like that," she says. "A little more complicated. We spend our lives with words—you know what I mean?" I do know what she means: we talk for a living, we're so good with words, we talk our way through anything, what can words do now?

None of this is making me feel better. I wish I could say to them, *now you are my family*. We used to say things like that: *friends are family, friends are better than family, you can choose your friends, you can't choose your family*. But that was the sixties when we said such things, and it's not the sixties anymore, and I don't feel it anymore. Besides, I'm afraid of making claims, Mother made claims, it drove people away.

All I can say is, "Now I feel what *family* is, now I no longer have one."

"You *had* family," says Kay. Kay, who brought dinner down from Berkeley that first week after Mother died, takes a sociological view (she's a sociologist): "You had your mother and aunt." She says this is something she's seen in her work, this closeness single women have with their family of origin.

"I guess. They made it less urgent to go out and make a family of my own."

"So, it makes sense, when you think what our mothers gave up for family. You had work, friends, relationships, family—work and love, isn't that what it's about?" What work, I want to say, a string of out-of-print books and articles, seems a sorry thing to throw a life at. Can't say this, of course, can't trash the kind of scholarship these women still do.

"But they weren't family I could grow old with." I look around the circle. Most of them managed to make families they can grow old with. C'mon, Gayle, you said no to that, two abortions is choice, neither was easy, both were choices I made knowingly, knowing myself—I did what I wanted so what's to regret? But it's a big thing not to have done, not to have had a child, who knew how big, who knew about this void, this *nothing where something was*. And what if it wasn't choice, what if it was fear, the family sadness, passed down like a bad gene?

I look around the room. The world feels newly divided into *family* and *not family*, a notion I'd refuse when Mother suggested it, but now I feel it's true. Family is who you go home to, where they have to take you in; home is where they know who you are, where you know who you are. From now on, the world is *not family* to me.

We move to the dining room, and food appears—people have been so good at feeding me. I put on a tape of Mother playing *Clair de Lune*. We go on talking, deep talk, sustaining talk—how I've missed these women. I look forward to the next night, when we're having dinner at Marilyn's. But the next night, the combination is different, the talk is dinner party chatter, gossip, words to fill the air— I can't stand it, I can't do it, I don't want to talk about anything but mothers, death, loss, Mother. I'm obsessed by it, possessed by it, I've gone too far in, I can't imagine ever coming out.

I am alone in this, no, not quite alone—Janet catches my eye. She too is quiet.

I wake up the next morning, feeling like an open wound. They've done nothing, these memorials, gestures at closure that close nothing. It's happening again like it happened before, I think I'm through the worst of it only to wake up and find it sitting on my chest.

But maybe this is the way it works, this slow, halting process that is grief, you lurch forward, fall back, forward again, each time a little further, maybe this is grief, making its way through.

In July, I go to England. Leave the house with Sammy and Joey, leave Nellie with Bob, just go. Alice Stewart, whose biography I dimly remember trying to write, is being awarded an honorary degree at Bristol; her brother John Naish is holding a family reunion at his country house. Alice has never been awarded an honorary degree, never had much official recognition, her views of radiation risk have not made her popular. This is a big deal.

I am still very wobbly and not sure I am up to it, but all I have to do is get myself on a plane and others will do the rest. I'm hoping this will get me back into the book.

We stand on the lawn of a sixteenth-century manor house. A magnificent old English oak frames the scene, its wide, arching branches cast a welcome shade. I feel like I've stepped into an episode of Masterpiece Theater, the upper-class British accents, women with wide-brimmed hats and filmy frocks, the sirs, the vicar, the baron. There are four generations of Naishes and Stewarts here, some very old people and some very young. Alice had seven siblings, they all had children, there are cousins and second cousins and in-laws and ex-in-laws. There are so many physicians in this family that they once filled an entire page of the British Medical Register. What would it feel like to have a family so big?

I am dazed from the long flight, my head's swimming with new names and faces. Alice's brother John, a stout white-haired gentleman with a cane, is regaling me with tales of Africa and Ceylon. He was there the years my father was in the Pacific, he was at Cambridge the years my father was at Yale, country doctors, both, he in this country near Bristol, my father in rural San Jose—what a lot they'd have to talk about.

Whoa—I spent a lifetime trying to put distance between us, now I wish him back?

It is poignant, seeing Alice. I was here in October for her ninetieth birthday, so were a hundred others, a world of people want to know Alice, this charismatic, crusty old anti-nuclear warrior. Alice *had* a ninetieth birthday, which my mother did not. Now it galls me that the time I spent with her, on her, is time I might have spent with Mom and Paddy. Now I know more about her than I know about them, and here's Alice, still going strong.

Alice is solicitous, sticks by my side. "Now you're an honorary member of the Naish-Stewart family," she says, raising a glass: "To the newest member of the family." I guess, as her biographer, I sort of am like family; I know more about some people here than they know about each other. But what a world of difference in that *like*.

I try to imagine how it would feel to have this many uncles, cousins, aunts, siblings, in-laws. Wouldn't the self feel more firmly secured, so solidly reflected in the eyes of others, wouldn't the memories be more firmly etched, all those relations there to remember, all those witnesses to one's progress through the world? all those kin with tales of other kin, stories passed down generation to generation, all that generation, stakes in the future, toeholds in time.

With Alice Stewart.

Surely the self would feel more self-assured, so many buttresses to the self, buffers against the void; and love, might love be less bent out of shape, others to cushion the *rubba-rub-rub* of me against her, her against me.

C'mon, Gayle, you know better than this, families can warp love, pulverize the self, you know that well.

I still need to talk about it, go over it. They are kind, they listen, the kindness of strangers. They ask about symptoms, diagnoses, treatment, they know about death, the medical side, anyway. I ramble on, Banquo's ghost at the feast, shaking gory locks.

I arrive home and spend the rest of July on Alice's book. To my surprise, my mind's right back into it—I'm surprised I still have a mind. I plunge in and find myself going an entire ten minutes without thinking about Mom and Paddy—work, the old bromide, works still. But then comes a voice, a gaggle of voices—*this is how you lost them, writing about Alice.* Then another voice, *look, they're gone but Alice is still here—write it, it's their book, too.*

I finish a draft, write a dedication to Mother and Paddy, send it off to the publisher. Maybe I'm through the worst of it.

Come August, I know better.

"A garage sale?" says Janet. I can tell from the way she says it that she thinks I'm really nuts. "But you hate garage sales! Why would you want to put yourself through that?"

"I know, I don't like garage sales. It's for them, they loved garage sales—it's a sort of...*memorial* garage sale."

"But you are going to have to sit there while people bid on their personal items, trying to bargain you down for things you hold dear."

"I'm not selling the dear things. Anyhow, it's not about money— if somebody wants something, they should have it. It's...to see that things get their proper homes. I can't explain."

Reggie next door will advertise our sale along with hers, but she keeps changing her mind about which weekend she wants to have it, so we don't fix on a date until late. Then I keep putting off coming down, reluctant to step into the maelstrom. Then Sammy's on the phone, "Gayle, get down here!"

I don't come until Friday night. I walk in and I see, none of it has gone away. It is all, every bit of it, still here, the garage loaded to the rafters, things on the rafters, and there in the center, Paddy's white wicker shelves draped with shawls, scarves, and beads, every-thing as it was.

What a scene, how to know what anything is worth. Reggie comes over from next door, shows me how it's done—"this goes in the 50 cents box, this is 75 cents." How on earth does she know? Thatcher, definitely Thatcher, not only the nose and hair, but the imperiousness; yet she is trying to help. It seems so important to get everything in the right box, I become fixated on this, shuffling things crazily from box to box, I do this for hours, until I finally make myself stop and go to bed. Then I can't sleep, not even with a pill. I give up and get up and read in the bathtub till the sun comes up. You'd think I was about to debut at Carnegie Hall, not having a garage sale on Clinton Road, I'm that nervous.

I come out front to find Sammy and Joey in crisis, blouses slacks dresses jackets strewn all over the lawn. They've strung a clothesline between the cherry tree and the willow and loaded it with clothes, but the twine broke and down it came, and here are people pulling up to the house, 7:30 on a Saturday morning—*nuts* they all are, nuts as Mom and Paddy. They swarm the driveway while we scramble around picking up clothes, searching for a place to hang them. Finally, we stick them in the branches of the cherry tree—and the tree is transformed, miraculously, to a great, exotic bird bearing the brilliant plumage of my mother and aunt, about to lift off.

None of the pricing turns out to matter. When somebody points to an item and asks how much, I just sort of assign a price according to whether I like the person or not—fifty cents, fifty dollars, not for sale.

"How much for that?" asks a guy, peremptory, pointing to a conch shell. I don't like his tone. I pick up the shell, it is perfect—salmon pink and glossy on the inside, flesh-colored and knobby on the outside, its rough whorl tapering to a delicate tip. I hold it to my ear, there's the sound of the sea. "Twenty-five dollars," I say, and he huffs away. Then a geeky little kid with thick, horn-rimmed glasses spots the shell and his eyes light up.

"How much?"

"A dollar." He looks thrilled.

"How much for the rest?" says his father, pointing to the box full of shells, and I see what an amazing collection it is: abalone shells, scallop shells, clam shells, tiger shells, sea fans and sand dollars and sun-bleached coral and driftwood and pieces of glass, smooth and shiny as gems, and mother-of-pearl, *pearls that were their eyes.* Years they spent, combing the coasts of California, Florida, Oregon, years, scouring the sands for a telltale glint, an iridescent gleam, I do it, too, scour beaches for shells—what are we seeking, scanning the shores?

"Not for sale," I say. Well, why put them out if they're not for sale? says his look. Okay, so I didn't till this moment know, I want these for myself. But I'm glad the kid got the conch, he's the right home.

"She got this at our garage sale," says Norma, picking up a weird, wavy purple bowl.

"And you probably got it at hers—want it back?" No, she does not want it back, but she does want the white unicorn and offers me a few dollars. Suddenly I don't want to let it go. A man who loved me once gave it to me, said it was one of a kind. "Not for sale," I say.

I get into the bargaining—when someone makes an offer, I come back with a higher price, fifty cents, seventy-five cents, a dollar. Then I catch myself—what *are* you doing? The point is to get rid of this stuff, not haggle for pennies and get stuck with it.

I see that some of the blouses in the cherry tree have brooches in the v necks, I pluck them off the branches and take them inside. The clothes are not big sellers; they were already out of style when Paddy and Mom got them at garage sales years before, though they do make people slow their cars and gape. Then along comes a slight, wispy, white-haired lady who sees a potential for outfits, she holds up a pink blouse against a pair of burgundy pants and a purple velveteen jacket—a quarter, a dime, my price comes down with each item. She's the right home. I point out other possibilities, this lime-green blouse with the avocado slacks, she scoops up an armful, then another, I help her to her car. A woman offers me five dollars for my mother's yarn basket and I huff, no way, there's hundreds of dollars of wool in this basket. She says she makes afghans for senior centers. I give her the whole lot.

Sunday afternoon, as the sale is winding down, I leave Sammy out front, nattering with the neighbors, and turn to Mother's closet. I've been wondering what to do with the clothes I couldn't bring myself to touch that first day I went through her closet, her turquoise silk jacket, her hibiscus red blouse, her black, beaded purse. Little Katie follows me into the bedroom, teetering on high-heeled shoes, wearing a huge pair of sunglasses and a poodle wig, and I realize, with Katie buzzing around, that the garage sale wasn't crazy at all. A neighborhood event, it's made the parting with things less lonely and grim; it's put my mother and aunt back into circulation, seeing that the things they cared about go to others who might care. "Beautiful things should be kept in circulation," said Paddy, handing me a gift cunningly wrapped in tissue paper, as her presents always were. "What a gorgeous antique ring!" I exclaimed, my grandmother's amethyst, a finely cut lavender stone set in silver filigree. "Yes, antique!" she snorted, "we became antique together."

Katie keeps finding things she likes and adding to her haul, reckoning the price I name against what's left of her allowance. When we finally come to tally it up, I can't remember any of the prices I've told her, but she remembers, and adds them up: $52.50. I think seriously for a moment, then I say, "Katie, for you—it's a gift!" I've found the music box that plays *Swan Lake*, and I throw that in too.

This must be what it feels like to be God.

Hey, Ma, we had a terrific garage sale—two days, all the neighbors. You'd have loved it! I have put the white unicorn back on her pillow.

But what I can't understand is how the house is as full as it was before—how can this be?

For the rest of summer, Bob and I make trips to Los Altos. Each time we drive away, the car packed so full that Nellie has to ride in my lap, I think I've made progress, but when we get back, it's all still there. A Sorcerer's Apprentice task, that movie Mother took me to when I was a kid, the guy sweeps and sweeps, the music goes faster, the waters keep rushing in. Now *my* garage is loaded to the rafters, my living room's stacked with boxes, my house and car reek of storeroom, things newly exhumed.

I do this with a sense of urgency—school's starting, time's seizing hold, the world's time, no time to think, and I'm not sorry for that. I have no idea what I'm doing with the house. Everyone says sell, sell, the market's up, prices are going crazy in the valley, it could all go bust. But there are still so many things in this house, couches, beds, tables, stuff in Sammy's and Joey's rooms, I think most of what's in their rooms is…mine.

Such a small house, she'd say, *nowhere to put anything.* But Mother—how can it have been so small and hold so many things?

HAUNTING

Grief is a mess.

— Eve Joseph, *In the Slender Margin*

The memorials are over, the public observances finished, the sympathy cards read and filed away. Friends have been patient, but their eyes begin to glaze. Time's up. Time to get on with it, get over it, get a grip.

But I'm not finished, I want to cry, I'm not even here. I'm elsewhere, dream-haunted, talking with my dead.

I'm back in the classroom, a piece of me is back, my mouth is moving, I don't know what's coming out. What my students are hearing, I have no idea, there's a wall between them and me.

In a dream I have, my father has died and I am looking for you. I must find you, find you and hug you and tell you that I love you, while *there is still time.* So I find you and draw you to me in a hearty hug, and you grin—then I see, it's not me hugging you, it is Linda from across the street; it's that photo of you and Linda, Linda giving you a hug...

I come to, face wet with tears, knowing that time has run out and you are no more. Why couldn't it have been me, giving you that hug?

You died in the full moon. The May moon, brighter than other moons. The man in black came and took you away. Out you went, out the front door we walked in more than forty years before, you a woman younger than I am now, I a child of ten. Out the same door you walked in and out a million times, fumbling for keys, balancing grocery bags, bundles, and later, your walking stick.

Be seeing you, he said.

I mark the moons since your passing. *Four, five, six.* A harvest moon, darker than other moons, it looms, huge and bronze, on the horizon. A tarnished moon, a menacing moon, too close to the earth.

I used to love this time of year, the nip in the air, the change in the season. I used to love the holidays, sparkle and tinsel and gaudy gestures against the dying of the light. But this year brings a chill. The days grow short, the sun feels weak, about to go out.

Mother, you dreaded the holidays. Now you no longer need to dread the holidays. Now that is left to me.

We divided the territory between us. You hated Christmas, I loved Christmas; you were sad, fretful, wedded to the past, I didn't have to be. Now that you are gone, the divide is down, there is nothing to keep me from becoming you. Is that all it was about, my energy, my drive, to prove I wasn't you—is that all *I* was about?

In a dream I have, I am standing at the kitchen sink, rinsing a cup. I have on your white cardigan, your old rag of a sweater. I look out the window onto the street. I see what you see, feel what you feel. I think, that was my mother's life, there at the window.

Only it's not me doing this, it is you—it is you, who are me.

All the good things are past, you'd say. *Man was made to mourn*, Grampa said that too. The family sadness, the family doom. Now I know you were right. The relationships that are left feel so thin and insubstantial compared to those that are gone. The living are like ghosts, the dead alone are real.

I search through my bookshelves for what is written about mothers. I scour the bookstores and libraries, looking for you.

"You'd need a thousand pairs of eyes to see that woman," writes Virginia Woolf of her mother. Yes, but her mother is simpler than my mother—there's a halo around that mother, a saintly glow.

"The loss of the mother to the daughter is the essential female tragedy," says Adrienne Rich, *Of Woman Born*. Yes, but this is *real* motherloss, I want to cry, no figure of speech.

I see, there's a whole new literature of motherloss. I read through this literature, looking for you. I find weak mothers, wretched mothers, manipulative mothers, I find strong mothers, heroic mothers who overcome adversities we were spared. But I never find you. I think all mothers in the world are simpler than you.

I find photographs of smiling mothers, hopeful mothers, beautiful mothers, but none so beautiful as you. I study the faces, all the lovely ladies gone to dust, all the daughters who will miss them forever, motherless daughters everywhere pining with grief. We are all of us *motherloss survivors*.

My generation, so resolved not to be our mothers, so determined not to be trapped by what trapped our mothers that we needed a new word for it—*matrophobia*, fear of or fear of becoming, the mother— my generation, an angry generation, so intent on making ourselves different, on making the world different, I see that we've moved from anger to elegy on the subject of mothers.

"When someone dies, you might as well accept the fact that you will be haunted by that person for the rest of your life," I read, "and that is not morbid. It invests the loss with permanent dignity."

Haunted, then, no hope of an exorcism.

In October, I find a bereavement group. It doesn't use the term bereavement, it calls itself a *transition* group, one of those euphemisms I've come to loathe. *Transition* to what? It does not say.

We sit in a circle, we are seven, motherless children, all. A circle of women I have conjured for help, a second circle, conjured for help.

"I'm a mess, I'm walking around not knowing why I'm alive."

"I find myself walking down the hall not knowing what I'm here for."

"Oh, I'm not distracted, I'm focused. My partner asks, 'do you want to go to dinner?' I say, 'my mother died.' My partner asks, 'do you want to go out, do something?' I say, 'my mother died.'"

Christ. These voices could be my own. But these women are nothing like me. Most are much younger than I am, the mothers they're mourning are my age. This gives me pause—what did I expect? I bet they're thinking this too. One says as much: "You were lucky to have her so long."

Lucky, again. I guess. What if she'd died when I was in my teens, we'd have been in the middle of a shouting match, or when I lived in New York, there'd have been a continent between us, or when I was so busy-important building a career, I'd have had trouble scheduling her in. But I don't *feel* lucky. I feel old, bereft, my life's come to nothing.

I want to say, it's not so simple, the longer, the luckier, it's not like that, because at my age there's a failing, a falling away. The story has more past than future, the story of your life, the story you tell yourself as you get out of bed, about who you are and where you're headed, you know full well where you are headed, you're next in line. So it's cruel, motherloss at midlife—just when you really need her, begin to understand her, she's gone. So no, I don't *feel* lucky, ought to but do not. These thoughts are rattling through my head. I don't speak them, I don't even feel I have a right to *feel* them.

Yet I could be dead, as the mothers mourned here are dead; I'm their age, yet alive. That bears some thought.

"I've been longing for my brother," is all I say.

"You can have mine!" snaps Miranda, a tall, willowy woman whose dark eyes flash anger. "He's a real shit. He wasn't there for us when she was dying, but now that there's property, he's in my face. You're lucky to be going through this alone." *Lucky*, again. But she has a point. I know that the wrong sibling would be worse than no sibling. But I know Bill would have been the right sibling.

"But you have a daughter..." I say.

Miranda has told us what a comfort her daughter's been. That's what I'd like right now, a grown-up daughter. But they don't come grown, they have to be grown, tended with care; I never had time. "She's been wonderful," says Miranda. "But, you know, I'm alone with this. I'm the only one who really feels Mom's passing. Also, I feel guilty, like I never had time enough to spend with either of them, like I was cheating them both. Now I don't have time to mourn."

Time, yes, that was always the problem, making time, having time to do the things I wanted to do. It's not that I was dead set against it, I thought I might have a kid, someday, but everything would have to be just right, right time, right place, right man, and it never happened; though I think if I'd really wanted it to happen, I'd have found one of those guys right enough. Truth is, I never found babies irresistible, not like puppies, though sometimes I'd see a baby and feel the pull, and who knows, if I could have picked one of those up as easily as I did Nellie, a puppy in a pet store, maybe I'd have yielded to impulse as fatefully as I did with her.

But I doubt it. I knew the meaning of *irrevocable*. Mother taught me.

You'll understand when you have children, she'd say, usually at some point when I'd made her the butt of my rudeness. It seemed such a heavy sentence—I'd feel what she felt, become what she became. Motherhood was sacrifice, self-sacrifice: it tied you down, then let you down, landed you with a spoiled brat like me. *Never have children*, she'd say, *they ruin your life*. Yet she'd also say that Billy and I were the best thing in her life.

So fraught, this mommyhood. For her as much as me. One day she opened the dictionary and burst into tears. That old family dictionary sat on the kitchen table, always within reach; leather-bound, gold-leafed, such was the respect accorded words back then. My mother loved to look up words, read their definitions out loud—but this time, her eye fell on something that made her cry. I peered over to see, and there, on the inside back cover, was a picture of a hobo on the railroad tracks, sack on a stick, and beneath it the words, "He Built the Road."

"My mother pasted that there when Grampa brought this dictionary home. We jumped on her for that, said she'd ruined the book—we were *horrible* to her!" She leaned back, snuffling and embarrassed, wondering, as I was wondering, where did *that* come from, that welling up of sorrow for a childhood cruelty so long ago, for she was in her eighties, and I—I would have been older than the mother she was grieving. Then, reaching for a tissue for the tears that would not stop, she sighed, "Well, I suppose that guilt will die with me."

No, Mother, it won't. Trust me, it won't.

"What I feel is…" A voice draws me back. Hedy, plump, pink-cheeked, the only woman in the group as old as I am, or nearly as old, is speaking tentatively, searching for a word, "…*invalidated*. That's what I feel since my mother died. I was a daughter, I'm no longer a daughter, but I'm not a mother—so what am I, *who* am I?"

Invalidated? I bristle at the word—invalid, as in an *invalid?* Hedy is a nurse, she's spent her professional life caring for others, nothing *invalid* about that. Don't the caring professions count? I want to say, but I don't trust my voice. Being a nurse, or a teacher—that counts for nothing? We who have not biologically reproduced—we're *invalid?*

Yet I know how she feels, like some umbilical cord to the universe, some vital connection, has been cut, some claim to existence voided out. And part of me fears she's right—what if motherhood really *is* the only game in town, our toehold in time. Something everybody else seemed to understand but me.

I make myself say it, force myself to speak—"Don't the caring professions count?" Nobody answers. I slump back.

I see, grief is a place you go alone.

October is the cruelest month, worse than April with its stirrings of memory and desire. The old year doesn't get it yet, the party's over, silly old tart still struts her stuff, flashes her finery, trailing gaudy streamers, orange red yellow, *vanity, vanity,* down they'll come with the first strong wind, down to earth where they will rot, the bite in the air a warning of this muddy end, *all is vanity.* October is the month when death is palpable, in your face. Yet I remember antici- pation once, exhilaration in the change, a schoolgirl skipping down the street kicks at leaves and sends them swirling, possibilities lay ahead, now I know too well what lies ahead, *all that lives must die,* and knowing this, a little of me does die, dies a little with the year.

Suddenly the dead are everywhere, skeletons lunge out of trees, skulls stare from store windows, empty eyes and idiot grins, they jeer, they mock, they're on a rampage, a *danse macabre.* All Hallows' Eve, spirits rising from the grave, roaming the earth, hungry ghosts, plain- tive ghosts, they want more than candy. This used to be the holiday I loved best, the frisson of horror, the tingle down the spine—not any- more. I have seen the bag of bones that took my mother's place, the death's head in her smile, I know it is no joke—these ghouls are not other than us, they *are* us, only a little further down the line. I see how it goes, the creature struggles, death wins in the end, no help for it, and no forgiveness.

It has touched me, claimed me. This is what *spooked* means.

Death is a fearful thing, says the play I am teaching. *Measure for Measure,* that death-drenched play.

I drag down to Claremont, I teach Tuesday, Wednesday, Thurs- day, I drag down, drag back.

I don't want to see anyone, don't want to be seen. I can't talk, can't listen, can barely make myself return the few phone calls I still get. I don't want to be in a classroom, I don't want anyone to see how old I am. I wish I could move to a new place where nobody remem- bers I was ever young.

Sometimes as the plane is landing, I look down and think, I wouldn't mind a little crash just now. If there were a way not to be, not Bill's way, that wound in the world, that smoking hole, just not to be. It never seemed possible while they were alive, but now that they're gone, I take it out and look at it, think about it as I never did before. But then I remember all those students I've dragged through *Lear, thou must be patient*, all of them knowing it was just words, *men must endure*—what a mockery it would make.

Nah, soon enough, over before you know it.

On days I'm not teaching, I drag around to banks, county offices, lawyers, accountants. The fallout from their deaths is staggering. Accounts need to be closed, titles need to be transferred, her house and my house must be re-registered with county offices, accountants are brought in for her income tax, my income tax, and for this new thing "the estate," records must be kept for the IRS, there are endless forms. Nobody seems to know how it all goes together. Lawyers are brought in, no two agree. A world of administrative detail opens and swallows me up—who knew death held this kind of horror too.

I begin to worry about money, which is odd since I have more of it than I ever had. But a form filled out wrong, a signature in the wrong place, could cost a lot. I need to pay attention, I can't pretend this has nothing to do with me, which is what I've always done. I'm nobody's baby now.

Bob helps with the paperwork, more patient with me than I was with Mother. The phone calls, the endless forms, make constant demands on his attention. My needs have become his needs, my sleeplessness has become his, he's losing hold of his work. He's not in great shape himself—he too, has lost a home, both of us, roots flailing in the air.

What I feel is…frozen. Like the novocaine aimed at my jaw hit my heart, seeped through the whole of me, my movements are on automatic, efforts, minimal. What I feel is…irritation. I need order, he is not orderly, I need space, this house is so small, *so small*, Mother's words become my own. Dishes pile up in the sink, on the counters, papers disappear under other papers, things get lost, I get frantic at loss. Each weekend we haul more things up from Los Altos, cram boxes into closets, stack them in corners, every room in this house is full—and this is with Bob's things still in storage. How would it be if he *really* moved in?

I want to scream, "What are you doing here now that they're gone?" I do not, of course, but I say it to Janet. We are walking in the hills, the late afternoon sun, low on the horizon, stabs my eyes. I tell her about a week last summer when I flew to France to be with him instead of going to see them, I eat my heart out over this. "I want to say, 'Why are you here, now that they're gone?'"

"Hardly a rational position," she says. She tells me when her mother died, nothing her husband could say or do was right. She says this irritation is probably about grief, not about Bob.

"But it was their last summer on earth—why couldn't I have spent it with them?"

"You spent a lot of time with them."

I tell her about the day Mother cried, opening the dictionary, her remorse for that childhood cruelty—"'My poor, dear mother,' she'd say, carrying that guilt around all her life, 'she made herself a doormat,' she resolved not to. Yet there she was, landed with a couple of brats who treated her like a...doormat. We were horrible to her, we took her for granted."

"Yup. That is what kids do," says Janet (she has two), "take moms for granted. Probably the better the parent, the more taken for granted."

"But I wasn't a kid."

We get to the top of the hill and I catch my breath, struck by the loveliness. A picture postcard of a view, the city, the bridges, the bay, white sails on the water like flocks of birds—a day like this is why everyone wants to live in the Bay Area. San Francisco is white as a bone, not a trace of fog through the Golden Gate, only the wide

expanse of Pacific. The eye of the world, and what it watches is not
our tears.

"You gave her a good death," says Janet.

"*A good death*—say that when you've seen one. It wasn't good,
I wasn't good, I was boxed into the old moves, grudging moves,
didn't take the term off—what was I rushing to that was so damn
important?"

So what would happen if you *did* slow down?" she ventures.
Now it's my best friend telling me this, *slow down*, feels like everyone is at me about this. "Would it be the worst thing in the world?"

"I'd be her. Pining for my unlived life."

But it has come to pass—I *am* her, pining for her unlived life
and my own as well. Time that was taut with expectation, time to
be rushed through on my way somewhere else, time has gone slack
as a worn-out old elastic, a girdle in a bottom drawer. Time is worth
nothing, now there's all the time in the world.

We are quiet, taking in the view. The bite in the breeze tells me
winter's not far off. Finally Janet speaks, choosing her words carefully. "Here's what I think. This is how you feel now, this is not how
you'll always feel. So maybe you should just…not think. Wait till
you feel better, then you can think. What do you think?"

She catches my eye. C'mon, says her look, what can I say? this is
what you'd say to me, right, same dumb-ass, useless advice? and the
edges of her eyes do a crinkling thing they do, like a wink.

"Right."

I seek, inquire, collect opinions. Does anybody know how long it
takes?

"It takes a long while."

"It takes longer than you think."

"After a year it seems to get better."

"It's hard to say how long it takes. Just when you think you've
got through it, you meet it around the next bend."

"You never really get over it."

"You don't get over it but you get used to it. You get so it doesn't hurt so much, the memories become pleasurable."

These are the things people say. I see, it will take as long as it takes.

What is shocking about death is the absence, the *nothing where something was.* Paddy said, when her Jack died, they came and took him away and that was that. He was there, then he wasn't, just like that. Years later, she'd shake her head in disbelief, that *nothing where someone was.*

Where do people go?

What is shocking about death is the silence. It's a terminated conversation that terminates a part of you. The thing about a relationship is that it's an ongoing conversation, a place you bring a part of yourself—*Wait'll I tell Ma.* But then Ma is gone, and where does that part of you go?

Do you get used to the silence? November 30 and April 6, Billy's birthday and deathday, I'd call. Always, those days, I'd call, no matter where I was, and always, she'd pick up the phone, no matter how late it was. "I knew you'd call," she'd say. Now nobody calls, a void where there was a voice.

It's that void I hate, that *nothing where someone was.* The things people say, *a good death, at peace, out of pain*—what a crock!

Dead loss, nothing more to say.

Get used to it, Gayle, it happens, has been known to happen. Two hundred thousand people die in a day, seventy million a year, many of them mothers.

Bob says I need to get perspective, take a longer view. "Remember the cave paintings we saw last summer?" How could I forget, that week I spent with him instead of them, the Dordogne. The reindeer, the woolly mammoth, the hand, on the cave wall, eighteen thousand years ago, scratchings that say, I was here, I passed this way. For that many generations, daughters have lost mommies, cried for mommies, all those generations and more.

But it's too chilling. Like the waves that swirled in and swept them away.

One day, we are walking along a beach, and I say, just think, bits of them might be here in the waves.

No, he says, the ashes swirl down, down, to the bottom of the sea, become part of the sediment on the ocean floor, they'll be lifted as a continent one day, millions of years from now.

I like the idea of Mom and Paddy rising as continents. *Of their bones are coral made.* But I can't take the long view right now.

In my bereavement group, we have brought photos.

Andrea's photo shows a round-faced woman with a pleasant smile and the same plump cheeks and freckled nose as her daughter. "My mother was a saint, we all loved her so much," says Andrea, biting back tears. She married young, loved her children, is missed by her children. A short, sweet story.

"My mother was the sunshine of the family. She was the center, kept us all together." Laurie's mother has hair curly as Laurie's, only white; she sits at the head of a holiday table, looking pleased with the children around the table.

They were such good mothers, of course they were, women who don't love their mothers don't come to groups like this.

When it's my turn to speak, what can I say?

I've brought too many photos. I've tried not to, but ninety years is a long time. Nearly the whole of the century. I pass them around.

My mother was a...*what?* I don't have a story, not even a term to fill in the blank.

"Beautiful, beautiful," the murmur goes around.

"She looks like Juliet Binoche," says Andrea.

"Like Isabella Rossellini," says Laurie. "Was she foreign?"

"No, she was born in Alameda, right here," I say, pleased at the compliments. My vanity about her looks, my absurd vanity about her looks. I say what I've said before, I don't know how anyone so bright and beautiful could be so unhappy. I say something about the pain my father caused her when he left her for the Younger Woman.

And here we are, on her seventieth birthday. She looks sixty, not seventy, blond, plump, glowing with health, gazing happily at the birthday cake, I am gazing at her, pleased that she's pleased. She has on the turquoise silk jacket my father brought back from China. This is probably the only party I ever made for her, and it was actually my boyfriend Norman who made it—he drove halfway across Los Angeles to get her that cake. But I remember that visit, she was making me crazy; she'd begun talking to herself, even when other people were in the room, insisted I take her to the station hours before she had to leave, fretting that she'd miss the train, her anxieties, my anxieties, they set me off.

"Who's this—your aunt?" Hedy holds out a photo of Mother, old, at the redwood table in the backyard, one of the last photos I have of her. She sits with a younger woman, holding hands.

"No. That's Maria." I should say who Maria is. "The Younger Woman." Silence. I should say more…How at some point, we started having Christmas with her and my father, and then after he died, we'd still go down to San Jose and have Christmas with her; how Maria would call Mother, crying, she missed him so much, and Mother would tell her she'd get used to living on her own; she had, it wasn't so bad. And she'd come up to Los Altos and take Mother out to lunch, just as my father had, opening the car door for her, handing her her cane, squiring her about. How the family reconstructed itself in strange new ways.

I sigh, feeling the enormity of things too complicated to say.

I go down to the basement, searching for my father's death certificate, for one of these endless legal forms. I riffle through the boxes and the sadness overwhelms me, these lives gone to ground under the house. I slump on the concrete floor, feeling like I might just stay down here and join them. Suddenly, I hear the sound of the piano. Bob is playing…something; I know this piece so well I can predict every note, though I don't know its name, the great, rolling chords of Schumann, or is it Chopin, draw me up the stairs, I throw myself on the bed, weeping, the rich, mournful music surrounds me, I drink it in.

Bob is all there is between me and a house full of dead people. I am suddenly so grateful that he is here.

But the next morning, I'm late, anxious I'll miss my plane, I can't find the lunch I fixed the night before—"Could you please keep your stuff on your side of the refrigerator," I hurl at him. He looks like he's been slapped, I want to take back the words, take him in my arms, but I'll miss my flight. I get to the airport and the flight's been canceled, I plotz down with my bags. Truth is, I don't care that the flight's been canceled, I might as well be here as anywhere, might as well be in the Oakland airport as in my house, my office, I wouldn't care if I spent the rest of my life in the Oakland airport.

I realize I need help.

I fumble in my purse for my address book—yes, I still have her number, the therapist I used to see, I've kept it through the several address books I've gone through in the years since we last talked. I dial and there's her voice on the answering machine, listing, as she always did, numbers where she can be reached. The hope I feel at the sound of her voice tells me this is the right call to be making, though I have no idea how it can work—Ann is in Pasadena, I'm in Claremont, forty-five minutes away by car, only I have no car in Claremont, and no time.

Later that day, she returns my call, tells me that before we talk, there's something she needs to say—she will soon be moving.

"Where to?" a rush of mad hope.

"Northern California."

I've been collecting names of therapists in Berkeley, where there are probably more shrinks per square foot than anywhere in the world, but I never called any because I'd have to tell the story of my life. I don't know the story of my life. The story is, my mother and aunt died and I feel like shit. I can't remember a time before.

But Ann knew me from before. A long time before, twenty years before, she saw me through crises. Two boyfriends, I dragged in to meet her, back in the days I still believed you could save a relationship if you hammered hard enough, and a relationship could save you; and she met my brother. I don't have to tell her the story of my life.

I find her office easily, a half hour across the Richmond–San Rafael Bridge, a drive that always lifts my spirits because it's the way to Mendocino. She greets me at the door, same cherubic smile she had always, only she stands less straight than I remember, her hair's gone gray, there are lines around her eyes and mouth that weren't there before—how can this be, she's only...my age.

I see her scanning my face. So. I've got old, too.

I plotz down in her chair and pass her some photos. She, too, is struck by the hearty, spirited mother in the photos. "So is this why we smile for the camera, do you think—to cheer up posterity?" She laughs, she laughs easily, I always liked that about her.

"But," she says, handing me back the photos, "the depressed mother of your memories, that's real, too. You're not making that up."

"No. Maybe. I don't know. I wonder if she really was so depressed— she was unhappy, but that's not the same as depressed, is it?" A look flits across Ann's face, I should ask what she is thinking, but I rush on—"I don't think she was depressed. She was always buzzing around with some project or cause."

"Maybe..." says Ann, cautious, "but don't go idealizing—it'll only make you feel worse."

"I can't feel worse." I slump back, the good feeling of seeing Ann again drains away. "As a matter of fact she told me I'd be sorry, which didn't help. But I could have been...kinder."

"You gave her a good…"

"…death. I know. Actually, I don't know. I didn't dare take the term off, left her unsupported in that, and…other things."

"Like what?"

"Like…her story of her life, I guess. She'd say she was lucky to be rid of him, free to devote herself to her music and us. I didn't buy it—I think she'd have been happier if she'd gone out to work, we'd all have been better off, I never said it but she probably knew I felt it, though I guess…we were the reason she didn't go out to work."

"I think mothers can't win," sighs Ann, who is a mother herself—"if they go out to work, they get blamed for not staying home, if they stay home, they get blamed for not going out to work. Something about that bond makes it hard to get right—first your life depends on her, then your life depends on separating from her, a lot can go wrong."

Cathected. I learned that word from Ann. Or maybe it was Adrienne Rich: "This cathexis between mother and daughter is the great unwritten story," *Impacted* is more like it, like a tooth. Or a toenail.

"Her needing so much didn't leave you a lot of space."

"I don't know, she wasn't *that* needy. In ways she was independent. Like the time she had her cataract operation, I offered to come down, she said, 'No, Honey, I don't want you underfoot, I just want to be in my own house, on my own.'"

"She was older then—what about when she was younger, when you were younger?"

"Yeah, she needed something from me I didn't have to give. She wanted me to say she'd done right by us, taking my father's support—but, Christ, why couldn't I have said it? she *did* do right by us!"

Ann is quiet. After a long moment, she says softly, "a lot of self-blame going on here. What about your anger?" She remembers my anger, knows it from the time before, "what she did to Bill…"

"So, do we know she did that to Bill?" I am quick on this trigger.

"The way she kept him with her, kept you with her, discouraged you from making ties that might take you away—it's not clear that was in your best interest."

This comes from a long time ago, I'm not sure I can do this now. Though it's true, no man I ever brought home was good enough, no man was as good as the man before, they became good once gone— "That Norman, he was so much fun," she said, after I'd moved on to Michael, that bullshit nostalgia, the good things are past. Yet this too is confusing because none of them *was* right, though probably if I'd brought home Mr. Right, she'd have found him wrong. Probably I would have too.

"But she *did* have our best interest at heart. There was nothing she wouldn't do for us—I knew it, Bill knew it. *Mom's cool*, he said, our last conversation, he was staying at her house. I asked him how things were between them—*Mom's cool*. Where we stood with my father was not so clear, but with her we came first—we were what she lived for, the center of her world."

That look on Ann's face again, like she's thinking something she's not saying. "Okay, so maybe it wasn't great to make us feel that important."

"It was a way of holding you."

I am so tired of this, we did this decades ago, did it to death— what they did, what you did, what is theirs, what is yours, what you might have been if they had been but can never be because they were not…do we have to go through all this again?

They fuck you up, your mum and dad, they may not mean to, but they do—how do the lines go?—*but they were fucked up in their turn…*

I know all this, have known it forever. *The talking cure*, this is called. As though anyone could talk their way to a cure.

But I need to talk, and I come back the next week, and the next, and we go round and round.

I need to remember, I don't want to remember…

Sunday night: "Hi, Ma, how're you doin'?" My weekly call, I'd put it off all weekend. Why did I ask? I could tell from her voice when she'd been alone too long, the way she said "hello," that dead, flat tone.

"Oh, all right, I suppose. Alive, if you call this living." That's what I dreaded, the drone, the accusation, like, what do you care, if you cared you'd be here, you'd save me from this.

I'd call on her birthday, evening by the time I got around to it— "Hi, Ma, Happy Birthday."

"Oh, well, the day's almost over." It dragged me down to think she'd sat there all day, waiting for my call.

The holidays were worst: "I hate Christmas, I hope this is my last."

"Soon enough," I'd snap, meaning, don't lay this on me, if you want me to call and come around, don't say things like this, I'd harden my heart, *another brick in the wall.*

Christ, probably all she wanted was a little company. I could tell from her voice when she'd had somebody there, it was strong and clear. "Well, Gayley, we had a wonderful day, Paddy was here…"

"She'd say"—I tell Ann—"'well, at least I never took drugs or drank,' and I'd think, *big goddam deal.* But you know, maybe it *was* a big deal, there were lots of women who did those things in Los Altos."

Ann says I keep slipping out of my own perspective. She points out how many of my childhood stories I tell from Mother's point of view. "Like that day she came and got you at school, taking you to Miami, you said, 'how hard that must have been for her to leave him with two little kids'—what about *you?* What did it feel like to *you?*"

"I don't know. It felt like adventure. Except…"

"Except what?"

"She forgot Whissy Bow-Wow. My little white dog, I took him everywhere—she forgot him."

"How did that feel?"

"I don't remember. I threw a tantrum, I'm sure."

My little white dog, I took him everywhere.

Ann says something about transitional objects, shrink-talk, I tune out. I can't do this, get worked up over a stuffed animal lost half a century ago, I cut in—"Yeah, well, she had other things on her mind."

"Try saying how it felt to *you.*" We're not getting anywhere.

"I don't know. How can I feel angry when I miss her so much?"

So I try, really try to send my mind back over the years, scanning for grievances I do not feel. She'd say she didn't go out to work or marry again on account of us, terrible claim, how could we make up for all we cost? Love was a word never said straight, a claim made against attachments to anyone but her, or so it felt, or so I heard, *never trust the outside world, never trust a man.* But that's only part of the story, it seems anything I can say about her, I can say the opposite…

There was a night near the end when I brought Keith's new poodle puppy into her room. I held the furry wriggling creature out for her to pet—her face lit up, she reached out her hand, then drew it back, told me to take the puppy out of the room, she was afraid of fleas. So like her, that contradiction. She had a capacity for fun, a giggle that bubbled up, irrepressible as a sneeze, but there were all these taboos: *It costs too much. It's not worth the trouble. I wouldn't care that much for any man,* she'd say as I mooned about the house. *Save your nerves, save your eyes, don't read so much, don't work so hard, don't spend so much on yourself, don't spend so much of yourself.*

I bought her a bathing suit for her eightieth birthday so she wouldn't have to skinny-dip with Sammy and Joey walking through the yard, but I forgot to take the price tag off. "They have a nerve, charging *that!*" she exploded. I tried to tell her that's what bathing suits cost these days, she made me take it back.

Life is a costly matter, I snapped, it takes all you have. The only way to be truly cost effective is to be dead.

She could be penny-pinching, mean-spirited, she could be large-minded, generous, and she could turn on a dime. She'd warn me against taking risks, yet she sort of liked that I did—"Oh, Gayley, you're a rascal," she'd say to some tale of derring-do. "You are doing with your life what I wish I had done with mine," she said as I was taking off to England to see Alice; considering how fearful she was about my transatlantic trips, it was a lot. So there I was, trying to be what she wanted to be while trying not to be her. It was confusing.

"She was a Gemini, if you want to know..." Ann does not want to know. She is quiet so long I think I've lost her. Finally she says, "You know, it's easier in a way when a parent is just plain awful, easier to separate when you have something solid to push against, when you can say, I don't want any part of this. How confusing, when your mother was so...confusing."

Confusing, yes. My best pal, my worst critic, all at once; girlish and giggling, sad and pitiable, a tower of strength, a sinkhole of depression. "Yeah, and it must be easier if they deserve the shit you dish out. She didn't deserve it, and I dished it out."

"Fifteen years ago, it was your father we talked about, your relationships with men."

"Ah, yes, that was the story then, my love life, my disastrous love life. My father's died since then…" I never talked about that with Ann, or with anyone—do we have to dredge that up, drag back through that? And Bill, does it lead back to Bill? Always to Bill.

"Looks like your father may have been the easy one," says Ann slowly. "All those years, I thought it was your father. I had no idea. She never let you go. It's like, she's bound you to her, like a—fairy tale."

Bound. The family ties, the ties that bind, *the family coil so twisted, tight*—is that what love is, a spell that binds? *Spellbound.*

A son is a son 'till he gets him a wife, a daughter's a daughter for the rest of your life. The rest of *whose* life—the mother's or the daughter's?—what does that mean?

A woman is her mother, that's the thing. So says Anne Sexton, one of those suicidal women poets I teach.

Her anger, my anger, her anxiety, my anxiety, her unhappiness, my unhappiness…Yes, but if a woman is her mother, what becomes of the woman when the mother dies?

But I got out, really I got out, I did things she never did—doesn't that prove I wasn't her? Then I remember what Adrienne Rich says about *matrophobia*, that the daughter who pushes hardest against her mother is guarding against a deep, underlying pull, afraid if she relaxes her defense, she'll lose herself entirely. So the harder I pulled, the closer I stuck, the closer I stuck, the harder I pulled, the harder, the closer, and I never got away. How is it possible, this final separation, when I have never separated?

I tell Ann about a night last summer when I was back in the house—I stood in her bedroom door, babbling and blubbering to the empty bed. "But Mother, you had *me* to grow old with, you had *me* to see you through. Now who do I have? I don't have—"

"*You?*" says Ann softly. "No, you don't have…you. Not now."

I'm back in the house, only there are lots more rooms, larger rooms, on many floors. It is full of things. There's a fruit stand with shelves that go up and up, the fruit will go bad if I don't do something about it. There's a piano, another piano, I count eight grand pianos. I wander up and down the stairs that were never there, wondering, as the spaces open up, where can I put my books, my work—what work will I do? I look out the kitchen window, there are carnival lights, a tilt-a-whirl, honky-tonk music—what am I doing here?

I have had dreams like this before, I'm back someplace I used to live, only there are all these rooms. Sometimes it's a place in Berkeley from my student days, sometimes my apartment in New York, always the rooms are full of things, crates, suitcases, some are my things, some left by the people there before, ceilings higher than they ever were, plaster crumbling off the walls, always it's up to me to set it right. Sometimes it's exciting—I could put this here, fix that, paint this—but mainly, the feeling is dislocation: I am back in a place which is familiar yet strange, where I am not at home but must make a home, it makes no sense to be back but I am back, and back for good.

In our bereavement group, a woman tells about her father's depression, her sister's cancer—she makes it through this litany of sorrows but loses it when she gets to her mother's house. When she tells us she's put it on the market, her voice breaks, she can't go on.

I understand, it's displacement, death is displacement, we all feel displaced. I still have the feeling, going back to that house, setting foot in the front door, this is the place where I knew who I was. This is the place I was somebody, I was somebody's baby. I'm nobody's baby now.

In ways I don't understand, the house is my mother.

I leave the telephone hooked up. It makes no sense to keep it on, but we've had that number so long I can't bear to shut it off. *415 967-1136*. We had it back when it was *Yorkshire 7-1136*. One night I dial the number and let it ring. Nobody home.

The group ends after six weeks. More displacement. I remember now, this was a *transition group*. Transition to *what?*

Sammy has been trying since September to rent the house, not the back rooms where he and Joey live, just the front. We put an ad in the paper and get lots of calls. People show up but nobody calls back. He doesn't know it, but the reason they don't call back is that they don't like the idea of sharing walls with this funny old duffer and his sidekick. They call me and ask, who are this Sammy and Joey? I tell them they're terrific, they've lived here forever, you'll love them. They don't call back.

We find a guy Sammy knows, or thinks he knows, who wants a room. I like the idea of renting only a room and leaving the rest of the house free. In case I want to come down. It's a daft idea, but I rent him Mother's room.

I don't come down, of course I don't, until my friend Judy in San Jose suggests we meet at the house for dinner. I haven't seen Judy since the memorial, five months before, when she spoke movingly of Mother playing Chopin. Judy, whose mother died a half year before mine, is, like me, re-living her loss in the passing of the seasons. She likes it that the evening we fix on to get together is November 1. "It's a special day," she says, "All Souls' Day, the time of year when the veil between the living and the dead is thinnest. A good day for honoring our dead."

The veil between worlds feels very thin indeed. A dream I had the night before, All Hallows' Eve, felt like a visitation. I was back in the house, Mom and Paddy were there, the three of us at the kitchen table. Paddy had on her royal blue blouse with the pink hibiscus, she was leaning forward, the way she did, so as not to miss a word. The table's a clutter, the house is full, Mother's posters are back up on the walls, Earthrise from the moon, the white gull soaring into the blue, Koko and the kitten, just as they were. I am taking books out of boxes, the feeling of when I'd come home summers from New York. But then I see the titles, *The Elizabethan Theater, Jacobean Drama*— really, the Renaissance? What am I doing back in the Renaissance, I left there a long time ago, and why am I writing a dissertation? We're together again, the three of us at the kitchen table, I'm so happy to have them back, but I can't write a dissertation, I did that already.

I need to talk to Judy.

But when I get to Los Altos, the renter is there. Sammy said he was away most weekends and I assumed he'd be gone, but not only is he here, he's moved Mother's furniture to the garage and filled the front room with his things. That wasn't the deal—he's rented a room, not the whole house.

I am furious, but part of me thinks, it's just as well, it makes a point—this isn't working. It makes no sense to keep this house. I can't bring myself to rent it, I can't afford not to—Sammy and Joey pay so little, it costs me to keep them here.

I tell Judy about my dream. "They were back, I was so glad to have them back—only, why was I writing a dissertation?"

"It sounds like you…that is, maybe you've…moved on?"

"I should let go of this house, you think?"

"It's not what I think that matters, Gayle, it's what you think."

Now the dreams start really coming, houses strange and familiar, houses with attics and cellars, rooms opening onto other rooms. I am moving back into the house, moving back into my old room, moving into her room.

"I don't want to let go, I have to let go."

"Of the house or your mother?"

"My mother is not in the house, my mother is not the house, the house is not my mother." We've been through this before, only this time, Ann says something new: "Maybe you ought to write about it."

Has she read my mind? I have, as a matter of fact, been doing something like that, not writing, exactly, just jotting things down, phrases, fragments, feelings…words, to quell the panic, words to stave off dread.

"Why would I want to do that?"

"It might help you sort things out. You know, it's important to get down the memories when you're the last of a family."

"Important to who? who's left?"

"*You're* left."

"I don't know enough about my mother to write about her. I don't even know how she met my father, what their marriage was like before me, how she really felt about having children. I know less about them than I know about Alice Stewart. I never asked, now there's no one left to ask."

"Don't tell it from her point of view. Tell it from your own."

My point of view, again. "Do I even know my point of view?"

"Find out as you go along."

"I can't remember. How could anybody with such a lousy memory write a memoir?"

"Fictionalize it, then. Make up a story."

"No, no, not a made-up story—what's the good of that? If I were to write this, it would have to be us, or what's the point?"

"Don't writers use fiction as a way of getting to the truth of things? I don't know—this is your field, not mine." Ann's gaze drifts out the window to the oak tree in the parking lot. Oaks are an endangered species in Marin County, but this one's survived, scraggly and dusty and hemmed round by pavement, but there it stands.

"*Lies*, that's what fiction is, a pack of lies. Cheap tricks, trumped up excitement, suspense to keep you reading, secrets that come out in the end—that's not how life is. There are no deathbed revelations, no wisdom through suffering, only flailing about. I don't even read that stuff anymore, I only read memoirs. I want true stories, ordinary people, everyday sorrows—I need to know, how do people get through this shit." I stop, suddenly hearing what I've said. I could be

Mother, haranguing me about novels, *come back to the real world*; so this is the real world, it sucks.

Ann looks skeptical, like, where am I going with this? I go on, "No, if I wrote about us, it'd have to be us, us as we were, the way I remember. Anyhow, anything my memory touches would be fiction enough."

"Okay, so not a fiction. Write about what we've been talking about in these sessions."

"Why would I want to re-live all that pain? Isn't the way to heal, to forget? Isn't it morbid to dwell in the past?"

DO NOT RESUSCITATE, said the signs by her bedside, on the telephone, on the refrigerator door.

"Maybe you need to realize that they're really gone. It's not something you can take in all at once. You have to learn it a little at a time. The way you'd learn about a lost limb."

"Go over it till I get it, you mean? Like what we're doing here?" Get used to it. Say it, shape it, find out what *it* is. Write the words— *catheter, gurney, chunky*. Write it out and the unthinkable becomes thinkable. Wear it out, wear sorrow out by writing it out. Rewire the system, restring the nerves.

"She'd hate this, she'd hate me."

"She won't read it."

"*Speak no ill of the dead*, they say, and I don't want to. Homage, or honesty? elegy, or etiology, an etiology of us?"

"Find out as you go along," says Ann.

Find it out, feel it out, write it out. Writing as exorcism. As un-haunting.

Typical. All those years I'd take my writing to your house, set up my computer in your front room, make it a barrier between you and me—and now that you're gone, I write about *you*. I never could find time to ask you about yourself, dear Mother, while you were alive— all that while I was writing about Alice. I pay more attention to you now than when you were here.

Typical, you'd say, that wry, bemused look of yours. So here I am again, talking with my dead. Maybe that's what elegy is, talking with our dead.

Come back, stay a little...

Ann says, slowly, tentatively, "You know, for some women, women who've had to defend themselves against a mother, death may be an important event in the relationship. Death may even in some sense be said to...*enable* the relationship."

MOVING HOUSE

Here...is where we run out of continent.

—Joan Didion, "Notes from a Native Daughter"

Indian summer, October is golden on the coast, winter feels far away. The road winds through the Anderson Valley, past fields with tumbledown barns and split-rail fences, like the hills behind Los Altos, or what those hills used to be, only here are apple orchards, not apricots. The road skirts along the Navarro River, the river widens at the sea, we wind up the riverbank, Nellie shoves her muzzle out the window, madly sniffing, ears flapping in the wind—which of us is more ecstatic to be on this road again, I don't know.

But when we get to Mendocino, our hearts sink. We hadn't anticipated what it would feel like to be here without Bob's house. "Should we drive past the house?" he says. "Sure," I say, "why not," though I can think of many reasons why we should not go back to that place that pained him so to lose.

I am nervous as we turn off the highway, jumpy as I felt the first time I drove down this road, this narrow, bumpy road through the pines. I'd known him only a few months, I had that trepidation you feel when you're just getting to know a person, just falling in love, and you're about to see where he lives, and what if you learn something you'd rather not know...but I walked in, and there was this gorgeous house, this gorgeous man with this gorgeous house. Well, *funky* might be a better word. It's a rambler, a house that's been added on to over the years—*eclectic*, you might call it, nobody planned it, it just grew. *Weatherbrow* is carved on a beam above the fireplace, and weathered it is, a house silvered as that beam, a shake roof so hoary with moss and pine needles, it practically disappears into the woods.

There's a FOR SALE sign at the end of the driveway—what a surprise, the house is still on the market, after all these months. And another surprise, as we drive up: where there were ferns and fuchsias and foxgloves are stumps and dirt. The owners have hacked back the vines and pruned the bushes to the ground—no wonder nobody's bought the place, it looks stricken. Pining for us, perhaps, as we have for it.

We walk around the back, peering in windows to see what else they've done. We find a flyer that lists a price. Way out of range, but...

It is late by the time we set off to the lighthouse, the walk we always used to take. The sun, low on the horizon, streaks the waves purple and gold, the grass glows as though lit from within, the air sharp with the scent of sage and sea, sea lions rowdy on the rocks below. I am walking fast, talking fast, I'd do cartwheels if I could—if we could get the owners to come down, if I could get myself to let go of Mother's house, if we could, if I could...

"*Slow down*," says Bob, unnerved that I'm racing off like this. "You know, this isn't the only house on the coast. If we're serious, we should look around."

So we spend the next day looking, and we know this is the only house for us.

Bob finds a book on how to be your own realtor and I make an offer. I come in with a price so low there's no danger it will be accepted, which is fine, since by now I'm losing my nerve. "*Do not*," say the grief books, "make a major move in the first year"—everyone says this. This is major, and it's barely half a year, this is not a move I'd make on my own, this is casting my lot with a man. *Never count on a man*, she'd say, and am I really doing this, trading her house for this house? She'd be aghast.

And does that make it a good plan or a bad plan?

We talk to a realtor about Mother's house. Debbie, a short bouncy woman with short bouncy black hair, is generous with her time, advising us on how to buy as well as sell, plunging us into a world of termite reports, septic tank inspections, negotiations, counter-negotiations. The distraction is welcome, after the doldrums we've been in, but the sums of money are astronomical. Bob and I go round and round, figuring loans, interest rates, monthly payments, calculating worst-possible cases—he is good at calculating worst-possible cases, I am amused to learn, who knew he was such a cautious man. There are many things I do not know about him, and I only dare contemplate this because we lived through some of the grimmest months of my life and pulled together rather than apart— it was not at all obvious this would happen; it becomes a sort of touchstone to me now, as the faxes start flying, offers and counter-offers whip back and forth. I hurl myself into it, then shrink back, he sets his pace to mine, revving up and backing off at a sign from me. We do this well together—if he pushed, I might bolt, that old fear, walls closing in, he may even sense this, having more than a touch of it himself; wary people, both, trust not an easy thing.

And so it goes, November and December, charging forward and drawing back. For days, I put it out of mind. Then I remember something Judy said that night we had dinner: "it's the risks I didn't take, not the risks I took, that I regret." *Portentous*, those words now seem, like the birds I find in Mother's things, the seashells and driftwood and fishing net balls pointing to the sea—it's as though a veil's been ripped away and things open up to reveal their meanings, as though the universe reveals itself, resplendent, *like shining from shook foil*. Yeah, right, says another voice, call forth the augurs, why don't you, pick through the entrails of a slaughtered lamb, cast the bones, as though the universe cares which way you move. But it's a surprisingly feeble voice—most of me is off reading omens in a universe radiant with meaning, a sacramental universe, sacramentalized by me.

In December, the owners come in with a counter-offer. Still

way too high, and I'm knee-deep in grading, so I let it go. I finish exams and papers and we take off for the Yucatán, feeling giddy and irresponsible—we climb pyramids and snorkel and walk the beaches, far from phones and faxes.

We get back and I make myself pay attention. The rains have started, it's a bad time to be selling on the coast. I sit down and fax a counter-counter-offer. After months of dithering and deciding and re-deciding and fearing that it might not happen and fearing that it might happen, the house is ours.

Valentine's Day, Debbie phones with good news. She is usually upbeat, but today she's really excited, I can hear. In spite of the rain, the Open House was packed, the rooms and backyard full. Its floors newly polished, walls fresh painted, heavy drapes down, this old house came through. "Good spaces, good light, established garden and pool. Make sure you see the inside," says the flyer. Debbie added that last bit because she's worried about the pink. It's been raining too hard for us to paint outside, and I'm glad. I like it pink.

She says we should expect offers by the middle of next week. She hopes for a bidding war, a *feeding frenzy*, the Silicon Valley realtors call it. She's found an apartment for Sammy and Joey that's walking distance to downtown Los Altos, quiet, with trees. "It's nice," says Sammy, "but not as nice as this." They'll be fine, he says, we'll stay in touch, though I can tell they're being brave. I try not to feel the sadness, hoping the check I wrote to cover their deposit and some months' rent will ease the pain a bit. As I watch them drive off down the block, their old Datsun low and lopsided with the weight of them and their earthly possessions, a knot in my throat, a sickliness of regret, another good-bye.

Bob and I have been emptying out the house, piece by piece, for weeks. Every single thing has had to be cleared out for the cleaning, painting, carpeting.

A few weeks ago, Debbie called with her weekly report.

"And by the way," she said "we found some boxes in the attic."

"We don't have an attic."

"Well, it's more like a crawl space, all sorts of things up there—Christmas ornaments, clothes, photographs. You're going to *love* it," she says, her indomitable cheer.

Oh-noo, I don't think I'm going to love it. I thought I was finished with the memorabilia.

I brace myself, and it is bad. All the things my mother couldn't deal with. Bill's high school yearbooks, his public speaking award. Porcelain china teacups and saucers, a saltshaker, very old, these would have been her mother's. The Poodle Rancho paperwork, pedigrees, receipts, contracts, this puppy for that stud—Paddy must have dumped this with Mother when she took off for Florida. And here's a box like a shoebox, only heftier, plain brown wrapper, an official document tacked to its side—*Edward Paterson*.

Mother, how could you?—Grampa in the attic!

This house is so small, I hear her mutter as she shoves him up the trapdoor, *out of sight, out of mind.*

But here, suddenly, are some photos I've never seen, portraits of my mother, my father, and Paddy, each captured at a moment they are opening a gift. *Christmas 1963*, Bill's writing on the back. Mother is taking a garment from a package, she holds it out, beaming, I can hear her chuckle—"Oh, just look at this!" Paddy is laughing, even my father looks amused at the present he's opening.

These photos startle me. Most of the family photos I know, old racks for old memories, but these tease the past into a different shape, make the light fall differently, reveal something about Bill, something important. No photo of him, that Christmas day, but he is palpably there, there in the way he set our parents at ease, made them forget they were having their pictures taken. *Billy Boy, Charming Billy, Sweet William*, there in the loving eye of the camera; now it comes back, his humor, his geniality, I had forgot. Such good photos, and he was, in 1963...he would have been fifteen.

Debbie was right—I *am* enjoying this.

Debbie and Bob are walking through the empty rooms, conferring about window hangings, carpeting, bathroom fixtures. They try to get my attention, but I am deep in the boxes. They give up and let me go.

Here's another photo I've never seen: Mother with a boyfriend, Uncle George we called him, a square-jawed, beefy kind of guy— he didn't last long, driven away by her bratty kids, no doubt. They are sitting on a picnic bench. She is dishy, bare-shouldered, wearing a strapless halter, curls piled high, legs crossed and shapely, high-heeled shoes. He has his arm around her, looking like he can hardly believe his good luck. She is holding a cigarette (she didn't smoke), she glances to the side, smiling, I can't read that smile—is she enjoying herself, or pretending to enjoy herself, playing at having a lover, secretly mocking the whole show?

I never can read her.

And here's a book, very old, no title on the cover, the binding so brittle it crumbles in my hand—a diary! But my mother didn't keep a diary. But then she wasn't my mother in 1922, she was a girl of fifteen.

I look for a place to sit down and begin flipping through the pages—and time rolls back to a time before me, a world opens up: Honolulu, the 1920s. They swim, they hike, they picnic, the neighbors drop by with mangoes, pineapples, bananas, she has a piano recital…

Bob is nudging me, it will soon be dark. Debbie wants us to drive around and look at other houses on the market, see how they're priced. I shove the diary in my purse.

I slump in the back seat, lost in the backroads of Los Altos, roads I haven't driven in decades, let Bob and Debbie do the talking. I trip out, remembering: this is the block the Todds used to live on, this is where Julie lived, and Julie's brother with the Elvis hair and the old cars, he'd take them apart and put them back together, revving the engines. No junk cars here now, these cars are high-end and high-polished, the yards are immaculate. This is the short cut I'd take on my way home from school, I see a schoolgirl skipping down the street, braids swinging wildly, in too much of a hurry to walk, kicking at piles of leaves, sending whirlpools of red, orange, and gold swirling into the air.

We are driving through the older neighborhoods near downtown, two-story wood-frame houses with water towers and fruit trees, vestiges of the vast orchards that once filled the valley. The branches are bare now, pinched, scrawny twigs stripped of life, but in a few weeks' time, they'll astound you, bursting into blossom, petals more fragile than a flower's, come to tell you, with their unspeakably sweet scent, that there's something in the world besides winter, then just as you're getting used to their unsettling beauty, they're gone and you're bereft, sure that the world will never again hold such promise. But then comes another surprise, when those hard little nubs nestled in new green leaf turn to burgundy-colored bings and dark purple prunes and rosy-rust apricots, the branches bend with their offerings, luscious, delicious, what gifts!—though unlike the petals, the fruit hangs around long enough for you to get sick of it, sweet turns to stickiness, ripeness to rot, a gummy pulp that messes shoes and draws flies, so you're glad to be rid of it, not like the blossoms, which you'd love to have last forever, but *forever* is just what a blossom can never do.

I am filled, suddenly, with gratitude for this place. Just as I am leaving this place.

Later that night, Bob and I return to the house. Decisions must be made on every single object in the yard, the driftwood, the Buddhas, the wind chimes, the potted plants, the wrought iron plant stands. Everything not rooted to the ground or nailed to the house gets thrown in the dumpster or dragged into the garage, where it will wait till we load it in the truck for Mendocino.

Bob spots the giant clam shell out by the pool—"Where did she get *that?*"

"No idea."

"A half shell for a Rubens Venus!" he laughs. This is the prize, as far as he's concerned—the rest, he's doing for me, but the giant clam shell, he really wants (yes, they are kindred spirits). He eases it onto a large piece of cardboard and drags it into the garage, along with the other things we're moving to Mendocino.

And so the old place is cleared out and cleaned up. With our things gone and the curtains down, it looks spacious. Relieved, perhaps, of the load of our lives, it breathes, sighs, expands.

The FOR SALE sign goes up, the stake in the front lawn, a stake through my heart. Debbie holds Open House, and she calls me, this Valentine's Day, elated at how fast the old house will sell. I tell myself this is good news, but it feels like a limb's been torn off, a piece of flesh hacked away. This house is so much a part of me that if you could scan a mind the way you can a brain, you'd find this house inscribed in mine, the shapes of its rooms in the contours of my consciousness, its beams, frames, rafters imprinted in nerves, sinew, bone, and surely you'd find our molecules in the soil out back, spun into the pinecones and redwood whorls, surely we are here for good.

I sit, fighting the desire to call Debbie back, tell her I've changed my mind. I stare at the pile of books on my desk, on top of which sits my mother's diary. So nearly not found.

I open the book gingerly. Will I find my mother in these pages, in this fifteen-year-old girl of the islands, thrilling to "the marvelous outdoors"? She thrills to sunsets, magnificent from their house on Palolo Hill, that suffuse the Pacific with a "flamingo flood" and transform Palolo Valley to "a basin of color": "I timed old Phoebus with Danny's watch and it took him just two and a half minutes to fall in the ocean, but he didn't drown because I saw him rise this morning!" She thrills to the storms, "flashes of lightning no more than two seconds apart...rosy red, pretty violet, blinding green. The valley was full of water and electricity and one simply couldn't have wished for a more advantageous and interesting position than here on Palolo Hill."

She hikes to the falls "through guava thickets, up cliffs, over rocks, down trails, by a beautiful running stream, waterfalls, deep gorges…Surf splashing up the cliffs 25 and 30 feet high, blowing off icy spray far inward, mountains of waves tearing at the beach…" She is fearless, this young lady: "The waves were monstrous, high as hills, over my head as soon as I stepped into the water. The raft seemed miles away, but I was determined to reach it…I was all in when I reached it, and swallowing a gallon of water…" The mother I knew was full of fears, but in Honolulu 1922, 1923, 1924, "Life is just one grand thing after another," a round of parties (the mother I knew didn't care for parties), beach parties, birthday parties, graduation parties, a Valentine's Day party. "I have the reputation of a flapper," she writes, and I remember, she did look like a flapper in the photos, with her beads and middy. "A wild time, I danced until my feet hurt, I tell you, it was fun, talk about laughing! All the snaps on the side of my dress came undone."

She writes poetry about sunsets, sailing ships, and the merry month of May, "when all things are blithe and gay." Then school is out and "we are knee deep in June." Mornings, she and Lydia help their mother scrub and wax the floor; afternoons, they laze about, eating candy and reading. They bake cream pies and mocha fudge cakes and coconut marshmallow cakes—they are not on diets, these young ladies!—they walk down the hill to town, to meet friends for a hot fudge sundae, then hitch a ride back. She takes the streetcar to her father's office at Lewers and Cooke, hardware and paint, drops in on him after the dentist—many trips to the dentist. Evenings, they take in a show, lots of shows—Gloria Swanson in *The Impossible Mrs. Bellew*, Charlie Chaplin in *The Pilgrim*, Anita Stewart in *The Woman He Married*.

She spices her writing with Latin and quotes from Shakespeare, she is proud to be the valedictorian of her graduating class, Queen

Lydia Lili'uokalani Elementary School, June 23, 1922: "Everyone re-
marked how extremely self-poised I was," what "an effective speaker,
and I got so many flowers I couldn't hold them all, five boxes of
candy, many congratulations." But her real love is the piano: "Do you
know that I should like to be a pianist? I hope that when I read this
at some future time, I shall be laughing at the doubts I hold now. My
new resolution: practice from 6:30 to 7:30 every morning." She makes
progress on Liszt's *Hungarian Rhapsody*, the *Moonlight Sonata*. She
has a recital—"I didn't forget a note."

"This is a wonderful place," she writes, though she and Lydia
long for "the bygone days in Lake County"—"kids days," they call
them, the swimming hole, the horse, their dog Jack. Lake County is
the paradise they have lost—young as they are, paradise has been lost.
When "Pa" tells them they're moving back to California, they're ecstatic. The morning before they sail, she writes, "Sunrise at 6:30, I am
bursting with the beauty of this place, tomorrow we sail, Jan 15, 1924,
thank heaven that this our last should be one of the most beautiful
mornings that ever dawned up on our rugged Palolo...I am completely thrilled!!! Adieu. When comes such another??"

Never, I want to cry—*stay where you are!* I want to reach back and
pluck the ship out of the water. *Look at you, swimming, picnicking,
larking about—can't you see, this place is paradise? Don't leave!* But I
guess that's the way it is with paradise—it's never *here* or *now*, always
then or *there*, in time that was or time that is to come.

I take off my glasses, the tears flow. I think, what was I up to
when I was fifteen? Dieting, binging, drinking, smoking, *sleeping the
day away* (*you only ever see dawn from the wrong side*, she'd say), speeding up the coast to hang out in North Beach dives, thrilling to Ginsberg's *howling for a fix*, writing poems about nuclear holocaust, not
sunsets and the month of May.

But maybe that was paradise, too. Paradise enough.

January 30, 1924, their ship docks in San Francisco, the bay
shrouded in fog. Six months later, "Lyd and I plug away at school

here in Santa Rosa, and once in awhile feel lonesome for our house high in the balmy tropics. We find neither teachers nor students so pleasant as they were in the islands." I could have told you that. Then comes a lot of moving around, Healdsburg, Sebastopol, Geyserville, towns I drive past on my way to Mendocino. They settle in San Francisco, she goes to Girls High, they pull together a life, but it's colder, lonelier, not like the *kids days* they long for in Lake County. She writes no more about straight A's or piano recitals.

But there is a place they go weekends and summers that calls forth the exuberant young lady of the islands, La Honda, in the Santa Cruz Mountains. "We rode to the tip of the mountain where we could see into the valley. The hay press was up there and we watched the men bail, a glorious Sunday... We returned from a horseback ride to the old Shingle Mill. We dismounted and, throwing the reins over the heads of our horses, allowed them to munch grass while we reclined by the side of the creek and played with buttercups. Sprawled in the tall grass among the buttercups, with Lyd by my side... and in the distance, the range of tall green hills in the purple haze of spring sunshine... Here is inspiration itself."

It's the Santa Clara Valley she's seeing through that spring haze, 1928, not far from Los Altos. I didn't know she had this kind of history with the place, I had no idea.

Then the writing stops. In the last entry, February 4, 1929, she has started classes at UC Berkeley. She makes an appointment to see an academic advisor, then, a lot of blank pages. Why did she stop writing? Later that year, the world plunged into Depression, but that wasn't till October, months later. I don't think that's why the writing stopped.

I wonder what that advisor said. "Cold and unfriendly," she said Berkeley was, a long streetcar ride from the far side of San Francisco to the ferry across the bay, another streetcar to the huge campus where she knew no one, it took hours, getting there and back. "A waste of time," her father said, told her to get a job. She stuck it out

My mother and her mother, 1930s, La Honda.

a year, then got a job. She regretted it all her life, not getting that degree. Was that why she wrote no more?

I lean back, trying to bring these images into focus, the slender young woman riding a horse through the hills, the stout, white-haired woman shoving this diary up the trapdoor, *out of sight, out of mind*, along with her son's photographs, too sad an ending for so exuberant a beginning.

For years, he was all we talked about. Something I'd say or something she'd say would set us off and we'd start crying, keening like a chorus in an ancient tragedy. We did this every time we got together, then every few months, then once in a year, then once in a while. In time, we learned to talk of other things.

Things have a way of working out, she'd say. I wonder if she felt they had for her.

I know this now. She made a home for us, a home I could come back to. She bore her losses gracefully as she could, made what family she could. She made a garden, turned a dead end into a park. There was music in this house, and in the course of time, we learned to laugh again.

And though she was no believer, she had a wonder in her. "Just think what a miracle it is," she'd say, taking a bandage off a cut, "how do they do it? the white corpuscles make the tissue here connect with the tissue there"—she'd hold out her finger for me to see—"the miracle of healing!" She'd go on in loving detail about the hunting habits of the cheetah, the reproductive life of the snail, gleaned from the latest nature documentary she'd watched on TV. She'd quote Lucretius on death, the futility of fearing death, *death is nothing.* She'd quote Heraclitus on change—*nothing stays the same, nothing so permanent as change*; she'd say this by way of consolation, not hopeless or self-pitying, just philosophical, like this is the way it is, get used to it. I never could see it as consolation. I begin to now.

And it's not true that she was no believer—she had a homebrew humanism all her own. A pinch of pantheism, a bit of Buddhism, a dash of Bolshevism, bohemianism, Beethoven, lots of Beethoven, mix and stir, it's a recipe requiring silliness, for whatever the sadness, there was always the silliness—*every cloud has a silly lining*, she'd say.

Count your blessings, she'd say, I'd tune out, write it off as one of those things mothers say. But I hear it now. *Appreciate it, Gayle.*

She had a way of saying things, an active, inquiring mind. Somebody should have told her, do something with it, make something of it.

I would have, if she'd been my student.

San Francisco is luminous, this spring day, lit with that special brightness of cities built on water. As I drive across the bridge, the bay is frothy, not its usual dull gray-green, but pale as a lime parfait, whisked full of light by the March winds. Something by Chopin (or is it Schumann) comes on the radio, something Mother used to play, and I'm filled, suddenly, with thanks to her for this day, for giving me joy of such a day, and it happens again, that veil ripped away...was it there all along, this resplendence, unseen by me as I rushed through on my way somewhere else? I am overflowing with thanks. Gratitude, *gracias, grazia, gracie*, the words are the same, aren't they? maybe there is grace for those of us who have no gods.

I take the 280 down the Peninsula, the road through the hills where I once rode a horse, where I now know my mother rode a horse. The hills are green, though in a few months' time, they'll be gold. I have heard these hills called tawny, tan, brown, but they are gold. You'd have to be Georgia O'Keeffe to paint these shapes, and even she could not capture the way the contours shift as the sun slips across the sky, darkening the hollows and lighting the tips with a gold-white sheen, nor could she catch the scent of sage and tarweed, that sweet spicy tang of California. South of Stanford, I come around a bend and see the foothills of San Jose, green as the Emerald City of Oz. The whole of the Santa Clara Valley is visible on this extraordinarily clear day, washed clean by the winter rains.

Am I really letting go of my home in the valley, this valley my father glimpsed on a produce crate and came west to find? This place holds nothing for me now, it is empty. Not empty, hardly empty—there's a clump of new structures by the freeway, I swear they weren't here before, cropped up like mushrooms after rain, huge as condominiums. Only they can't be condominiums—Los Altos Hills is zoned for single dwellings. The city fathers couldn't have predicted these plywood palazzos, bloated to fill full-acre lots, faux Tudor, faux Victorian, faux Tuscan.

I exit at Magdalena, the road to our house, something gypsy-mournful comes on the radio, romantic, yearning, *Malaguena*, something she used to play, *Malaguena, Magdalena*. I pass a row of plum trees in bloom. "How lovely, the blossoms," I hear her say, her pleasure in the blossoms, her last time out, a year ago. I cross the expressway, formerly the railroad tracks, pass Andronico's, formerly the Rancho Market, where the BookMobile parked Saturdays, the parking lot now clogged with SUVs, Hummers, Porches, Mercedes, BMWs, Jaguars. A car zooms up on my tail, low-slung and purring, I hit the brakes, my usual response to tailgaters—IMRICH, says the license plate. I guess you have to be fast to get that rich, license plates in the valley boast IMFAST, IMSMART, STARTUP, EUREKA. Bob tells me there was one time when every top manager at Apple was taking cabs to work because they'd had their licenses suspended for speeding. He follows these things, he reads *Wired*, wired is the way they drive. I mean, I'm a fast driver, or I used to be, now everyone in California is on my tail.

When people say *The Valley* now, they no longer mean the San Fernando Valley, where the Valley Girls come from, or the great Central Valley that Joan Didion calls California's "real valley," the agricultural heartland of the state, but Silicon Valley. Come here and strike it rich, *EUREKA*, the state motto, *I found it*, I struck gold, I came, I saw, I conquered, I devoured—boundless the desire, boundless the state, or so they assumed.

It was you, Mother, who gave me this way of looking at things, so don't blame me for moving on. I'm only doing what your father did, what my father did, what you might have done if you hadn't had us, head for the open spaces.

I turn down our block, there's an odd assortment of people standing in the driveway, Linda from across the street, Debbie the realtor, and Inge, her hair a brighter shade of red. They are chatting like old friends, when up drives a rickety, wood-slatted truck and out jump Inge's ex-boyfriend and ex-husband and Jenny, back from Jamaica and back for good. They hoist the couches onto the truck, along with the kitchen table—my eyes follow the table as it bounces down Clinton Road on the back of the truck.

Later, Jenny and Inge and I go downtown Los Altos to Mother's favorite Chinese restaurant, and after dinner, I show them some photos. "She look like that when she die," says Jenny, pointing to the young dark beauty. So she saw it too—I thought it was only me who saw it, the young face through the old face, I thought it was a trick of tears. But Jenny saw it too.

I show her the photo I've been saving for her, Mom and Paddy standing by a plump, matronly woman. "Look on the back—it says *Marie Cohen.*" Jenny peers, puzzled. "That's who she thought you were!"

"*That* what Marie look like?"

"She had a friend named Marie Cohen, she used to talk about her, she was very fond of her; I'd forgot."

"Different color," laughs Jenny. Yes. But I see the similarity, the round, bosomy, motherly form.

Later I return to the house and let myself in. I wander through the rooms, an old ghost prowling the premises. I walk into her bedroom, no place to sit, no reason to sit, it is empty of presence. I wander out to Sammy's room, which used to be my room summers when I came back from New York, I remember what it felt like, arrived the night before from that gray northern city, to wake up and step outside to a burst of light and color...

Don't know what you've got till it's gone, that song won't go from my mind, *they paved paradise, put up a parking lot...* I press my face against the window, smudge the glass with tears. We had so much, Mother, how could we not know? We seemed always to be fretting to be somewhere else.

I wander out into the yard. In the middle of the patio stands a Buddha without a head. Somebody tried to drag it from the bamboo thicket where it lived all these years, and in moving it, decapitated it. I try to haul it over to the side, but it's too heavy, so there it sits in the center of the patio, still poised and dignified, though without a head, a string of weathered jade around its neck. I slip the beads into my pocket.

I walk over to the pool and kneel, trailing my hand through the water. There's a full moon, the water ripples, the moon dances. Are you on the moon now, are you, perhaps, the moon, *Clair de Lune*, a spirit come back to play upon the water, a skinny-dipping spirit.

We are lucky it's not raining, this weekend of the Big Move.

First, to the U-Haul on El Camino, pick up the truck, then to Mother's. Bob heads for the giant clam shell, the prize, as far as he's concerned, maneuvers it up the ramp and into the truck, strapping it in. Our breaths steam. In go the boxes, then the furniture, which we pack in carefully. Into the truck go Paddy's white wicker shelves, Mother's desk, the bookshelf Ted built. Each thing we take feels like a piece of the past I get to keep.

It's midnight when we get on the road. Bob drives on ahead, I follow in the Honda. "Keep me in sight," he says, and that's easy to do, the truck has only one taillight and lurches dramatically—we're not at all sure about this truck, not sure it will make it to Mendocino. I'm glad to have to keep him in view, I don't want to look back, turn to a pillar of salt, like Lot's wife—*Flee this valley, don't look back, lest ye be consumed*.

We turn off the freeway at Cloverdale, the road to the coast. Bob picks up speed like a horse scenting the barn, the truck sways wildly around the bends, I can barely keep up.

It's strange to see the Los Altos furniture dropped down into the splendid rooms where Bob used to live. Everything is so much grander here, the high, angled skylights that let in moon, stars, trees. Her things find their places easily, the cherrywood chest, the shoji screens, the dragon-knobbed music cabinet—they look better here, they can breathe.

The next day, we stand on the deck and watch the sun disappear into the sea. Twilight floods the sky, lavender glows from beneath the horizon, turns purple, indigo, midnight blue. A pair of hawks glides into view, they hang, suspended, then, dipping, reeling, they soar away. I raise my glass—"*To the ancestors*. Their frugality, their generosity." I think of that dedication I once wrote, *to Agnes, Paddy, and*

Jack, who gave me a place to stand—I had no idea how literally that would translate. A place to stand. For now, at least, though we see, from our deck, Cape Mendocino jutting out to sea, the westernmost tip of the continent, you can go no farther west, famed, geologically, as the point where three tectonic plates converge. Seismographically active, this California, permanent as change.

Bob is planting apple trees. I watch as his shovel cuts through the ground, sinking easily into earth soft from the rains. The dark soil makes me think of a grave, but it also makes me think what it means to set down roots. He plucks a plump, pink worm off the shovel, places it gently in the grass, where it wriggles away. I love it when he does this—he tosses snails off of sidewalks and rescues spiders and sow bugs with his bare hands. "You have the soul of a Hindu," I say, realizing it's something I could say of anyone I've loved.

He does great Nellie imitations, too, gets down on the floor and does this cycling thing she does, the way she rolls over on her back, pumping air with all fours, it looks like doggie aerobics though probably she's just scratching her ass. What a clown she is, what a pair of clowns—who knew he was a silly man, who knew how much that would matter. Her begging techniques have become more accomplished with his spoiling, too, and I'm not even sure she still loves me most.

He's the only man I've been with who doesn't make me feel walls closing in.

"Perhaps that's because you've got two sets of walls," comments Janet, doing that crinkly thing with her eyes that's like a wink.

On Tuesdays I fly down to Claremont. I teach Tuesday, Wednesday, Thursday, fly back Thursday. I fly down, fly back, same as before, same as always.

Yet not the same.

I am teaching a course on the 1950s. I go to the library and check out some college yearbooks, 1953, 1958, 1963. I want my students to

I'm not even sure she still loves me most.

see how they'd have looked if they'd been at this college those years, skirts puffed out by crinolines, sweaters pulled tight over torpedo bras, pearl chokers at the neck, that prissy sexiness, that fifties tease. They giggle as the yearbooks go around. "Laugh away," I say, "you'd have worn these too."

"High maintenance," says Monica, pointing to a hairdo puffed up high. Her own hair is a long sandy braid that disappears into a sweatshirt hood.

"*Beehive*," I say, dredging the name up from a distant past. "Held together by hairspray. The hairspray gave you cancer, we later learned." I look around and see their hair, tousled, tufted, spiked, blue, pink, and orange. I feel, as I often feel with them, like I've stepped out of a time capsule. They look worlds away from me, a galaxy from my mother. But are they?

I tell them what it felt like to wear petticoats like that, layer on layer of flouncy white crinolines that weighted you down and tripped you up, catching in car doors, requiring washing, whitening, starching, ironing. I tell them what it felt like to cinch in a waist to that hourglass shape, to stuff a burgeoning body into a girdle so tight you could barely sneeze.

"Yeah, we don't have to wear a girdle," says Stephanie, a tall, rangy redhead whose collarbones and hip bones protrude alarmingly. "We don't *get* to wear a girdle! We have to *be* skinny."

"It's like, we've internalized the girdle," says Alexandra, who is also model thin, short, black, curly hair around a gamin face.

They're right—my generation of women may have been defined as bodies, but at least we got to *have* bodies. Marilyn Monroe and Sophia Lauren would be sent to the fat farm today. Merry widow bras and cinch belts may have whittled us down to size, but it was sizes larger than these kids get to be, with their show-all midriffs and skinny-tight jeans. Some tell me they've been on diets since they can remember, some say their kid sisters are on diets, too.

Waif-like, wasted, that's the look, judging from the ads they bring in. "Why would anyone want to look like *this?*" I hold up a glossy, full-page ad from the *New York Times*: a girl, all bony protuber-ances, glares, sullen, sunken-eyed, like she's just been beaten or raped. "Why does this look become trendy just as women are beginning to take up space? *You've come a long way, baby*—so, have you?"

"Backlash," says Stephanie. We've read the book.

"Big business," says another.

"Who profits?" We talk about the interests that prey on female insecurity, the diet industry, the fashion industry, cosmetics, cos-metic surgery. Annais brings in the Martha Stewart wedding hand-book—weddings aren't the informal backyard events they used to be, that anyone with a Universal Life Church license could perform; these cost the earth. Literally. I try to get them to think about how this consumption wastes the planet, but nature is something that, when you grow up in southern California, you know mainly by reputation.

They're hard to read, these young women, a strange mixture of entitlement and insecurity. They talk knowledgeably about *raging hormones*, they use words I barely knew at their age, let alone would say in class—*orgasm, clitoris* (I do a double take when one announces that the masturbation workshop has been changed to Wednesday). They throw around words that didn't exist in my day, *anorexia, disempowerment, heteronormativity*. At the end of the semester, I ask them to write about their lives, and I read about drugs, drink, sexual abuse, date rape, and a level of loutishness in guys I've seen only in bad movies. I read about eating disorders, depression, anxiety, PTSD, OCD, ADD, ADHD, an alphabet soup of ailments, and the medications they take for them. I read about nose jobs, breast implants, and forms of self-mutilation, cutting, shredding, tearing, burning, unheard of in my day.

I read no rhapsodic descriptions of sunsets or "the marvelous outdoors," and I have a thought that's heresy for a feminist: what if it's *worse* for women today? But then I remember the loneliness of my mother's life, the *holier than thou* across the street who snubbed her for being without a husband—there were no support groups to turn to those days, no networks or hotlines, women kept their sufferings to themselves or drank them away or took them out on kids. If they were lucky, or smart, they found their way to music, to some art form that spins sorrow to sustenance, to a saving grace.

I am suddenly so grateful to have moved through time at the time I did, when I could wander the world on a bike or horse. The world my students inherit is scarier, uglier, and who knows but what I'd have been a casualty of these times, some drug or disorder would have got its hooks into me. And yet these kids have resources we didn't have. They have each other; they value friendships in a way we were slow to learn. They have their mothers, there's a camaraderie it took Mother and me decades to build, the gap between generations has shrunk—too much, I think sometimes, a little more separation might do. They have classes like this, books that had not been written when I was in college, they have teachers, too…me, I'm a resource.

"How lovely it is here," I hear her say. We were walking across campus, graduation day, 1985, a day so clear you could reach out and touch the mountains. The San Gabriels are starker than the hills of home, rock and crag that jut almost at right angles from the desert floor, but on days like this, you see the beauty. We walked down the path lined with orange trees, past elegant, old Spanish-style dorms, till we came to a courtyard with a fountain at the center and an arbor, wisteria vines with trunks thick as banyans, their flowers purple, pendulous, swarming with bees. Like a medieval cloister, this courtyard, an enclosed garden, that's how they pictured paradise in the Middle Ages, *hortus conclusus*, a place for peace, for contemplation.

"How lucky you are to be here," she said. "This is a place where you're somebody. Appreciate it, Gayle. I was never anybody anywhere." It was the only time she ever came to graduation, that day in May, the scent of wisteria mingling with the blossoms and the bees. She met my students, they buzzed around, said nice things, their parents said nice things. "These are darling girls," she said, "charming young people" (which was not always the way I saw them)—"you can help them, Gayley, inspire them. It's not easy to be young."

You are the greatest teacher, said the card on her refrigerator door, a kid's drawing, sun flower sky tree balloon, *Happy Birthday, 1982*, it came from one of her piano students. It stayed on the refrigerator door, yellow and curled with age, it was there at the end, alongside the DO NOT RESUSCITATE sign, it's there now, somewhere in my basement. She said it was *forever*, was fond of quoting whoever it was who said a teacher's influence is for eternity.

I don't know about *forever*, but I know I like working with these kids for the time we're here. I like it that this college is a sort of sheltered place, a place they can find their voices, get to know a professor and I can get to know them. This place works well for some of them, for some of *us*, I should say, a little ecosystem that allows unique and fragile life forms to survive and thrive. I wonder, what if she'd lived in one of these dorms instead of having to take that long ride to the huge, unfriendly campus across the bay, what if she'd made the kinds of friends my students make, read the books they read—what a difference it might have made.

I think of that line from Robert Frost, *home is where when you go, they have to take you in.* Tenure's a bit like that. They have taken me in, and what an opportunity it is, I've got their attention, I can tell them a thing or two. I think about Mother's words, *a place where you're somebody.* I'd say it differently—*this is a place where I know who I am.*

I'm no longer counting the years till retirement. I don't want another terminated conversation. It's an ongoing conversation, teaching, a conversation that goes on not just in the classroom, but in my head—*wait'll I tell them this, wait'll I show them this.* It's part of the babble that sustains the story of a life, a conversation I don't want to end just yet.

There are more students hanging around my office these days. They come in with outrageous stories, funny stories. I love it that they're reviving the student chapter of NOW, that they're making consciousness-raising groups around eating disorders. We plot strategies. When, at the end of the semester, Stephanie and Annais and Monica invite me to dinner, I take the extra trip down, we share a bottle of wine, tell our life stories, I watch them graduate, I get all choked up. I'm afraid there may not come another group I'm so fond of, but each year I fear that, and each year there comes another. Teaching is a bit like having a family that never grows up, never grows old, fools you into thinking you're not growing old either. Oh well, there are worse delusions. Time tells, in the end; whatever we tell it, time has the last word.

It's an odd business, teaching—you never know what gets through. Sometimes they'll write or come back years later and say, "I'll never forget when you said..." and they tell you something you can't imagine ever saying, and you think, well, okay, if that's what you got out of the course, it's good you got something.

I see them differently now. They're not an intrusion on my work, they *are* what I've done. They're what I've done instead of children, and that's okay—I'm better at this than I'd have been at that. Like everything else, it cuts both ways. The art is in making the choice you can live with.

I say to them, *you're extraordinary.* Do something with it, don't let it get away.

Each Tuesday, I fly over the valley, nose pressed to the window, tracing the way back. Strange compulsion, to trace the way back: San Francisco, the city where I was born, Stanford, the red-tiled library where I wrote my dissertation, and a few miles south, the cluster of buildings that's downtown Los Altos, easy to spot by the sharp angle San Antonio makes with the expressway. I follow the expressway south to Clinton Road, find the patch of green at the end of the road, the park that was my mother's gift. I stare down, scanning the scene for a clue to where they have gone, it moves back, and away.

You can see from the air that this really is a peninsula, a slender strip of land bounded by bay on one side and ocean on the other. It looks fragile, precarious—it doesn't feel that way when you're on the ground, it feels like solid land, but from up here you see, it's surrounded. The bay itself looks shrunk, not the grand body of water it seems from the shore, but an embattled bay, encroached on from all sides, one-third the size it once was, ringed round by population and pollution. If women hadn't fought for it, there'd be no more bay.

Impossible, this both-ways view, from the air and from the land, bird's-eye view, worm's-eye view—you have to see double to see this way.

More and more there's a yellow stain clinging to the foothills of San Jose, that sleepy agricultural town where my father had his practice, now the capital of Silicon Valley. Freeways crosshatch the valley floor, houses march up the hills, quarries gouge hillsides, slashing the conifer forests of the coastal range, gashes visible from the air, though not from the roads below. Towns once separate are now squished into an urban stew. Silicon Valley stretches all the way to Gilroy, soon it will reach Salinas, Los Robles, Los Angeles—it will all be Los Angeles someday.

And you can see from the air that this is a state starved of water. They've drained the groundwater and dried the lakes, dammed the rivers and strangled the streams. Where there was water is parched, cracked mud, where there was fertile basin is dust, it's a scarred and stricken landscape I see below, and it's not only the water that's strained past capacity, everything is on overload, highways, housing, energy, schools, tempers. Seven million people lived in California the year I was born; if I live as long as Mother, I'll see that multiplied by ten.

After forty minutes in the air, there are mountains again, the San Gabriels that make the Los Angeles basin, a stony soil, a yellow mange of dying pines, a haze on the horizon—a forest fire? No, it's the air that hangs that way, a grimy film, now you see it, now you don't, now you taste it, acrid in the mouth, tight in the chest, eighty degrees and haze, says the captain's voice (they never say *smog*), a normal day in LA.

Why isn't this declared a national emergency?

They were not endless, those ridges upon ridges of redwoods rising from the sea, those marshes and wetlands filled with swans, herons, flocks of geese so thick they darkened the sun. We thought it was boundless, *the earth abideth forever*—wasn't that the promise? the generations come and the generations go but the earth is forever. Well, not any more, not in California. And with each forest felled there went a world, with each meadow and marsh and creek and river lost, there vanished ecosystems and the delicate life forms they sustained, and we let this happen after we knew better, gobbled it all up.

The only thing constant about the California of my youth, writes Joan Didion, is the rate at which it has disappeared. Was made to disappear. "Silicon Valley is now the center of the world," I read somewhere, "the greatest creator of new wealth and employment in human history." The *Valley of Heart's Delight* become the *Valley of Dollars*, milk and honey turned to money. Never mind that where there were orchards, woods, grasslands, are now twenty-three Superfund sites, places so poisoned that the federal government had to intervene to clean them up.

Let it go, Gayle.

Is it only nostalgia, this longing for a valley that is no more? Of course it's nostalgia, but there is real worry, too. This was one of the most fertile valleys in the world, a Nile River delta of a valley, a fertile crescent; soil this rich takes eons to make. Now farmland in California is disappearing so fast that the state will soon have to import its produce, that waxed, mealy pulp that passes for produce. *Never cut down a fruit-bearing tree*, advised a rabbi, long ago, a precept for right living still.

They left a piece of orchard in Sunnyvale, so kids can see where an apricot comes from.

Get used to it, Gayle, everyone else has. Nobody on this flight between the Bay Area and the Los Angeles Inland Empire is even looking out the window. The cloud-capped Sierras to the left, the Pacific to the right, the whole grand panorama of California below, nobody's looking. Nobody cares about the valley of your youth, nobody remembers, nobody knew it existed, until its crop turned to cash. You'd have to go back in time to find my valley now. The Santa Clara Valley had no Jeffers, no Steinbeck, to memorialize it, to mourn it. What has not been written might as well never have been.

Let it go. Leave it behind.

I mark the moons since your passing...*ten, eleven, twelve...*It is May again, month of your birth, month of your death, the month you loved best.

I find, to my surprise, that I am thinking about other things. I find that I have mixed feelings about thinking about other things. If I go on with my life, does that mean you are truly dead? *Life goes on, life is for the living*, too cruel.

We *are* guilty, we the living. We get on with our lives, we leave you for dead. No wonder you're vengeful in the old tales, you're mad as hell.

But then I remember the tales that tell us we do you wrong to mourn too much, we bind you with our grief—you *want* us to let go.

Listen. The dead want nothing from us, they care neither for our tears nor joy. It's easier to imagine them angry than to imagine them dead, but they are truly dead. I talk to them, I imagine them approving, or not, I take care with their photos, their possessions, I honor their memories, I know that they are dead. I do these things for me, the living, not the dead.

Twelve moons after she dies, the full moon falls on May 10. The May moon, brighter than other moons. I've watched the full moon slip, each month, a little more out of synch with the anniversary. Bob and I walk down the road by our house, the trees and fields are drenched in silvery light, the earth pungent from the heat of the day. There are not many warm nights in Mendocino, but on a night like this, I smell the hills of home, complicated by the salt tang of waves.

I think of the lines I found in Paddy's desk, the lyrics of a song she scrawled on an envelope:

I love you California,
You're the greatest state of all,
I love you in the summer, winter,
And in the spring and fall...
I love your grand old ocean
And I love your rugged shore...
It is there I would be
In the land by the sea,
It is home sweet home to me.

Me, too, Paddy, through the old-fashioned rhyme, I feel it too, *bred in the bone*, this love of the land. It's not true that everyone in California is from somewhere else, some of us were born here, born of mothers who were born here—to us, it's not real estate, it is home.

I guess I should be glad there's some California left—move north, since there's no more west, isn't that what everyone's doing? I guess I should feel lucky that the craziness in Silicon Valley gave me a way out of Silicon Valley—that, too, is what everyone's doing, using the money they make from the valley to get away from the valley they've ruined by making the money. Such an absurdly in-flated price I fetched for Mother's house, I could buy this piece of paradise, follow the winding roads back in time, past slope-roofed barns and split-rail fences, north to Mendocino. A private solution, I know, and not one I approve of, but it's what there was. But the north coast is precarious, too, a slender strip of cliff-lined beaches and estu-aries and woodlands of oak, pine, fir, redwood that fights for its life against loggers and developers.

I find a poem Paddy wrote for me, a birthday card, June 23, 1952:

> *May Gayley Girl with her*
> *brush and her braids,*
> *her pencil and pad,*
> *and her innocent ways,*
> *sketch and paint and*
> *give to the world,*
> *her love and her art,*
> *caring naught what*
> *it pays.*

The blessings of these women! to have two such women dote on me, to be the apple of their eye. I accepted my centrality in the universe as a birthright.

"Don't you take it too hard," said Paddy one night when I drove her back to her place and came in to chat. She gestured at the hang-ing on her wall, a Japanese silk, pink and white blossoms on blue, told me she wanted Cindy and Alfred to have it—"The rest of what I have is yours, instructions in the file cabinet."

"Oh, Paddy, not for a while yet."

"You never know," she said, "maybe soon. And don't you feel too bad, you hear?"

"What do you mean, don't feel bad?"

"Yes, for a day or two," she shrugged. "But not long. It really isn't very important."

She died a few days later. Later, after we'd moved her things out, I drove down to her place to turn in her keys, and they told me there'd been people in to the front office, asking for her. I gave them the obituary I wrote for the *Los Altos Town Crier*, praising her generosity, her work for a better world, referring donations to the Southern Poverty Law Center. They posted it in the lobby for all to see. They gave me a form that asked her forwarding address.

Forwarding address—what an idea! I gave my own.

Now when I get a piece of mail with her name on it, there's a stab of pain, but then I think, no, it's right that it come to me, for where else does she reside now but with me? So I get requests from every environmental and social justice group known to man, catalogues for vitamins and herbal remedies and Paula Allen wigs. "Grow your own tomato tree," one catalogue boasts, and I remember, she tried. It didn't survive. Her potted plants did, though; they're on my front porch.

I see that I've made shrines everywhere—Paddy's ducks on my bathroom shelves, Mother's Buddha, the one that kept its head, on a kitchen sill. Maybe there are ways for those of us who have no gods.

On the anniversary of Mother's death, May 20, I am back in Berkeley, raw, teary, desolate, longing for chocolate. I justify my trip to See's, telling myself it's a commemorative visit, and the smell of chocolate as I set foot in the candy store brings back my weekly trips to See's and the comfort food we all ate while she was dying.

I spend the evening writing, it's better than weeping. I guess lots of people do this, write about a person they've lost because they can't bear to think that person is really gone, that she, in her amazing, absolute uniqueness is absolutely gone. *Come back, stay a little.* I find the right word and it feels like I've salvaged a piece of them— I can leave it a little, let the pain go into the words, know that it's still there, it will always be there, but I don't have to carry it around all the time.

Later that night, Janet comes over and we walk in the hills. It's a clear night, the lights of San Francisco, the bridges, even the Richmond oil refineries are dazzling. I tell her this is the anniversary, though the moon's no longer full. "Yes," she says, "the *yahrzeit.* The Jewish calendar is lunar, did you know?" I did not. I love it when she tells me I've gone and rediscovered something Jewish; I'm not sure it proves I'm at heart really Jewish, as she'd like to think, but it pleases me to let her think so.

"Just think, a year," I say, walking her to her car. "She's been gone a whole year."

"Yes, but *you're* still here. That's sort of neat," she says, as she drives off into the night.

LOST AND FOUND

Why save a letter, take a snapshot, write a memoir, carve a tombstone?
—ANNIE DILLARD, *For the Time Being*

SUMMERTIME, the year rolls round again, as years will do, fog clings to the branches of the redwood tree out back. Aunt Mabel planted that tree; it towers, stories higher than this small house she and Uncle Ted left me, here in Berkeley. That tree and a wild tangle of juniper and bougainvillea are all that's left of their garden, and a lawn more dandelion than grass. I really ought to do something about this yard. But I am deep in the boxes, deep inside.

I am excavating the boxes in the basement. Everyone's things have landed here, everything that's survived their many moves and mine. Of all that living, only these things remain and this house that's now the end of the line. The things they cared enough to save become the things I care enough to save, the shaping of the story falls to me.

I dig down through the boxes, sifting through the shards and fragments of our lives. There are things I need to know, things still missing, lost so long I'm not sure what they are. And Bill, always Bill, at the heart of the heart, always and ever, Bill, barefoot boy with dog, have I written him out of the story? I see that I have. But he wrote himself out, removed himself long ago; now, I, complicit, erase him too. To erase the blood guilt of it, not my brother's keeper.

I drag up a carton from deep in the basement, too heavy to lift, the cardboard crumbles as I tug, papers spill out on the stairs, theater

programs, newspaper clippings, book reviews, snapshots, the beginnings of a poem. My twenties are in this box, my thirties, forties, too,
dozens of letters from lovers, friends I barely remember, signatures
I can barely decipher. I skim through these letters, entire dramas
play themselves out, so urgent, so forgotten, they hold no interest
for me now.

I am looking for family. God, was she right, then? family is all
there is.

A letter from my father, his voice drifts back across the decades,
thanking me for my hospitality, telling me of the arthritis in his old
dog, in himself.

Now what was so wrong with him? I drink in his kindness, his
concern; it cuts me to the heart, his effort to reach out. He tells me
how much he enjoyed his visit with me, what a lovely town Claremont is, how could I not love it there, how lucky I am, I take it the
rest of the way, the way it would have gone—you don't know how
lucky you are, have never known, have never appreciated. Or so I
imagine, these grooves are deep—*you spoiled brat, you.*

(Yes, but kids don't come spoiled, says Ann—someone spoils
them, then calls them spoiled.)

I approach his steamer trunk with trepidation, the musty old
trunk he hauled his every move, his many moves, since World War II.
I drag it up the stairs. I dig down through the photos, they are tied
in packets, arranged alphabetically, *Bali, Berlin, Cairo, Catalonia,* how
orderly he was, in everything but his life. He'd come back from these
trips with slides of castles, city walls, ruins, never any people—I'd be
bored, then guilty for feeling bored.

Skip these. Go for the letters. Her letters, 1944, 1945, 1946, her
writing on the envelopes, *Captain Jack Greenberg,* a PO box number
in San Francisco, a long row of numbers. He is in New Guinea,
though she doesn't know where he is, she has only that long row of

numbers; where the troops were was kept secret. She is in Palo Alto with her sister, her father, and me.

I feel like a voyeur, peering into these inmost, private places. There are answers here. Yes, he *was* with us when I was born—he left in January 1944, I was six months old. He's not at the front, he's behind the lines, on the healing, not the killing side of war, treating MacArthur's wounded. But it's a dangerous place, the Pacific, US forces invade the Philippines, seize Iwo Jima, prepare for the invasion of Japan.

I open her letters carefully, the paper rips at my touch. Some are handwritten, so faded I can barely make them out, most are typed—egads, the old Underwood even then, that print is distinctive as her voice. They're *long*, seven or eight pages. She is keeping him apprised of events on the home front. As Hitler is murdering his way through Europe, as London is blitzed, Japan torched, she tells him of the really momentous events going on, 1944, 1945, 1946: my first words, my first steps on the beach at Santa Cruz, my first birthday, my second birthday. She drives us around to every poultry farm in Sunnyvale looking for an egg to make a cake. "I would have given anything if you could have seen G tonight after dinner, sitting on the ground by a tub of apricots, one in each hand, G in a blue dress, the green leaves, the vivid shadows, the yellow cots. I wish I could really draw word pictures…I've never felt so unequal to any task in my life…" But her writing *is* up to it, every bit up to it, her images are vivid, her sentences step along, never miss a beat—where'd she learn to write like this?

We are living in a small house on Alma Street, Palo Alto, Grampa, Paddy, Mother and me. An old oak tree shades the house, blanketing the yard with leaves and acorns, keeping it cool in summer but damp in the winter, bad for Lydia's arthritis. Paddy, whose name was still *Lydia* those days, wants to move to Miami, but she has a job in Palo Alto and a singing teacher she likes. Grampa wants to retire, but war wages are good. Dining out with Marie Cohen the other night, who

Where'd she learn to write like this?

Miss Biggerstaff, Big Canyon School, Lake County, 1912.

should walk into the restaurant but Vyacheslav Molotov. Molotov in Palo Alto, poultry farms in Sunnyvale, the four of us piled into a small house by the railroad tracks, trains rumbling by, Grampa's radio blaring, Paddy at her singing, Mother playing the piano, what a caterwauling, yet she seems content. Life lies in the future, not in some crudded-up old past.

The baby is a lot of laughs: "She is the type of baby that gives one many laughs," my mother writes. "Everything is a game with her...She seems to think me quite funny...I hope I'll always be as amusing to her as I am now!" She is amused to watch herself turn into a doting mother: "Just look at this letter. It's all about Gayle. Marie would say I've joined the class of doting idiots." The date is June 6, 1944, D-day, the day Allied troops land on the beach at Normandy. She thanks him for this darling baby, for "this amazing little creature who has been on this earth such a very short time yet who knows and says so many things, has learned so many words, this vital, impish little creature, constantly demanding attention or bearing watching, running to me dozens of times a day with a different story on the tip of her tongue. I hold my breath as I stare into her eager little face, trying to read her lips, then her mind, and we both usually end up in utter confusion. But often I get the idea, since our impressions are much the same…"

I hold my breath, reading this. I've never felt so close to her. I see our bond in the making—I see how a woman becomes her mother, and it no longer seems a curse but a blessing.

He, at war, has long periods of idleness, but for her, "there's no let up, caring for the world's most active baby." When he complains of boredom, she reassures him: "it won't be forever, and who knows you may sometime look back at the peaceful nights you had in New Guinea if G ever keeps you up as she did us the other night, from 1 till 4 AM. Must go now. G is saying 'Bottle broke,' and she's right. She threw it on the floor."

Enchanted as she is by this impish creature, she's exasperated, too, bored, impatient to get back her life. "It is utterly impossible to apply myself to anything…have you ever had to play horsey with your shoe strings and other tasks about that level all day long? Marie says only a moron could enjoy it. It is difficult to explain, so I won't try too hard…" She tries to keep a few piano students, to study Russian, to read a biography of Shostakovich; she volunteers at the Democratic headquarters, enrolls in a psychology course to help her understand the terrible twos, but it's a struggle: "You've no idea what tyrants these two year olds are. It is impossible to write, read or practice when I am here alone with her…The pottie situation is a mess. There isn't any other word for it. But we're carrying on."

A delight of a baby, a terror of a baby, a tyrant of a baby, a strong-willed and stubborn baby on her way to becoming a very spoiled child. A Mephistophelean laugh as I upend her purse and pour the contents on the floor—"she has your laugh," she writes, "pure mischief, the little devil," but she's an angel, too, "a little elf": "She says, 'Caterpillar is whissy, mommy is whissy, whissy mommie,' as she hugs me and kisses me." "She is an adorable little hellyun, Jackie. She's difficult to describe because she is so full of devilry and impishness... Then there is her other side—the sweet, open smile, and the innocent expression.... And her energies are boundless....it must be your energy, not mine."

Photos fall out of the envelopes, black-and-white snapshots, a scowling infant wielding a spoon like a scepter, an angel baby, adoring, reaching for her hand, they make me see double, these photos, a blessing, a burden, a gift, a stone around her neck—you have to see double, to take these in. Ambivalence, I see, comes with the territory, the mother country, of course it does, how could it not.

No secrets here, only testimony of love, theirs for each other and for me. "If only it would end soon," she writes, "this endless separation, I miss you so. Good night, darling, I'll dream about happy days to come, with you and Gayley by my side as we skim over smooth roads, past redwood groves, over mountains, along the seashore. And no dread of parting."

But wait, there are secrets. An unmarked envelope, a photo of a naked lady, not my mother, not Maria, a whole series of this lady and her baby. Not secret, exactly, only secret from him that I knew.

...angel baby, adoring, reaching for her hand.

While he was overseas, a woman appeared at the door, a nurse he'd knocked up on an army base on his way to New Guinea, an infant in her arms: *Where is the doctor?* Mother didn't know where he was, she had only that PO box and a row of numbers—weeks went by when she got no letters. When did she tell me this? I can't remember, it must have leaked out in conversations at the kitchen table, as secrets did in our family. I never got the whole story, I didn't want it, I don't want it now. Her letters are here in the trunk…not mine to read.

He said he was sorry, men do such things in a war. She tried to forgive him. But it made a rift. A casualty of the war, their marriage, a minor casualty, but not minor to us.

Go way, go way far way—my first words to him. I was two and a half, and who was this stranger in uniform, come to boss me around? I'd ruled the roost, Paddy and Grampa at my command, Mother's family of origin become *my* family of origin, a tight little band—and who was this man, trying to make order of our nice little mess?

They waited some years to have another child. While she was pregnant, there were anonymous phone calls, a woman saying he was sleeping around. The Other Woman, another Other Woman? All the while she was carrying Bill.

He did not know I knew these things, he and I never talked, not about this. *He* talked. He told me about the walled cities in Spain, the roads the Romans built as far north as Scotland, the routes the Crusaders took, the castles they built. I tuned out. I locked into the position I held, easier than trying to imagine him, the sorrows he'd buried along with his past, his many losses. He'd lost his mother when he was three, his father a few years later, then William, the brother he loved most. Dead by his own hand.

He doted on the little girl I was, but did not know what to make of the woman I became, edgy and brusque and fiercely partisan to my mother. He'd have loved to have had a daughter who brightened his old age with grandchildren and laughter, but I never learned that kind of love from him; he had no knack for family, neither did I. He'd have liked us to talk, I think, but we neither of us knew how. Anyhow, the TV was on too loud to talk, louder as he got deafer, and Maria, too, went deaf from the blare.

I'd trek down to San Jose, a dutiful daughter, but Maria was always there. The house felt more like hers than his, formal and fussy in an old-world, over-decorated way—*provincial Italian*, Mother called it. But the yard was his, a half acre on a creek, one of the few creeks in San Jose that hadn't been cemented over, oak trees and chaparral lined the lot. He'd take me on the tour of the fruit trees he'd planted, walk me around from tree to tree, the cherry trees, the one that bore fruit and the one that did not, the fig tree that wouldn't grow, for all he tried to get it to grow (he loved figs). He'd grumble about the birds, squirrels, raccoons, possums that ate the fruit, the gopher that devoured roots, but he hadn't the heart to put out traps.

He had a sweetness at the end. He was touchingly grateful when Mother and I came to see him in the hospital. Maria sat by his bedside, singing him songs, bringing him treats—I think he even gave her a proper ring. I was with him the night before he died, Maria was with him all that day, but she'd just left—he died among strangers, wired to machines, in a hospital he'd worked in thirty years. He'd been asking to see his doctor, but it was a weekend and there were no doctors. He'd never have given such slipshod care.

I never really mourned him. Always there were more urgent things to do, books that needed finishing, classes that needed teaching, I'd just met Bob.

Now it all comes back, the fig tree that wouldn't grow, the creatures he hadn't the heart to kill, his kindness with patients, old people, old dogs, with us when we came to him with a hurt…The good doctor, the kind father.

But there was that other father, the father I walled out.

He and I sit at the kitchen table, Mother and Paddy are there, and he decides that the mat needs cutting. (The mat?) He grabs it from me and begins hacking away. I doubt that this needs doing, but he is so sure, he takes it into his hands, those capable surgeon's hands, but it is too much, he clutches his side. *Do you want me to call 911?* I shout, but he's gasping, choking, he can't speak…

I cry out and wake myself up, wake Bob up, too. I never used to dream about him and now that I do, I dream he is dying. What the dream brings back is his stubbornness, his maddening certainty—he was so sure he knew what needed doing, even when he didn't, yet he was trying to help. What the dream brings back is his impatience, that revved up quality he had—he moved faster than anyone else in the family, his metabolism set to a higher speed, he turned the heat down when we wanted it up, he stood while we sat, tapping his foot, jangling his keys, always the sense there were places he'd rather be.

It served him well, that drive, propelled him out of the Lower East Side, through City College, University of Chicago, Yale, and those were the years Yale medical school let in five Jews a year—he never told me, I read it in a book, he said nothing of that time or of any other, left it all behind. His forebears had been walled into ghettos, forced to wear markers, forbidden to leave cities or move around, and in California, he found a land without walls; but he brought walls of his own.

So we sat at the kitchen table, the week after Bill died, he and I and Mother, crying, going over what we'd done, what we'd failed to do, and I never asked, tell me about your brother, tell me how you got through that, how can I get through this now? William was a secret I wasn't supposed to know, there were so many secrets, I couldn't remember what I was supposed to know, but I remembered about William. "I must have done something wrong," he cried, "terribly wrong, but what he did was wrong, *wrong, wrong, wrong*"—he said it over and over, said he wished he was dead, over and over. After that, he never spoke of Bill again. He buried my brother William along with his brother William, in a place too deep for words.

He killed himself for a woman, Maria told me he told her, this was after he'd died, after we'd dropped all pretense about who knew what. She said he was sobbing, practically spat out the words—*for a woman!* A dancer, a Rockette, the kind who broke hearts. *Women are like streetcars, miss one, another comes along*, he told Bill. Bill was fifteen when he told him that, and even then he knew it was full of shit.

A lazy hippie, my father said he was, said it to his face.

People should be careful what they say. Sticks and stones may break your bones, but words can really kill you.

Families can kill you, too.

In the last photos I have of Bill, he and Dad are in Dad's backyard. The trees are bare, the sun is weak, January, 1977. Bill holds a mug of coffee. He is twenty-eight, handsome, bearded, looks like a young Alan Bates, not as dark as my father was, but intense like him, and defended—you can see from the set of his jaw, the way he stands, rocked back on his boots, heels dug in, he is defended. Dad looks

The last photo I have of Bill.

like a little old Jewish man, hair thinning, nose broadening, getting a paunch. He stands with his left side toward Bill, his good ear. They look nothing alike, except for the posture—Dad's is defensive, too.

Dad's dog Saturday sits in the foreground, white hairs in his dusty-gold muzzle.

Bill would die first. Then Saturday. Then Dad.

What are they talking about? Probably Bill is trying to tell him about his trees, the fig tree that wouldn't grow, the peaches and cherries that the birds ate all of—he knew about trees, he had a feeling for the soil, what sun, what shade, each plant required, when to water, prune, and pick. Nobody taught him, he just knew. Probably Dad is not listening. Or not hearing. He was by this time quite deaf.

Fifteen months after I took this picture, Bill drove his car off the twisty part of the road to Half Moon Bay.

Sweet William, do I have to take you out now, try and see it through your eyes. Green eyes, almond-shaped, those eyes that looked out on so much of what mine had, yet saw so differently. From behind that beard (you needed that beard, your face could conceal nothing), you looked out and saw a gentler, kinder reality. You believed in plants, animals, people, and you knew how to capture what you saw on film.

Brother Bill, barefoot boy in poncho. You had a calm, quiet patience, you needed it, I guess, growing up in a household of helpless, histrionic females. You knew how to fix things, how to make things work. Oh yes, you tried to show me how to work the camera, you explained more than once the f-stops and apertures, but it did no good; the photos I brought back from England made the Lake District look like mudholes. The photos you brought back from Kauai—the deep red magic of the canyons, the blue-black gleam of the lagoons—it took more than a light meter to capture that.

Odyssey Orchards is where I wish you'd stayed, a hippie commune in the Central Valley near Davis. An old farmhouse falling in on itself, junk cars in the yard, a couch on the sagging front porch, its stuffing sprung out, chickens cats dogs babies naked in the dust, a sun so strong the melons grew visibly larger from dawn to dusk, crenshaw casaba cantaloupe persian honeydew. The girls picked the melons, topless in the fields, the locals drove by and gaped. A fig tree so full it was a menace to parked cars, figs splatted juicily on hoods and tops, giant sunflowers like a kid might draw, flower house tree hills sky.

GREENIE'S VEGGIES, said the sign, ALL ORGANIC, ALTERNATIVE FARMING. It was possible to believe in alternatives those days.

I'd drive out summers from New York, city-slicker sister in a Mustang convertible, taking care to park out of range of the falling figs. I'd read all day, then you and I would sit on the porch and drink our way through a vat of carrot wine you produced from an unexpected surplus of carrots. It wasn't my scene, exactly, though I could understand—if I'd had to choose between Odyssey Orchards and the MadAve job I'd just escaped, I'd have moved here, too. I could feel the pull, those summer nights, earth pulsing with the sound of crickets and warm, grassy smells, the pungence of fruit drying, fruit stewing, fruit rotting, so like the valley of our youth.

"So what do you intend to do—let yourself get drafted and blown to smithereens, like poor Tommy down the block?" I walked into the kitchen just as she hurled this at him. He was back from Odyssey Orchards, I was back from New York, we'd coordinate visits to Mother's so we could spend time together. He had a harder time coming home than I did; I could bring work.

"I don't know, I have to see."

"You don't have to see, you have to do something, and soon— here, read this," she shoved a conscientious objector pamphlet at him. There were CO pamphlets strewn all over the table.

"Lay off, Ma."

"Or do you intend to move to Canada, never see your family again?"

"It'd be quieter in Canada." He left the table and said little the rest of the day. He didn't fight back the way I did, and she didn't let up—when she got something into her head, she pushed, even when she didn't know what she was talking about.

Yet she was never hard on him the way Dad was. One time he brought home a film he shot with his friends in the Davis dump. He and his doberman romp through the rubbish, he spots a garbage can, lifts the lid, grins, gives a broad wink—and out leaps this gorgeous babe, his girlfriend Jan, leggy and dazzling as a Las Vegas dancer, which is what she'd been before she came to work on the farm. Mother and I thought it was charming, Dad wrinkled his nose, said it looked like *The Grapes of Wrath*—why could he not see that his son's romance with the land was a version of his own, the valley he'd glimpsed on a produce crate and come west to find? Education had been his way in the world, and there was Bill, back in the dirt, refusing his offers to pay for tuition; all he saw was the dirt. Nor could he see it was fear, not laziness, that made Bill drop out, first out of Berkeley, then Davis. I saw it, heard it, too, the tightness in his voice, the panic when he hit a hard place, "I couldn't hack it, Gayle."

Bill was at home in the sixties, but the sixties ended, his people disappeared, shaved off beards, got jobs in the city. He moved to Pasadena, got a job with the Rose Bowl parade, the Tournament of Roses, designing the animation systems that made the Baskin Robbins bunny hop, the American Eagle flap its wings. He was making things, learning things, he had buddies he worked with, I thought he was fine; and, amazingly, we were only forty-five minutes apart, what with the new 210 freeway, after having a continent between us for so many years; and we became part of each other's lives for the first time since I'd left home. He got to know my friends, had an affair with one, or two, barefoot boy with cheek, got on well with Norman, and so did I, a short, bearded Marxist historian who made me laugh, who looked enough like Al Pacino to get asked for his autograph. I was making forays into normal life, Norman and I were talking marriage, though it never felt quite real. I'd watch how other people did it, try to imitate their moves—only Bill knew what I meant by this, only he of all the world.

Then he met a woman from the islands, the kind he always fell for, the kind who broke hearts, he pulled up stakes, followed her to Kauai. He'd be a photographer, he'd photograph the islands. He ran through his money and then some, he came down hard.

I was in England with Norman. When I got back, Bill was in Kauai, down and out. I talked him into coming back, met him at the airport, drove him to Pasadena. His boss at the floats wanted him back, he could pay off the money he owed, no big deal; the family he'd lived with wanted him back, he could have his old room, rent-free; everyone wanted him back, no big deal.

He went to Mother's, where he'd left his car. I drove him to the airport. "Gayle, can I move in with you?" he said as he hugged me good-bye, a hug so tight I could smell the fear, I pushed it away, afraid of the feeling, that old nerve, that old panic, *walls closing in*—please don't ask, *don't clutch*. My place was tiny, a room I slept in and a room I used for work, how could he stay in the room I used for work?

"You'll be fine in Pasadena," I said. I thought he would. The family with the room for him lived just across from the Rose Bowl, and they had room in their hearts as well as their house; they'd just lost their son. "It makes no sense to be out here with me, so far from where you work—you'll be fine, you'll see, nothing bad has happened."

A month passed, he didn't come back from Mother's. Another month, and another. We were on the phone a lot.

"You need to get back here where your life is."

"I know."

"Well, aren't you?"

Silence.

"Why aren't you?"

Silence.

"You gotta get back, Bill, it's no good your hiding out like this." We'd been over this before. "How's Mom?"

"Mom's cool." Long pause. "Dad wants me to go back to school." That catch in his voice when he spoke of college. There was something about money owed, taxes he couldn't pay, he was embarrassed to ask Dad.

"I know. It's no good your being there—just pack up and leave. I'll be here." (Did I say, "I'll be here"?)

"I dunno, Gayle. *I'm losin' it.*"

"Well, okay. I'll see you." I hung up. Spring break came, and I went to England to be with Norman.

And that was that.

I made myself view his body. Dad drove me to the mortuary on El Camino, I made myself look. No mark on his face, no disfigurement, only a set to his jaw, as though braced for a blow. I stood there a long time, trying to take it in, knowing that if I didn't, I'd spend the rest of my life expecting him to turn up like the not-dead brother at the end of one of those lying Shakespeare plays. I did, anyway, expect him to turn up, for years, I thought he'd walk through the door.

Dear Mom, the note left in his briefcase, the briefcase left in the closet, in case he changed his mind, a short note, a childlike hand, I can't go on, can't live with myself, would you rather see me crazy, on drugs, an alcoholic, it's better this way, it said, or words to that effect. I read it through once and never again. It's there somewhere in the basement, I will not dig it out. It said, "Gayle, go on being happy." It did not sound like a blessing.

We'd talked about depression, but I thought we meant the same thing by the word—you go down, you go up, later the same day or maybe the next day, down and up like a ping-pong ball, I had no idea about the kind that just goes on and on. We'd talked about suicide, not often, but the subject came up, but I thought it was an *idea* we were talking about, not anything anybody would *do*.

It does no good to blame, but I do blame—I blame myself, I blame them, we all of us blamed each other and ourselves. Not out loud, of course—out loud there were no recriminations, well hardly any. There were the words I overheard her say to Paddy, "I think this might not have happened if she'd come back," but I knew that already. There was the night she threw my father out of the house for something he said about Bill, physically, literally shoved him out the front door, she never told me what it was he said. But mostly we were gentle with each other, we had to be, we all hurt so much.

She said it must have been the drugs he took, the LSD. She told me she never took a glass of wine or an aspirin while she was pregnant with him, or with me, she was that careful. But she said she'd been unhappy those months she was carrying him, she cried a lot, those anonymous phone calls, she wondered if that did him harm. She said, "Maybe I should have left that man." But she did not dwell on that, neither did I.

I went to see his therapist in Pasadena.

"Your mother tried to kill herself?" It was a question, not a statement.

"No. She talked about it. She never tried."

"She did," he said. "I think she did."

"I don't think so. I'd have known about it."

"You weren't around. Bill dealt with it—there was something about an ambulance, a hospital," he said, still not quite sure.

"I don't think so. There's no way I wouldn't have known."

"They might have kept it from you," he said, but he couldn't be sure. He tried to find the notes he'd kept from their sessions, they were lost.

But I don't think this could have happened without my knowing— they were not good at secrets, my family. I think this shrink had translated my mother's words into images, as perhaps Bill had done. I never asked her. Nor did I ever say she should not have said those things about killing herself, can't go on, I'll end up crazy. I was old enough to know that words were words, to sense that a person might say a thing so as *not* to do it, but Bill was too young, he hadn't had time to harden his heart.

All night, it seems, I've been sitting on the floor, shuffling through his photos, Bill on a tractor in the field, Bill in the melon patch, Bill on the porch of the old farmhouse. All night I have been picking up his photos and putting them down, Bill by the Baskin-Robbins bunny, Bill with his doberman—what can I do with these?

They fuck you up, your mum and dad, they may not mean to but they do. They fuck you up, your siblings, too. I was there before he was born, dug in and greedy for growing room of my own, five and a half years' head start, a bossy, clever older sister, successful in the terms our family understood. So Mother was with Paddy, except that she had only a year and a half head start, and Paddy, being Paddy, survived. But Bill, lone male in a household with two fighting females pitted against each other yet bonded against a powerful, absent, but ambiguously present male—what way had he to grow? Some little girls would have welcomed a baby brother, I wanted a dog. So I became part of the family doom for him, as he for me.

Only later did we become pals, apricot fights, singing along to the Hit Parade, camping out in the living room, lunatics giggling at something only we could find funny, only we against the whole wide world, and later, we became friends, best friends. But even then I let him down. Probably it was the thing he needed most, the thing I could not give—*Gayle, can I move in with you?*

Back in the boxes go the Baskin-Robbins bunny, the twenty-foot tall grinning eagle, that whole world that died with him. *Deal with it?* I don't even know what that might mean.

I crawl into bed, stiff, cold, weepy, the sky is light, I sleep a little, I think it's a sleep, I hear laughter, light, bubbly, gurgly, a little kid's laughter, I follow it but it's faint, it is gone—*Billy, come back!* I wake out of the dream, if it is a dream, heart pounding, face wet with tears—*Billy*, I'm crying, *I'm sorry, so sorry*.

There is a kind of grief that acts out as craziness. A week after he died I found myself in bed with a man who looked a lot like Bill, bearded, boyish, an earthy kind of guy. By the time Norman got back from England, there was this other man. Then I fell madly in love with someone else and broke off with Norman. Then I went back to Norman but did not let go of the new man—so there was this new triangle; then I left Norman and met another man, so now there was the new man and *another* other man, and they went on for years, these shifting triangles, and I think it was this: Bill was the one man I'd counted on never to leave, so I had to make sure there were two men around in case one left. I thought we'd grow old together. *Never trust a man, never trust.*

It was during this time that I was trying to get pregnant, these days I couldn't stand to be alone a single night: I'd have a baby and I'd name it Bill. And each time I flipped, or flopped, back to the other man, I was sure this was the Right Man; then I'd start drifting back to the other man, just as sure that he was right, keeping two around in case one left. Then I did get pregnant, only not with the Right Man, though he'd *seemed* right enough at the time, an agony of indecision, an agony of a decision. Then the man I was not pregnant with lunged at me as I got out of his car; I'd just told him I was leaving him (for the third time). I grabbed at the car door, the window shattered, British sports car piece of shit, he threw me down into the broken glass, I was bleeding, knees, hands, face streaming, my glasses broken, he kept hitting me, he was drunk and murderous and I didn't care, I was a broken thing already. Drama enough to last a lifetime, and maybe

I courted the drama so as not to feel, but far from deflecting pain, this made worse pain—it hurt, being beaten up in a parking lot, it hurt, that abortion, not the physical pain so much as the death of a possibility. I was thirty-eight, I knew there'd be no more.

For years after he died, I'd dream of a man walking down a street, a boyish, bearded man in a work shirt. I'd see him and my heart would leap and I'd know it was him, know that he was somewhere in the world, it's just that we hadn't seen each other in a long time. I'd follow him, he'd be walking away. Only once did he stop and say a few words, his voice unmistakably, penetratingly Bill's—"I couldn't hack it, Gayle."

It made sense, the way dreams do. Only it doesn't make sense, it has never made sense, a few bad moves, some thousands of dollars, nothing to die for, I still do not see, always in the dreams he is walking away. Anyone looking at the two of us growing up would have put money on me to be the one to do a thing like that, and I'd have thought so too—he was the sane and calm one. He was that hardest of things to be, a gentle male, a man without meanness or bluster— what room was there to grow?

Then the dreams stopped.

Only this, years after that summer of sorting out, not long ago, I jerked awake, gasping for breath, heart pounding, the flap and stir of beating wings, as a large, winged creature lifted up out of a small, cramped room. I felt it more than saw it, the whoosh of wings, the air gusting, eddying, a creature huge and feathered like a bird from myth, not like a harpy, not bent on retribution, or only a little, intent mainly on getting away, an angel, maybe, though not like any angel you've ever seen, nothing human about it. I bolted out of bed, sobbing, knowing it was Bill, lifting himself up and out.

So do I return in my dreams and try to rework the story, make it come right, trying to say to him, perhaps, as I said to Mother, fly away, get out of here, find some place you can be all you should have been. But he is beyond me, nothing human remains, somewhere I can never reach, even in a dream.

This is the part that can never come right, the part I wanted never to write. I wanted to write only about the women, the women who came through, I kept putting this off, pushing it back, the words slow and halting and wrong, and what good do words do anyway, yet not to tell seemed worse.

Brother of mine, *bone of my bone, flesh of my flesh*, I thought I knew you. I thought when you said, *I'm losin' it*, it was only the sort of thing people say. How lonely you must have been, driving those hills, trying to summon the nerve to do it, the nerve not to do it, how lonely those moments, I can barely think, even now, decades later, I can hardly bring them to mind, coming fast 'round the bend, bracing your body, making yourself jerk the wheel hard, the moment you might have pulled it back, I don't think you wanted to die.

Oakland, 1949, says the writing on the back, my father's writing. Billy has that blissed-out, Buddha look babies have, volley-ball cheeks and pudgy thighs, Mother is trying to get him to sit up on the bed to have his picture taken. She looks sullen, pouty, irritated with my father as he takes the photo, interacting more with him than the baby, not that madonna look she has in photos with me, she never had that idyll with Bill. This would have been not long after that night I remember, the night we brought him home to that house where his life entered ours, where memory began for me.

There are not so many photos of her and Bill. The pictures not taken, they tell a story, too.

Oakland, 1999, a lifetime later, my lifetime, not his, I drive across town to find that house. I've found the address on a driver's license in my father's trunk—I'm surprised it's so close, but there it is, Thirty-Seventh Street, not far from where I live. I'm surprised that it exists at all, sealed off in memory as it's been, this block I ranged, a fire-breathing dragon, my first Halloween.

I get out of the car, whoosh of traffic, MacArthur Boulevard, Broadway, the 580 freeway, slap and tear of tires on asphalt. The block would have been quieter in 1949, less down-at-heels. Can I find the house without looking at the number? Yes, easily, it's the only stucco on a block of wood-frames, a small gray duplex; a few steps up the porch, I ring the bell.

Nobody home. There's a park at the end of the street, I can see it from the porch. I walk down the block, the name comes back, Moss-wood Park, the smell is familiar, the sharp, fresh scent of redwoods, there's a swing set where children swing, benches where mothers sit watching children swing, mothers watching children, all these years later, the amazing patience of mothers.

I slump down on a bench. No gates of memory open, no images flood me from the past, only an enormous sadness.

But if I close my eyes, I see a woman walking down the street, pushing a pram, wearing a long, trim jacket with high-heeled shoes, that smart 1940s look. A young woman trying to get a footing in the world, not easy in those shoes, trying to balance the baby with the man who'd no sooner come back from war than he wanted to be off again, ambitions for himself that were even then being disappointed, as hers were, too. These two held between them a new life. Then another. No wonder it was not so well done.

Yet I blamed them so.

So incautious are people, stamping out replications of themselves before they know what is there. It was what people did, it is what people do, it is not what everybody ought to do. But brave, braver than I've ever been.

And maybe it wasn't them, or us, or me—maybe it was the times. The Depression that made them so distrustful, the war that pulled them apart, the fifties that hit women like a stun gun, the sixties, the drug culture; maybe it was the seventies, when the counterculture

A woman walking down the street, pushing a pram.

went mainstream and left Bill so alone. Maybe it was old history, racial memory, pogroms, massacres, famines, terror encoded in the genes, Jewish melancholy, Irish melancholy, the sorrow of our kind.

Brother of mine, my only, I could not imagine, I cannot imagine, I could not follow you to that last place, where the rubber left the road.

Boxes from the cellar pile up around the piano, bringing a whiff of earth and mold. I sort, sift, read through the day and night, I read till I can read no more, stumble upstairs, fall into a sleep, fitful, full of dreams. It's July, I think, though I'm not keeping time, I'm deep in the boxes, deep inside. I am obsessed by this, possessed by it, I am taking possession, or is it taking possession of me?

A photo of my father in a field full of poppies, an infant in his arms. It's a lovely photo, a rare moment when he looks content to be where he is, pleased with his baby boy. It belongs in his album— where *is* his album? It's not in the closet where I keep the albums I've made for Mom and Paddy. I find it under a stack of mail in the hall, most of its pages blank.

That's wrong—he belongs with his family. He was not much with us, but he was there, in a way—there with a checkbook, tuition, my dentist bills, there with a camera, always with a camera, and those were the days cameras took time and fussing with. The photos are his gift, I see that now, a gift of love—I see how he's given us form and presence and color, almost as though he knew somebody might need these images as stepstones back into the past, he having so thoroughly jettisoned his own.

It got easier to love him as he got old, easier still, now that he is gone. Easier to find in people what there is to love when they're no longer there to confuse you.

A restless man, a wandering man, a satchel and camera slung over his shoulder, he traveled light. On to the next castle, the next port, the next woman, he traveled best alone.

Only once did he take me along. I was fifteen, we quarreled the whole way. But there was a magical moment when he pulled the car over on a country lane in France and said, "Here, take the wheel!" A sports convertible like all the rest, it heaved and lurched till I got the feel of it—"*Drive!*" he said, I caught on fast, the surge of the car, the open road, he gave me that. He taught me about work, how it could save your life—I got that from him, I did not get it from her. He said he was glad I'd done something with my life that wasn't about money. That was the closest I ever got to a father's blessing. It was more than Bill got.

His last trip, he took alone. Maria was in the front yard, when up drove an airport limousine and out he came with a suitcase.

"Where you going?" she yelled.

"Istanbul!" he gave her a peck on the cheek, got in the limousine, and rode away. Maria was on the phone to Mother who was on the phone to me—he was seventy-four, deaf as a post, a terrible driver. He drove all the way from Istanbul to Paris, he was gone three months, we thought we'd never see him again.

I dig down in his trunk and find some photos from his travels, a winding street in Lisbon, a solitary Roman column on the coast of Spain, a pyramid in Mexico—how could I ever have found these boring? I see what good photos they are, the composition, the care, now that I've taken so many lousy photos myself. I fit them into his album.

So *that's* where you've gone. *Way far away.*

I think sometimes I might set out in search of family, go back east, hunt up lost kin, find the family my family left behind. It is strong, this longing for blood.

Family. I see why you'd want one, I see why you would not. To no one else do you matter so much, no one else has that kind of stake in you, though no one else can drive that kind of stake *through* you. They have you, they hold you, no one holds you as they do, to have and to hold. It's a lot about *possession:* you are bigger because you *have*, more important because you *belong*, belong to, possess, aug-mentation by possession. *Mine—my* kid, *my* kind, *my* clan, *my* people, possession legitimized, *legitimate*, as we never were. Blood and law, *the ties that bind, so conventional*, Mother would say, tribal ties—you'd think they'd have come up with something better by now.

And yet they were my kin, my kind, my family, there's no more where they came from. When a family dies, a world dies with them, and a language dies, the family names, *Teddy Bear, Grandfather Gruff,* the fond names, *Silly Billy*, *Gayley Goose*. The family stories, the jokes no longer funny with nobody there to get them—remember the time when…? no one remembers. Silly things that Bill and only Bill would get. Like the day he found a bowl of something green and fuzzy, in my refrigerator—"Jesus, Gayle, what you got growing here? you're worse than Mother!" and we laughed, for it was just like her, she couldn't stand to throw out food, so she kept it around till it was no longer good, then she could throw it out. Only he would get this, only he in all the world.

But no. It's not blood I want, not DNA, not the genetic material passed from organism to organism, that's not where the life is, but in bonds built through living, relationships, affiliations forged through life and time.

On my refrigerator door, where my friends have photos of their kids, I have kids, too, Annais, Ellie, Tiffany, Sarah, Amy, Eva, Etienne, Karen, Kelsey, Lindsay, Lauren, Claire, and some whose names I can't quite bring to mind, graduation photos, class photos, and scenes from *A Midsummer Night's Dream*, photos that go back decades. Daughters of the mind. Except that my kids are always the same age, never grow old, never grow up, though I do—my face has more lines, my dresses are less form-fitting. But I like the older face better than the younger face, it's less anxious, more at home. That part of the story turned out well.

Friends, too, are there on the refrigerator door, along with an ex-lover or two become a friend, and Bob. But this is not that kind of story—I grew up reading stories like that, happy ending with a man, unhappy ending with no man, this is not that kind of story, I swear. No man should ever be the end of a woman's story, what a disaster that would have been, marry the handsome prince and there an end.

Still, Bob is here, we are here, that matters more than I can say.

On my refrigerator door, I have kids...Annais, Ellie...

I go down to the basement, I almost never find the thing I'm looking for, but I do find things I had no idea were there.

Bottles with notes in them—"this was your grandmother's perfume bottle," "this was your grandmother's rose vase," "Great Grandfather Heuser's whisky bottle." Paddy has written, in her elegant old-fashioned hand, the birthdates and death dates of my grandfather, Edward Paterson, and my grandmother, Christine Heuser, whose stories I will never know. Messages in bottles, a fact here, a date there, Paddy left me this information to do with what I would. She knew I'd be listening. I don't know how she knew, all the noise in my life, but she knew.

My mother's Latin grammar. *Gallia est omnis divisa in patres tres*, she has written on the flyleaf. She'd quote these words, just up and say them, out of nowhere, as though Gaul's three parts contained the sum of wisdom; Billy and I would roll our eyes and laugh.

Things have a way of turning up, she'd say. I'd be searching the house for something I'd left on the kitchen table—"Hey, Ma, have you seen my..." "Well, Gayley, it was there yesterday, it's there

somewhere, if you children would only pick up after yourselves…
Well, don't worry, *things have a way of turning up.*" But it did not turn
up, it had vanished into the jungle growth on the kitchen table,
never to be seen again; I'd stomp down the hall. "Well, Gayley, I just
don't know, *things have a way of disappearing.*" Any contradiction between these two positions would go unnoticed. So her voice goes on
in me, with its contradictory messages.

My father, too, a lust for life and a melancholy too deep for
words, a wandering Jew who set down roots in the valley, the healer
we came to with a hurt, the womanizer who broke our hearts. And
Paddy, my shy, unassuming aunt, stage center in those Gilbert and
Sullivan roles, having visits from the FBI. And Bill, I thought I knew
him, I knew him least of all. I marvel at clarity, I stand in awe of
clarity—I have always wondered how people can say such clear and
certain things, can be so sure of what they say, when it seems to me
infinitely complex, the world, and getting stranger, always there are
two possibilities, two or more—and how fortunate I am to have
found my way to poetry, where you can speak paradoxes and not
sound mad; poetry, the language of logical impossibilities.

There's a legacy here, a what do you call it, a *patrimony?* I reach
for the old family dictionary, I look up the word *patrimony*, I read,
"that which is bequeathed by the ancestors." From *pater*, father. But
what is the word for the mother's bequest? I look up *mater*, I find…
matrimony? "matrimonium, maternity legalized." That's it, then,
what the mother bequeaths is…matrimony?

I don't think so. There is no word for this legacy of hers.

It is summer, we are in my backyard, Bob and I are about to rush off,
Mother appears on the porch, insisting that before we go, we have
something to eat. As we sit down to the meal, bees descend, she huffs,
indignant—so many bees! Bob asks her to turn down the Shostakovich.

This is dream nonsense: we never eat outside in my yard in Berkeley, she never had music playing in the background, she's like Bob that way. And besides, in the dream, she is in her fifties and I am in my fifties, the age I am now.

But she is very much there, doing what she always did, fussing that before we rush off, we have something to eat, and I, instead of being irritated, walk over to her and put my hands on her ears and run my hands down her shoulders. I don't think that's even a thing we do with humans, it's a thing I do with Nellie, a gesture of affection, reassurance, *possession*—yet it seems right in the dream. Then Bob and I are in bed, my old bedroom in Los Altos, he is wrapped around me, his leg digging into mine—what a heavy bone, what a bony person. I wake out of the dream and we are in Mendocino, he is curled around me, his leg lies heavily on mine, my leg's all numb and tingly, but I am infinitely grateful for the weight of him.

I wish I had hugged her to me, I wish I had held onto Bill, I want to cherish those I love, hold them, cleave to them. You can't do this, of course, go around grabbing and clutching at people just because you know we're going to die, you have to take them for granted, have to but cannot. In the midst of life we are in death, in the midst of death we are in life—how do the words go?

Memento mori, think on the end. Seems like something we need to remember, seems like something we need to forget. Know it, forget it, deny it, remember it, how can all of these be true, see the now point as a moving point, solid and real but vanishing, too, present and passing, just passing through. You need to see double to see this way.

I return to the house, the apricot orchard is back, branches bending with the luscious fruit, gardens opening onto other gardens, and there, in this paradisiacal place, she is walking, a plump, white-haired woman with a little white dog, and I am so glad to have her back, then I'm in the swimming pool, a bulldozer bears down, grinding, shuddering, shoveling dirt into the pool, it will bury me alive...

The chambers of a house, the chambers of a mind, shelves high, deep, and cluttered, some too high to reach, wires tangled, crusted, some dangerously live wires, so many boxes I haven't got to the bottom of, boxes I'll never go into, things that are missing, that will always be missing.

I am trudging across the dunes looking for a place to swim, a cold sea, a leaden sky, a rough coast, northern California, and there on a bluff, gazing out to sea, stands my mother. She is my age, hair tied back, scarf fluttering in the wind. She turns to me, a long, sad look. I want to say, I understand the sadness now, you were right, Grampa was right, *man was made to mourn*. I get it now, the losses accumulate, sorrow cuts grooves, I get that now. But I can't say it, can't give in to that sadness, even in a dream. I say, instead, "Are you all right, will you be all right up here?" Here where I must leave you now.

She turns away, looks back out to sea.

When I think of my mother, it's that look of hers I remember, that way she had of gazing elsewhere, dreamy, yearning, as she played. *Clair de Lune* is my mother, *The Moonlight*, the *Appassionata*. How well they knew, the old masters, how well she knew, that transmutation of longing to beauty, to a saving grace.

I reach for a pencil and pad, catch the images as they dissolve— put it away, Gayle, put the pain in the words, leave it behind.

I read somewhere that the task of mourning is to transform ghosts to ancestors. Good ghosts, friendly ghosts, I transform you to ancestors.

Rest, perturbed spirits. All of you. All of us.

Words, words, how many days, months, years have vanished into these words? So much for my resolution to live each day as though it's my last, take more time with people, get out into the world—I've done it just like before, just like I always do, canceled appointments, not answered the phone, not shown up to things, then wondered, where's my life. On bad days, those raw, skinless, weepy days I wake to without warning, I know it's just words I do, all I ever do, move words on a page. But on good days, I find the right words and it's a comfort and a celebration, soothing words, shaping words, saving words, and I have a mad hope, as my printer cranks away, that I'll see them there, dancing on the pages, I'll have conjured them back— I think, okay, I missed it the first time around, maybe I'll get it this time.

Writing for those of us who need more time, writing for those who need a second chance. Memoir as repair work, as reparations.

Now these words are your monument, these words are how you'll be remembered, if you are remembered—my writing is your resuscitation, the sole repository of you. But it's my words, not your words, *mystory*, not *yourstory*, it's a made-up story as surely as if I'd set out to write fiction. There's a terrible tyranny the living have over the dead—we speak for you, steal your voices, feed on you, batten, ghoul-like. Memoir as grave robbing. Have I ever known your story, do I know it now? *This is something you know nothing about*, your last words, strike me now as profound: I could not imagine your death any more than I could follow Bill to that last place, though I was there with you in the room—and your life, have I imagined it? It is pure projection, this project, the meanings I spin out, that we all spin out around *that undiscovered country from whose bourn no traveler returns*—but maybe it's true, as Whitman said, that death is different from what we suppose, and luckier.

The impulse to elegy, to explanation, is about *us, we the living*, for our ends, our purposes, for though this is something we know nothing about, we know this: the dead are not *other* than us, they *are* us, only a little farther down the line. So we bring to bear on them all our need to make sense of our lives, for I have to make sense of that dissolution, the worlds they take with them, I cannot

not resuscitate, it's my own life at stake. I who am up and breathing, I who am *pre-deceased*, must find my story in their stories, stitch the narrative threads together from what remains. A scrap afghan, *a thing of shreds and patches*.

Not much but not nothing, something where nothing was, something saved from the dumpster, snatched back from the fire, put back into circulation, appropriation but appreciation, too. A garage sale, then, memoir as…garage sale?

It will do for now, it will have to do, this mourning book, this long good-bye.

Bob calls and says I should get up to Mendocino while there's still some summer left. Keith calls and says I should come back down and see them. He says the lawyers I sold to have cut down the cherry tree and gutted the house, but the house still stands. Reggie's next door was a teardown like the other little ranch styles on the block, bulldozed to the ground. But my mother's house still stands.

I get on the freeway, fighting the urge to drive south, a homing creature with no direction home. Against all instinct, I turn north. 101 north through Marin, Petaluma, Santa Rosa, rushing to beat the rush, it's a lifelong habit, this pushing against time. There's a lot more traffic on this freeway than there used to be, billboards and car dealerships line the highway, houses march up the hills, the oaks are dying, the blight is creeping north.

But north of Healdsburg, the traffic thins, and 128 to the coast is a road carved from my youth, orchards and meadows and split-rail fences. I slow for the redwood forest, hard to slow down when everyone in California is on my tail, I pull over to the side, a logging truck thunders by, sawdust flies off felled trunks. The ground yields, soft and mulchy to my foot, I breathe in the moist, sharp scent of the redwoods, trees tall as ancestors, taller than the tallest cathedral in Christendom, sun filters through the canopy like beams in a cathedral nave. *Sequoia sempervirens*, these trees are called, *forever living, forever green*. I don't know about *forever*—I know that just off the road may be scars and stumps, the end-of-world carnage of clear-cut.

At river's end, the road winds up the bank, up the coast highway, past the town of Mendocino to our house. It's not the old house but each time it feels more like home, the giant clam shell by the front door, ferns and fuchsias and foxgloves, a trumpet vine sends scarlet flowers to the top of a redwood tree. Bob waves as I pull up. He is working well, this house lets him work, it lets me work, too, we work well together.

I write now in a room filled with your things, in the presence of birds, pink and ivory birds on your black Chinese screen, purple birds on your pearl gray rug. I sit on the deck and watch the gulls dive and play, the geese form Vs that un-form and re-form, the sleek sassy ravens chortle and caw and fly so close I hear their *whrrrr*, the small brown birds make a welcoming chirp—and I feel their presence with a kind of wonder. I'd like to say I am better at living in the present, but I don't know—all those days I felt trapped in Los Altos, I was longing to be in Mendocino, and now that I'm here, I cast myself back there.

But maybe that's always the way it is, this shifting between, that's where we live, here and there, now and then, the now point as a moving point, just passing through.

I see them now, two ancient ladies in bright flowery blouses and broad-rimmed hats, they sit under the cherry tree, waving *good-bye!* I turn and wave and drive off down the block, back to my life, they wave wildly—*good-bye, good-bye!*

I will forge in my imagination a place to return to, the cherry tree in bloom, the beam of their smiles.

ACKNOWLEDGMENTS

It surprised me, when I came to name the people I have to thank, what a long list it is. Since a major impetus for writing this book was the acute sense of loneliness and abandonment that came with losing the last of my family, along with the fear that my friends had heard enough, it's heartening to see how many have stepped forward to read parts or all of this memoir.

Those who were there from the beginning with exceptionally helpful readings include Janet Adelman, Ann Rosalind Jones, Roberta Johnson, Wendy Martin, Trish Moran, Kay Trimberger, Judy Dunbar, Frances McConnell, Elizabeth Minnich. Early versions of the book were also read by Hedy Straus, Richard Fadem, Rena Fraden, Gail and Bob Tager, Cindy Brady, Diana Russell, Dorothy Wall, Cynthia Greenberg, Dan Eaves, Suzanne Lacke. Coming in at later stages were Elizabeth Abel, Georgina Kleege, Marilyn Fabe, Michaela Grudin, Karen Greenberg, Karen Wunsch. Readers with comments about specific chapters include Judy Newton, Christina Gillis, Claire Kahane, Ilene Philipson, Mardi Louisell, Barbara Epstein, Carol Ockman. Special thanks to Jean Naggar and Ann Coffey, whose support went way beyond the text. And to the Mendocino Writers Conference.

But the losses accumulate, try as you may to freeze time in prose. Some of the major players in this book have moved on in the years it took me to bring this project to completion, not only Janet Adelman but several of the stalwart band who rallied around me on Clinton Road: Keith Webber, Bob Hayes (Sammy), Cindy and Alfred Brady, Louise Mumby. Let this book be a loving tribute to their memory. To my students at Scripps College, I owe a debt of gratitude for keeping me steady on through some grim years, especially to those who shared their life stories in our creative nonfiction class, too numerous to name. Special thanks go to Lisa Sharihari, class of 1998, who I'm pretty sure left the flowers by my office door, and Ellen Rissman-Wong, class of 1979, who has "honorary membership" in my family for her genealogical digging, and can probably tell you more details about it than I can. And to Annais Fern and Ellie Irons for the photo.

Deep and heartfelt thanks go to Judy Edmondson (Jenny), who saw me through the darkest days, and Becky Ballinger, who sustained my teaching life at Scripps. A special thanks to Vicki Ratner, the only physician at my mother's bedside and one of my oldest friends. And to others, Carol Neely, David Claus, Toni Clark, Larry Thornton, Nancy Ware, Mike Zeller, Valerie Miner, and Helen Longino, whose friendship has mattered enormously through the years. Thanks also to Tom Withers, Linda White, Kaaren Gann, and Vicki Nelson— Vicki, for chiming in at the last with words I needed to hear. And it's not entirely true that I have no family—there are cousins in the Midwest (Pierre, Miriam, Liz, and Robert Fabien) who I've had the pleasure of getting to know since I began this project, and a surprise second cousin, Gene Fidell, who recently surfaced in New Haven, who tells me there are more; such are the mysteries of blood. Nor is it entirely true that the valley has had no writer to memorialize it. Yvonne Jacobson's *Passing Farms: Enduring Values* is a moving commemoration; and a recent account of growing up in Los Altos, *California Apricots: The Lost Orchards of Silicon Valley*, by Robin Chapman, is delicious in its evocation of the town I remember.

Some lines of poetry and prose are unattributed in my text. "This cathexis between mother and daughter" is from Adrienne Rich, *Of Woman Born*. "The family coil, so twisted, tight," is from Rich's *In the Wake of Home*. "Death is the mother of beauty" is from Wallace Stevens, "Sunday Morning"; "shining from shook foil" is from Gerard Manley Hopkins, "God's Grandeur"; "A woman is her mother" is from Anne Sexton, "Housewife"; "They fuck you up, your mum and dad" is from Philip Larkin, "This Be the Verse"; "The staring unsleeping eye of the earth" is from Robinson Jeffers, "The Eye"; "You'd need a thousand pairs of eyes to see that woman" is from Virginia Woolf's elegy for her mother, *To the Lighthouse*.

"Home is the place where, when you have to go here, / They have to take you in," misquoted in chapter 4, is from Robert Frost's "The Death of the Hired Man." Another line I take liberties with—"all that is constant about the California of my childhood is the rate at which it disappears"—is from Joan Didion's *The White Album*; and another—"to die is different from what anyone supposed, and luckier"—is from Walt Whitman's *Song of Myself*. "Silicon Valley is the center of the world" is said by Mike Malone, *The Valley of Heart's Delight: A Silicon Valley Notebook, 1963–2001*, though there are so many versions of this statement as to make it commonplace. "Consider it not so deeply" is Lady Macbeth's advice to Macbeth; it worked no better for him than it did for me. "Rest perturbed spirits," "that undiscovered country," "all that lives must die," are from *Hamlet*. "Pearls that were his eyes," "of his bones are coral made," are from *The Tempest*, which was of all Shakespeare's plays, most on my mind as I wrote, for the possibilities of redemption it holds out, the transformation of sorrow into "something rich and strange."

My aching sense of death as a terminated conversation was eased, to some extent, as I read the stories of others. The many grief memoirs I read, along with books by Hope Edelman and Virginia Stem Owens, provided solace and sustenance. The works that moved me most were Blake Morrison's *When Did You Last See Your Father?*, Mark Doty's *Heaven's Coast*, Sandra Gilbert's *Death's Door*, and *I've Always Meant To Tell You*, a collection of letters that women imagine writing their mothers, edited by Constance Warloe (this is the book with photographs, referred to in chapter 5). The line I quote, "When someone dies, you might as well accept the fact that you will be haunted . . . ," was, I thought, from that collection, but I cannot find it there or anywhere; thank you, whoever said it. It's my hope that *Missing Persons* may provide readers with the kind of consolation I found in the words of others.

And as always and ever, love and gratitude to Robert Jourdain, who lived these events with me, nurtured me and this book, without whom, I don't know what.

ABOUT THE AUTHOR

GAYLE GREENE is professor emerita, Scripps College, Claremont, California. She has written widely on Shakespeare and published several books on contemporary women's fiction and feminist theory, two of which, *Making a Difference: Feminist Literary Criticism* and *Changing Subjects: The Making of Feminist Literary Criticism* (both coedited with Coppélia Kahn) have been reissued by Routledge. Her biography of radiation epidemiologist Alice Stewart, *The Woman Who Knew Too Much*, was reissued by University of Michigan Press in 2017. *Insomniac* (University of California Press; Little Brown UK Book Group, 2008) is a first-person account of living with insomnia and an exploration of sleep science. Part memoir and part scientific investigation, it was Amazon's number one pick for March 2008 and was shortlisted for the Gregory Bateson Book Prize by the Society for Cultural Anthropology for being "interdisciplinary, experimental, and innovative."

Born in San Francisco, native daughter to a native daughter, Greene grew up in the Santa Clara Valley when it was still the "Valley of Heart's Delight," a place so paradisiacal that people flocked from miles around to see the blossoms in the spring. *Missing Persons* takes place in the years when the vast orchards were being dug up and paved over for tract housing, strip malls, and freeways, when the "heart's delight" was transformed to Silicon. She now divides her time between the Bay Area and Mendocino.

Her web page is gaylegreene.org.